HATE MAIL FROM CHEERLEADERS

AND OTHER ADVENTURES FROM THE LIFE OF REILLY

RICK REILLY

SPORTS ILLUSTRATED BOOKS

HATE MAIL FROM CHEERLEADERS

AND OTHER ADVENTURES FROM THE LIFE OF REILLY

For Cynthia,
the life in Reilly

Contents

Introduction

BY LANCE ARMSTRONG

I'M A SUCKER FOR COMEBACK STORIES. STORIES ABOUT PEOPLE who get handed a bag full of coal and turn it into a diamond necklace. I like stories about the guy who gets knocked over 100 times and then wins the race on the 101st. ¶ You know, Rick Reilly kind of stories. ¶ Like the one he wrote about Dick Hoyt, who was overweight and had a quadriplegic son with cerebral palsy. And then one day the son gets a computer he can work by moving his head, and one of the things he types is, "I want to go for a run"—or something like that. And next thing you know, the dad has pushed, pulled and pedaled the son through more than 200 triathlons, more than 80 marathons and a bunch of Ironman triathlons. And it's humbling, for a guy like me who's run a marathon, to realize those guys would've totally kicked my ass.

Or like the one about the nine-year-old Little League cancer survivor. The other team walked the slugger in the bottom of the last inning of the championship game just so they could strike out the cancer kid. These are the same kind of people who try to run me off the road on my bike. At the end of the column, the kid says, "Someday, *I'll* be the one they walk." Very cool. My kind of kid.

11

I guess I like those kind of stories because I hear about them every day. In my work with the Lance Armstrong Foundation in fighting cancer, I hear amazing comeback stories all the time. They give me goose bumps. They give me hope. They give me inspiration to fight harder. And with the way the U.S. government is dragging its feet on cancer research, it takes all the fight we've got. But then, that will just be another great comeback story, won't it?

I guess I like those kind of stories because I'm one of those stories.

That's the main reason I'm a Rick Reilly fan. His columns aren't the normal stuff you get in the sports pages. He never seems to write about wins and losses, and which shortstop hit for what average on turf, lefthanded, after eating a burrito for lunch. It never even seems to be so much about sports as it is about people. You know, the blind hockey fan going to her first real game. Reilly's daughter driving him crazy on Take Your Daughter to Work Day. Sort of un-sportswriting.

They're often these amazing stories of struggle, will and victory. I have no idea where he finds them, but they're irresistible.

Rick is kind of a bizarre person. Very different. And sometimes that's a good thing. For instance, I see so many writers out there who take information they get from a source—*any* source—and go with it. Never bother to check out the credibility of the source or find out what ax he may have to grind or double-check his allegations. They don't check those things out because it might ruin the sensational aspect of what that source has to say. Truth be damned. But I never hear that about Rick's stuff. He's got integrity, and that's sometimes a rare commodity in journalism.

I remember the first time he interviewed me, during the 2001 Tour de France. He was asking me questions I'd never heard before. Like, *When are you happiest?* and *Have you ever peed on anyone during those mass roadside pit stops?*

I also remember that column he wrote that week. Hate to say this, but it wasn't about the bike. Or the race, really. It was about struggle, will and victory. It ended with this scene about the moment that week when my then-wife Kristin and I were about to open this envelope from our doctor, telling us what the sex of our baby would be. To me that column seemed a little bigger than sportswriting. A little better.

Not that I'd ever tell *him* that. No, I much prefer to torture him.

One time, for instance, I brought him along on a little training ride in

Austin. He'd never ridden with clips before. I showed him how to clip in and we took off. I made sure he was pretty much toast within 15 minutes. So I brought him back to the parking lot, got off my bike and watched to see when it would occur to him: He had no idea how to get off the bike. He was trapped.

"Hey!" he hollered. "How do you get your freakin' feet off the pedals?"

I laughed. "*Now* you ask?"

All you have to do is kick your heels out sideways and you come right off, but I wasn't about to tell him. God, it was hilarious to see him trying to untie his shoes as he pedaled. Or kick forward. Cursing me the whole time. Finally, his circles got smaller and smaller until he just fell over sideways. Klunk.

Hey, I said he was different, not smart.

Foreword

BY RICK REILLY

O.K., EVERYBODY, GO AHEAD AND GRAB A SEAT. That's great. Now I guess you're all wondering why I called this press conference.

Well, see, I've spent half my life at press conferences but not *once* have I gotten to stand at the podium and be the big enchilada. You know, show up late, call only on people I like, and strut off in the middle of it. Besides, who's going to stop me? It's my book.

O.K., questions, questions. Tom.

Tom Brokaw: *What's with the weird title?*

Oh, right. *Hate Mail from Cheerleaders.* Well, when I first started writing the SPORTS ILLUSTRATED column every week, I did one on cheerleading.

I said, "Cheerleading's not a sport! There are 10 or 11 sports for girls at every high school. If you want to play a sport, get in between the lines and play a real sport! But wearing a circle skirt and a tight sweater and facing away from the field going, '2-4-6-8' is not a sport."

Well, this went over like anthrax brownies. We broke a record for hate mail on it, but hate mail from cheerleaders really isn't bad at all. It's sort of like getting pelted with rolls of scented Charmin. It's always on pastel paper and usually includes a picture of the squad. And they write, "I hope you die" with a little heart over the *i.*

Love your top, Katie. Go ahead.

Katie Couric: *Have you been lifting?*

Oh, well, thanks. Yeah, a little.

Walter.

Walter Cronkite: *You ever get any scary mail?*

Well, whenever I write about guns or my opposition to the war or anything to do with Detroit, the mail comes with lots of cutout magazine letters and blood. But mostly people seem to enjoy proving they're much more clever than me. Of course, that's not hard—sort of like taking Stephen Hawking two falls out of three.

Oprah.

Oprah Winfrey: *Does it bother you when people come up to you and say, "I love your column because it's the perfect length for my morning you-know-what?"*

Yes. Yes, it does. And I hear it all the time. And that's why I always have a pair of surgical gloves with me, in case they want to shake hands.

O.K. Grantland.

Grantland Rice: *I see other sportswriters doing not just one column a week, but three or four, and doing daily radio shows and TV shows. And yet you only do one little bitsy-witsy 800-word column a week. How do you justify that?*

Next question.

Damon Runyon: *Why won't you answer Grantland's question?*

See, here's what you people don't get. I work all week just trying to find one decent idea. Sometimes I'll write three and four full columns, but you only see one because the others either: a) sucked, b) were un-fact-checkable, or c) were made moot by the fact that Mike Tyson just shot the president.

And then there's all the "balk" columns. You know, ones I start and give up on because they turned out to be worth only half a column, or one paragraph, or one line.

Like these gems:

World's Shortest Books: (*Darryl Strawberry's 10-day Method to Beat Drugs*)

If Every-day People Could Use Athletes' Excuses (Surgeon, after patient dies: "I don't know. I just came out a little flat. You can't get hyped up every single day.")

If Life Were Fair: (Terrell Owens would be in front of a microphone somewhere saying, "Number 673. Whopper, no onions?")

Yes, George.

George Will: *Can I go to the swimsuit shoot with you?*

As if! No, but if somebody else takes you, be sure to meet François the Buttduster. No trip is complete without hanging out with François, who is French and gay and applies body makeup on the models with a French feather duster. He'll be dusting down Heidi Klum's derriere, going, "Oh, Heidi, your skin, eet iz so parfait!"

And because the shoots are always at some remote beach, François gets to stand face-first toward the models and hold up the beach towel for them to change bikinis behind. The veteran models comfort the new models with, "Don't worry. It's just François. He's gay!"

But you always want to get beers with François afterward because he's *not* French and he's *not* gay, either. I think he lives in Bergen Park, N.J. We'll be like, "Frankie, what does Elle Macpherson look like naked?' And he'll be like, "Dude, fuhgeddaboutit!!!"

Fact is, I almost called this book *François the Buttduster*, but which photo shoot would you rather do: a whole day with Frankie or a whole day with three cheerleaders so hot they melt your fillings? *(Pause.)* Exactly.

O.K., last question. This is kinda weird, but I guess it's you, Rick.

Rick Reilly: *Is there lunch?*

Working press only, leech.

1

Your Team . . .
My Team . . .

SEPTEMBER 29, 2003

YOUR TEAM SUCKS. ¶ MY TEAM IS IN THE FIRST YEAR of its annual five-year rebuilding program. ¶ Your team is full of thugs, criminals and perverts. ¶ My team is colorful.

YOUR COLLEGE COACH wouldn't suspend his star players even if they stored the stolen stereos under his desk.
MY COLLEGE COACH believes in due process.

YOUR QUARTERBACK is dumber than a bottle of peroxide. He wouldn't know the playbook if Elmo read it to him.
MY QUARTERBACK relies on his athletic instincts.

YOUR ANNOUNCER is a shameless, drunk homer.
MY ANNOUNCER is the last of a dying breed.

YOUR TEAM'S FANS are the kind of single-toothed, liquor-soaked, foulmouthed vermin that real vermin cross the street to avoid.
MY TEAM'S FANS fans are fiercely loyal.

YOUR DEPARTING SUPERSTAR sold out teammates, fans and the city that supported him for 20 years just to grab an easy ring.
MY ARRIVING SUPERSTAR isn't afraid to chase his dreams.

YOUR OWNER is a silver-spoon billionaire who bought a championship just because he could.
MY OWNER is part of the capitalist system that made this country great.

YOUR PITCHER is a headhunter.
MY PITCHER controls the inside of the plate.

YOUR NBA COACH was a weed-smoking hippie who does nothing more than roll the balls out every day to one of the greatest rosters in league history.
MY NBA COACH lets 'em play.

YOUR SLUGGER is a steroid-dripping cheat.
MY SLUGGER has made a major off-season commitment to reshaping his body.

YOUR SUPERSTAR is a selfish and arrogant narcissist who can't even stand his own teammates, much less his fans.
MY SUPERSTAR is focused.

YOUR CHEERLEADERS are uglier than the primates at the Tehran Zoo.
MY CHEERLEADERS reject the old, chauvinistic notions of spirit leaders.

YOUR COLLEGE'S BASKETBALL COACH is a perverted lush who has rubbed up against more coeds than a sorority-house beagle.
MY COLLEGE'S BASKETBALL COACH understands the importance of student-body support.

YOUR STADIUM is a bandbox with more tricked-up features than a plastic surgeon's waiting room.
MY STADIUM is neoclassic.

YOUR SHORTSTOP hasn't had a decent year since David Wells was a size medium.
MY SHORTSTOP is primed for a breakout season.

YOUR NASCAR DRIVER is a No-Doz-addicted maniac who is out there putting lives in peril.
MY NASCAR DRIVER is racin'.

THE PARENTS ON YOUR KID'S SOCCER TEAM are ref-baiting loudmouths who need to get a life.
THE PARENTS ON MY KID'S SOCCER TEAM are fully engaged in the lives of their children.

YOUR COACH is a bloodthirsty, chair-heaving madman who ought to be hand-cuffed for emotionally and physically bullying his players and staff.
MY COACH is old school.

YOUR DRAFT CHOICE is a complete bust.
MY DRAFT CHOICE is still getting comfortable with the intricacies of the system.

YOUR FIGURE SKATER is *so* gay.
MY FIGURE SKATER enjoys the pageantry and tradition of the sport.

YOUR COLUMNIST hasn't had an original idea since fifth grade.
MY COLUMNIST is a devoted reader of *Mad* magazine (with thanks).

Postscript: YOUR BEST-OF BOOK makes every column its own chapter and adds a lot of pointless postscripts in a status-seeking quest to fill 300 pages. MY BEST-OF BOOK is substantial.

2

Worth the Wait

OCTOBER 20, 2003

WHY DO THEY COME? WHY DO THEY HANG AROUND to watch the slowest high school cross-country runner in America? Why do they want to see a kid finish the 3.1 miles in 51 minutes when the winner did it in 16? ¶ Why do they cry? Why do they nearly break their wrists applauding a junior who falls flat on his face almost every race? Why do they hug a teenager who could be beaten by any other kid running backward?

Why do they do it? Why do all of his teammates go back out on the course and run the last 10 minutes of every race with him? Why do other teams do it too? And the girls' teams? Why run all the way back out there to pace a kid running like a tortoise with bunions?

Why?

Because Ben Comen never quits.

See, Ben has a heart just slightly larger than the Chicago Hyatt. He also has cerebral palsy. The disease doesn't mess with his intellect—he gets A's and B's—but it seizes his muscles and contorts his body and gives him the balance of a Times Square drunk. Yet there he is, competing for the Hanna

High cross-country team in Anderson, S.C., dragging that wracked body over rocks and fallen branches and ditches. And people ask, Why?

"Because I feel like I've been put here to set an example," says Ben, 16. "Anybody can find something they can do—and do it well. I like to show people that you can either stop trying or you can pick yourself up and keep going. It's just more fun to keep going."

It must be, because faced with what Ben faces, most of us would quit.

Imagine what it feels like for Ben to watch his perfectly healthy twin, Alex, or his younger brother, Chris, run like rabbits for Hanna High, while Ben runs like a man whacking through an Amazon thicket. Imagine never beating anybody to the finish line. Imagine dragging along that stubborn left side, pulling that unbending tire iron of a leg around to the front and pogo-sticking off it to get back to his right.

Worse, he lifts his feet so little that he trips on anything—a Twinkie-sized rock, a licorice-thick branch, the cracks between linoleum tiles. But he won't let anybody help him up. "It messes up my flow," he says. He's not embarrassed, just mad.

Worst, he falls hard. His brain can't send signals fast enough for his arms to cushion his fall, so he often smacks his head or his face or his shoulder. Sometimes his mom, Joan, can't watch.

"I've been coaching cross-country for 31 years," says Hanna's Chuck Parker, "and I've never met anyone with the drive that Ben has. I don't think there's an inch of that kid I haven't had to bandage up."

But never before Ben finishes the race. Like Rocky Marciano, Ben finishes bloody and bruised, but never beaten. Oh, he always loses—Ben barely finishes ahead of the sunset, forget other runners. But he hasn't quit once. Through rain, wind or welt, he always crosses the finish line.

Lord, it's some sight when he gets there: Ben clunking his way home, shepherded by all those kids, while the cheerleaders screech and parents try to holler encouragement, only to find nothing coming out of their voice boxes.

The other day Ben was coming in with his huge army, Ben's Friends, his face stoplight red and tortured, that laborious gait eating up the earth inch by inch, when he fell not 10 yards from the line. There was a gasp from the parents and a second of silence from the kids. But then Ben went through the 15-second process of getting his bloody knees under him, his balance back and his forward motion going again—and he finished. From the roar you'd have thought he just won Boston.

"Words can't describe that moment," says his mom. "I saw grown men just stand there and cry."

Ben can get to you that way. This is a kid who builds wheelchair ramps for Easter Seals, spends nights helping at an assisted-living home, mans a drill for Habitat for Humanity, devotes hours to holding the hand of a disabled neighbor, Miss Jessie, and plans to run a marathon and become a doctor. Boy, the youth of today, huh?

Oh, one aside: Hanna High is also the home of a mentally challenged man known as Radio, who has been the football team's assistant for more than 30 years. Radio gained national attention in a 1996 SPORTS ILLUSTRATED story by Gary Smith and is the hero of a major movie that opens nationwide on Oct. 24.

Feel like you could use a little dose of humanity? Get yourself to Hanna. And while you're there, go out and join Ben's Friends.

You'll be amazed what a little jog can do for your heart.

Postscript: I'll never forget the e-mail that tipped me off to this story. A mom from a rival high school wrote, "I have just come from the most amazing sight." She said that as the parents watched Ben limping along, with a hundred kids running alongside him, they realized what they were seeing and "every one of us—even the men—had tears streaming down their faces." Ben's a sophomore at Presbyterian College now, and he's staying active. He recently rode a marathon on a recumbent bike. He heads up the Ben Comen Living Without Limits Foundation, too—and guess who headlined the foundation's first "fun run"? Kevin Costner.

3

Chillin' with the Splinter

JUNE 30, 2003

HUNG OUT WITH TED WILLIAMS THE OTHER DAY. Pretty cool. ¶ He's spending his time in a one-story cement building in a warehouse district next to the Scottsdale, Ariz., airport, frozen, upside down, waiting for science to bring him back from the dead.

"Uh, we don't say 'dead,' " says the voluptuous redhead giving the tour here at Alcor Life Extension Foundation, America's largest cryonics company. "We say 'the end of his first life cycle.' "

On the wall are photos of people hoping for a mulligan, with little plaques underneath that read, for example, FIRST LIFE CYCLE: 1925–1997. SECOND LIFE CYCLE: 1997–___. But there are no pictures of Teddy Ballgame hitting for any cycle.

"We cannot verify if Mr. Williams is with us or not," says a little bearded doctor named Jerry Lemler, a former Tennessee psychiatrist who is the head of Alcor and looks exactly like the late poet Allen Ginsberg. "We protect the anonymity of all patients."

O.K., the greatest hitter who ever lived is here, according to his daugh-

25

ter, Bobby-Jo Ferrell, and the former curator of the Ted Williams Museum, Buzz Hamon. They're still upset that when Williams *didn't* die of heart failure a year ago next week, at 83, he was packed in a crate of ice and flown to Alcor, where Lemler and his staff drilled holes in his skull to insert temperature probes (that's gonna hurt later on) and started freezing him—

"Not 'freezing,' " interjects Lemler. "We put you in a glasslike matrix." O.K., they put him in "a glasslike matrix," meaning they replaced more than 60% of the water in his cells with a kind of human antifreeze so his tissue became as rigid as glass (but didn't actually freeze) while they gradually dropped his body temperature to -196°C. Some old sportswriters will tell you that is just a little warmer than Williams was with them. From there, they carted him into a kind of stainless-steel morgue—

"Please," says Lemler, "we call it the 'patient care bay.' We house 58 residents in our patient care bay." O.K., into the "patient care bay" with the rest of the "residents," who were having another in a string of *very* quiet days. Anyway, they tucked him in a waterproof sleeping bag, opened up one of the 10-foot-tall stainless-steel cylindrical tanks filled with liquid nitrogen and lowered him in. There are seven of these babies, and they look like giant thermoses, except they burp and hiss with the liquid nitrogen, which keeps Williams a Boston Blue Sox.

Friends and relatives lay flowers at the base of the tanks, which makes the whole place look like a cemetery built by KitchenAid.

What's even creepier is that they hang the bodies upside down—"in case there's ever a leak, the brain would be the last exposed," explains Lemler. How's that for irony? Williams, one of the greatest big-game fishermen ever, is hanging upside down until his next life cycle begins. Somewhere a whole lot of marlin are giggling.

Worse, the Hall of Famer shares his tank here at Coolerstown with at least two other bodies and probably eight severed heads—

"Not *severed heads*," interrupts Lemler. "Neuros."

All right, he shares his tank with eight "neuros," which are bodiless people who hope science will be able to grow back everything below the neck, hopefully in the shape of Pamela Anderson or Tyrese. Either way, it's going to be a bit of a shock to Williams if he suddenly wakes up in there.

Is this what Williams wanted, to be the most famous "cryonaut" in history, living with eight or 10 tankmates in an overgrown martini shaker?

Doesn't matter now. Ferrell sued her brother, John Henry Williams, to get her father's body back and cremate it (talk about a climate change!) but settled for $215,000. So Ted Williams will live in suspense until either a) science thaws him out or b) Lemler runs out of cash and sells the whole shop to some unwitting buyer.

Honey, are you sure there's Creamsicles in these things?

And what happens if Williams pulls a Lazarus—

"Reanimates," says the redhead.

Oh, God. O.K., what happens when the poor bastard "reanimates" and finds that all his friends are dead and Eminem's grandkid is president and all his stuff has been auctioned off on eBay? And who's going to be the one to tell him that the Red Sox *still* haven't won a World Series?

Plus, what's he going to do for money? True, Alcor stores the stuff the "residents" want for the second time around in a one-cubic-foot box one mile under a Hutchinson, Kans., salt mine.

You know: CDs, photos, stuff like that. No cash, though, so the undead better have some Microsoft stock hidden in there with their Billy Joel CDs.

Still, if in, say, the year 2500 scientists *could* reanimate Williams (hey, they already do it with embryos and sperm), reverse the aging process and get him back to, say, 20, his age during his first year in Boston, then a world we can't imagine would suddenly have a gift from us: one of the greatest athletes of our time. Now *that* would be a comeback—

"Well, not really a comeback in the sense—"

Oh, shut up.

Postscript: It got weirder. There was a rumor that Williams's kids were hoping to use Ted's DNA to clone him. Can you imagine Ted Williams on the juice? He'd hit .502! But Williams' three kids agreed not to use his body for cloning, and two of them also signed papers saying they too would be frozen when they died. Sadly, that day came in 2004 for Williams's son, John-Henry, who now hangs with Pop.

4

Four of a Kind

SEPTEMBER 24, 2001

THE HUGE RUGBY PLAYER, THE FORMER HIGH SCHOOL football star and the onetime college baseball player were in first class, the former national judo champ was in coach. On the morning of Sept. 11, at 32,000 feet, those four men teamed up to sacrifice their lives for those of perhaps thousands of others.

Probably about an hour into United Flight 93's scheduled trip from Newark to San Francisco, the 38 passengers aboard the Boeing 757 realized they were being hijacked. The terrorists commandeered the cockpit, and the passengers were herded to the back of the plane.

Shoved together were four remarkable men who didn't much like being shoved around. One was publicist Mark Bingham, 31, who helped Cal win the 1991 and '93 national collegiate rugby championships. He was a surfer, and in July he was carried on the horns of a bull in Pamplona. Six-foot-five, rowdy and fearless, he once wrestled a gun from a mugger's hand late at night on a San Francisco street.

One was medical research company executive Tom Burnett, 38, the standout quarterback for Jefferson High in Bloomington, Minn., when the team went to the division championship game in 1980. That team rallied around Burnett every time it was in trouble.

One was businessman Jeremy Glick, 31, 6' 2" and muscular, the 1993 collegiate judo champ in the 220-pound class from the University of Rochester (N.Y.), a national-caliber wrestler at Saddle River (N.J.) Day School and an all-state soccer player. "As long as I've known him," says his wife, Lyz, "he was the kind of man who never tried to be the hero—but always was."

One was 32-year-old sales account manager Todd Beamer, who played mostly third base and shortstop in three seasons for Wheaton (Ill.) College.

The rugby player picked up an AirFone and called his mother, Alice Hoglan, in Sacramento to tell her he loved her. The judo champ called Lyz at her parents' house in Windham, N.Y., to say goodbye to her and their 12-week-old daughter, Emmy. But in the calls the quarterback made to his wife, Deena, in San Ramon, Calif., and in the conversation the baseball player had with a GTE operator, the men made it clear that they'd found out that two other hijacked planes had cleaved the World Trade Center towers.

The pieces of the puzzle started to fit. Somewhere near Cleveland the passengers on Flight 93 had felt the plane take a hard turn south. They were now on course for Washington, D.C. Senator Arlen Specter (R., Pa.) believes the plane might have been headed for the Capitol. Beamer, Bingham, Burnett and Glick must have realized their jet was a guided missile.

The four apparently came up with a plan. Burnett told his wife, "I know we're going to die. Some of us are going to do something about it." He wanted to rush the hijackers.

Nobody alive is sure about what happened next, but there's good reason to believe that the four stormed the cockpit. Flight 93 never made it to Washington. Instead, it dived into a field 80 miles southeast of Pittsburgh. All passengers and crew perished. Nobody on the ground was killed.

In the heart of San Francisco's largest gay neighborhood, a makeshift memorial grew, bouquet by bouquet, to the rugby player who was unafraid. Yeah, Bingham was gay.

In Windham, a peace grew inside Lyz Glick. "I think God had this larger purpose for him," she said. "He was supposed to fly out the night before, but couldn't. I had Emmy one month early, so Jeremy got to see her. You can't tell me God isn't at work there."

In Cranbury, N.J., a baby grew in Lisa Beamer, Todd's wife, their third child. Hearing the report last Friday of her husband's heroics, Lisa said, "made my life worth living again."

In Washington, a movement grew in Congress to give the four men the Presidential Medal of Freedom, the highest award a civilian can receive.

At a time like this, sports are trivial. But what the best athletes can do—keep their composure amid chaos, form a plan when all seems lost and find the guts to carry it out—may be why the Capitol isn't a charcoal pit.

My 26-year-old niece, Jessica Robinson, works for Congressman Lane Evans (D., Ill.). Jessica was in the Capitol that morning. This Christmas I'll get to see her smiling face.

I'm glad there were four guys up there I could count on.

Postscript: The attacks came on a Tuesday and I started making calls Wednesday. At first, the whole column was about the rugby guy. But the rugby guy's mom added, "And I think he said there was a baseball player, too, who stormed the cockpit." And so I'd tear it all up and write it again. And then I'd find out about somebody new who was in the group. I wrote four entirely different columns that week and this one is the last. From talking to relatives and wives, I knew so much about that flight I felt like I could've written a book. In the end, somebody wrote a movie instead—United 93.

5

Parental Discretion Advised

APRIL 2, 2001

TWO FATHERS STAND WATCHING THEIR KIDS. ¶ "WELL, THE wife and I have finally come to a decision," says the one with the Reebok headband. ¶ "Yeah?" says the one in the Nike cap. ¶ "Amber's gonna concentrate 100 percent on tennis from now on. Her coach says she's gotta pick one sport right now, or she'll get left behind the other girls."

"She looks like she's got good quickness," says the cap.

"Her kinesiologist says she's quicker than Venus at this age," says the headband, beaming.

"We've decided the same thing about Ike and golf," says the cap. "If he's going to stay ahead of the other kids, he's got to specialize now."

"His hand-eye looks good," says the headband.

"His physiologist says his muscle fibers twitch faster than Tiger's!"

"Golf's fine, I guess," says the headband, "but our financial planner says for girls, tennis is it. With Venus and Serena pushing the global marketing envelope, our yearly income should be seven figures!"

"You mean *her* income."

31

"Right. Her income."

"Ike's psychologist has told us he's gifted in lots of other sports besides golf, but there's no time," says the cap. "You don't want to be spinning your wheels."

"Course not!" says the headband. "You don't want to be shut outta the best camps—"

"And the best leagues—"

"And the national teams."

"I mean, yeah," says the cap, "it looks like my wife will have to quit her job just to drive Ike to all his golf tournaments, but there's no Tiger without Earl, right?"

"Tell me about it!" says the headband. "I'm working three jobs just to pay for all this stuff—Amber's pilates are *killin'* me!—but it's all about the kids, man."

"I hear that. Like, Ike's media tutor won't be cheap, but it'll free up his afternoons for his bunker workshops."

"Hey, you're gonna have expenses," says the headband. "We ripped out the bedrooms upstairs and put in an indoor tennis cage, but whaddya gonna do? The little girl across the street has a live-in volleying partner!"

"God! That's just plain overparenting!"

"Criminal!"

"The wife and I feel that if we put in the hours and the money now, Ike will be good enough to go straight to the PGA Tour out of high school and not waste time going to college. Not that college is a *bad* thing."

"Nah, not really *bad*," says the headband. "But Amber's career strategist thinks she can do Wimbledon by 14. *That's* what's important. Did you see the MLS kid whose parents let him miss a game the other day because of his prom?"

"Sounds like *somebody's* got their priorities mixed up," says the cap. "I mean, I'm sure Ike will be a little disappointed he'll have to leave home and move in with the Leadbetters soon, but some decisions a father has to make for his son."

"I know, I know," says the headband. "I'm a little bummed that Amber won't get to play lacrosse or basketball or, even, I don't know, piano, but how can she do that and put in the 13 hours a day that will get us to the level we need?"

"*She* needs."

"*She* needs, right."

"Hey, I only wish my dad had done this for me," says the cap.

"Hell, yeah!" says the headband. "I know this dad who's renting a house on a lake this summer. Says he and the family are just gonna fish and skip stones!"

"What a waste of time!"

"I mean, what are you gonna do with your kid for two weeks on a lake? I wouldn't know what to say to Amber for two weeks!"

"Most summers from now on, Ike will be playing the mini Asian tours, to build up his tolerance for travel and foreign foods. He'll need it when he gets his Gulfstream IV."

There's a pause.

"Which one's yours, anyway?" says the cap.

"The little one in the pink diaper near the incubator," says the headband.

"Beautiful. Mine's in the blue. With the nurse and the bottle."

"Got creatine?"

"Hey, it's never too early to start, am I right?"

6

Scales of Injustice

JULY 2–JULY 9, 2001

P EOPLE FOR THE ETHICAL TREATMENT OF ANIMALS (PETA) has new billboards out that claim fishing is cruel. I totally agree. The last time I went, all I caught was a sunburn, three hooks in the back of my thigh and hell from my pals for forgetting the Off. ¶ Unfortunately, this is not what PETA means. PETA means fishing is cruel to the *fish*. Seriously. PETA plans to put up billboards across the U.S. and in Canada that show a Labrador retriever with a hook in his bloody lip. IF YOU WOULDN'T DO IT TO A DOG, the signs say, WHY DO IT TO A FISH?

And, of course, the answer is: Because fish do not bring me my slippers.

Look, I wailed for the whales. I fumed over fur. I emotionally clubbed myself over the baby seals. But I'll be damned if I'm going to weep over a walleye.

PETA says fish feel pain and that to snag one with a steel hook, drag it along for 50 yards or so and then haul it out of the water so it suffocates is sick. "Why do we throw a Frisbee to some animals and a barbed hook to others?" PETA asks on its website.

And, of course, the answer is: Because fish really suck at catching Frisbees.

PETA thinks it's evil to eat fish, too. But why should we stop eating them when *they eat each other*? Besides, they had their chance to evolve. They could've crawled out of the primordial ooze with us, but they didn't. They decided to stay behind and swim in the water they pee in and go around never blinking. When fish lift their scaly butts past us in the food chain, they can eat us. Until then, pass the tartar sauce.

PETA even says catch-and-release is cruel. They say the harm and stress caused by being caught and released is sometimes enough to kill the fish later on. As if the fish go straight into therapy after being caught.

Fish: I'm telling you, Doc, I was just minding my own business when I got hauled into the sky, examined by some weird beings and then thrown back!

Fish psychiatrist: Lemme guess. A UFO, right?

I mean, what's PETA going to do? You'll be sitting at the counter in the deli, and suddenly, the PETA police will come running in, shouting, "All right, back away from the tuna melt and nobody gets hurt!" My God, we're talking about *fish* here. Fish have a brain the size of a corn kernel.

Professor James Rose, a University of Wyoming neuroscientist, studied fish for years and determined that they lack a neocortex (parts of which process the brain's response to pain), much like Cubs fans. Besides, if fish are so smart, why can you catch a fish, throw it back and then, two hours later, *catch the same fish*? I mean, do you really want to save something dumber than Robert Downey Jr.?

Didn't Jesus fish? He seemed like a pretty sensitive guy. When He zapped up all those fishes for 5,000 people, what do you think He did with them, throw them back?

I know, I know—I hate hunting. But sitting in the back of a pickup, taking a rifle with an infrared scope and killing a deer from 1,000 yards away is not nearly the same thing as standing up to your spleen in icy rushing river water, trying to cast the perfectly tied fly into the perfect eddy to catch a rainbow trout. Is it our fault that the trout falls for it? Tell you what: I will get behind hunting when hunters come up with a shoot-and-release program.

Why does PETA stop at fish? Where does PETA stand on the plight of the worm? And plankton? And the million micro-organisms that are crushed by your boots every time you go on a nature hike? Have these PETA vegetarians ever gotten close to a broccoli to hear its screams as it's violently yanked from its birthplace and boiled to death?

Fishing is cruel? I always thought fishing was one of the most peaceful things you could do. What are fathers and sons supposed to do together, knit sweaters out of each other's navel lint? What are we supposed to read, Hemingway's *Old Man and the Parking Lot*?

I'll tell you one thing. Before I agree to this whole fish-human truce, somebody had better have a long face-to-face with the sharks about it. I say we send a bunch of PETA members down right away.

Postscript: You sometimes get the feeling the folks at PETA have a little too much time on their hands. Their latest effort is a push to get Merriam-Webster to change the definition of "circus" to include a reference to "captive animals." Oy. One of their biggest supporters is Pamela Anderson, though she hardly practices ethical treatment of animals. Did you see what she did to Kid Rock?

7

Earning Their Pinstripes

SEPTEMBER 23, 2002

S O, KID, YOU WANT TO BE A NEW YORK YANKEES BATBOY? Hang out with Derek Jeter? Ride in the parades? Great. But, first, maybe you'd better take a look at a batboy's typical day. ¶ 2 p.m.—Pete Shalhoub, 17, shows up for a 7:05 game and starts setting up the dugout. Sure, most of the players won't be arriving for at least two hours, but so what? Pete'll be here two hours after the players have left, too.

You think batboys still only run out and get Johnny Blanchard's bat? Get real. Pete and the six other Yankees batboys-clubhouse boys are valets, cabbies, maids, deliverymen, shrinks and short-order cooks. And they're not 12 years old anymore. They're all 16 and older because the average sixth-grader doesn't do well when he's also working 75-hour weeks.

Some nights Pete has to show up at 3 in the morning to help unload the road-trip truck, do laundry and set up players' lockers. That takes four hours. Then he goes straight to high school in Jersey City, and then right back to the Stadium, where he'll work until about 1 a.m., go to bed at 2 and get up again at 6 the next morning to go to class.

"It's like I tell him," says Joe Lee, another member of the crew. "In this job you've got to sleep twice as fast."

3:45 p.m.—One of Pete's 1,000 jobs is mixing Gatorade for the dugout. That can be dangerous. A few years ago former visiting team batboy Joe Rocchio made green, not knowing volcanic Cleveland Indians star Albert Belle drank only red. Belle spit it out, knocked the jug over in the dugout, and Joe had to clean it up. Glamorous job, no?

4 p.m.—When players arrive, batboys start hopping. They're each player's little Jeeves. "Anything they ask for, they pretty much get," says Pete. That includes everything from, "Go get my wife a birthday present" to "Go get my brother-in-law at the airport." From going to a player's home to pack his bags to making dinner reservations. One player asked Lee to go to the ball-park every day during a 12-day road trip and idle his car for a half hour. "Keeps the engine clean," the player said.

Of course, there *are* rewards. When Jason Giambi was with Oakland, he sent an A's batboy to McDonald's. Giambi got three hits that day, so he kept sending the kid for the rest of the season. When Giambi won the MVP, he tipped him $5,000.

4:30 p.m.—A new kid shows up, the winner of a contest to be a batboy for a day. He's lucky he doesn't get the initiation Craig Postolowski got. To start, Jeter sent him off to look for the key to the batter's box. Then Joe Torre told him to go get the knuckleballs ready. Then Don Zimmer needed the lefthanded fungo bat. Finally, when Bernie Williams asked him to get a bucket of steam from the shower to clean home plate, he realized he'd been had.

5:45 p.m.—It's Pete's day to shag flies in the outfield and run the balls back to the batting practice pitcher. This is a gas. There's other cool stuff too. Some nights the clubhouse is lousy with celebs. You get to be in the team photo. And players have been known to lend batboys their sweet sleds for the prom. Of course, two years ago Manny Alexander of the Boston Red Sox lent his car to a batboy. Problem is, the kid got pulled over and police found steroids in it. Oops. Always check the glove compartment, Kid.

7:05 p.m.—Tonight Pete works balls for the home plate umpire. Another guy works the rightfield line, snagging foul balls, and another works bats in the dugout. (The rest are stuck in the clubhouse.) Problem is, sometimes a kid will be so tired from lack of sleep that he'll be out there nodding off in front of 50,000 people. "I've done it," says Lee. "I'm just glad a line drive didn't wake me up."

10:30 p.m.—Game's over. The real, nasty work starts. "Everybody thinks this is when we go home," says Pete. "But we've still got two hours of work to do." They pick up dirty uniforms, vacuum, straighten lockers, make food runs, empty trash, clean and polish 40 pairs of shoes. And they've got to do it all while dodging flying jocks, socks and towels thrown at their heads by millionaires. *Fwomp!*

12:30 a.m.—O.K., everything's done. Pete's spent, but he'll be in bed before 2 a.m. for once. At least he saw some baseball. The boys who worked the clubhouse have to watch the highlights later.

So there it is, Kid. And remember, don't ask for tickets, autographs or a raise. With the Yankees, you get the minimum, $5.15 an hour, even if you've been on the job 10 years. Hey, don't forget your boss is George Steinbrenner!

So, you want the job? Kid? *Kid?*

Postscript: Here's my attempt at the first-ever Yankees batboy joke.

Rookie Yankee batboy: Hey, is it true the batboys here get World Series rings?

Veteran Yankee batboy: How would I know? I've only been here six years.

8

Vision of Happiness

DECEMBER 30, 2002 — JANUARY 6, 2003

OR YEARS "MIRIAM FROM FOREST HILLS" HAS BEEN one of the great hockey callers in New York sports-talk radio. "Ya gotta beat that goaltender top shelf!" she'd insist. "Why don't these guys *know* that?" ⁊ She lives for her New York Islanders, having missed only two of their radio broadcasts in the team's 30-year history. In her tiny apartment in the Forest Hills section of Queens, N.Y., score books and audiotapes of Islanders games are stacked floor to ceiling, so many that she has only half of her single bed to sleep in.

Yet she had never attended an Islanders game.

When the team's vice president of communications, Chris Botta, found that out not long ago, he vowed to get her to a game and offered up two guest passes, hers for the taking. There was one detail.

Miriam is blind—has been since birth.

Living with her cat, Joey, and on a fixed income, Miriam had always thought that going to an Islanders game wasn't only too expensive, it was also inconceivable. This is a woman who waits for six-for-a-dollar sales on the spiral notebooks that she uses to keep score in Braille. This is a woman who sticks her radio between cans of chicken soup on the windowsill to get better reception.

"The Islanders are a way for me to talk to the sighted world," says Miriam, a 51-year-old native of Queens who has ruddy cheeks, short gray hair and gray eyes she doesn't hide behind sunglasses. "It's something safe [to talk about], you know?"

It's how she kids the cop on the corner. "What happened to your silly Rangers last night?" she'll chide him, as she crosses the street with her white cane. And he'll kid back, "Yeah? They'll still kill your Islanders next week!"

Sports gives her a family—the radio audience of Joe Benigno's 1-to-5:30 a.m. show on WFAN. She calls in regularly to be with them. It's a family she knows, like the floor plan of her apartment, but has never seen: Doris from Rego Park (she's had some health problems) and Bruce from Bayside (he likes cats) and Short Al from Brooklyn (his wife passed away recently).

So that was enough for Miriam—until Botta wouldn't take no for an answer. He offered to pick her up at her apartment and take her to Nassau Coliseum, home of the Islanders. Suddenly, Miriam was about to go to a place where she'd *gone* for 30 years but had never actually *been*. "I think she was a little worried," Botta recalls. "For 30 years she's had this ideal of what it was. She was afraid that actually going there might ruin it for her."

Miriam swallowed hard and went.

As soon as Botta walked her up the steps into the arena, she started noticing all the things that don't get through the little speaker in her radio—"the smell of the hot dogs and potato chips and coffee," she says. "And the fans chanting the same things I chant at home: 'Let's go, Islanders!' It was great to know there are people out there doing the same things I do at home."

She touched the arms of the men whose voices she'd spent thousands of nights with—Howie Rose, the Islanders' TV voice, and John Wiedeman, the radio voice. She sat in the team's sky-high radio booth and tried to make herself believe she was really *there*. "It's so weird to hear the fans' voices *beneath* you," Miriam kept saying that night.

She hugged Islanders legend Clark Gilles. She held the hand of star center Michael Peca, never letting go through the whole conversation. She got to ask superstar scorer Alexei Yashin how to say, "Will you help me cross the street?" in Russian, a phrase that would come in handy in her heavily Russian neighborhood.

She was given an Islanders jersey, much too big, and she wears it almost every day, constantly feeling the embroidered logo with her right hand. She got an ISLANDERS MEDIA sticker to put on her ski jacket. Botta took her into the Nassau Coliseum club, got the crowd's attention and had the host of the postgame radio program introduce the famous "Miriam from Forest Hills, here for her first Islanders game ever!" The patrons gave her a standing O.

So who cared if the Islanders lost 3–2 that night?

Botta saved the best thing for last. He took her onto the ice, where her heroes have fought for 30 years. Miriam bent down and scooped up a handful of the ice shavings carved by the players' skates and brought it to her face.

We forget sometimes what sports mean in this country. We get lost in the players' salaries and the standings and who's going to pay for a new arena. But sometimes, for people like Miriam, the playing of the game is a joy in itself, win or lose. For them, it's a place where a square peg can fit into a round-hole world.

After 30 years, somebody cared enough to look into a cramped little apartment and take her to a part of that world she never dreamed she'd reach—let her smell it and hear it and touch it. And when the night was over, on the ride home, a giddy Miriam turned to Botta and said, "You know, everything was just like I pictured." Botta just grinned.

Some Christmas gifts you keep forever.

Postscript: This is one of my alltime favorites. Miriam was tough and sarcastic and wonderful. When I first walked into that apartment, I saw stacks and stacks of hockey scorebooks. But when I opened them, they were empty. "There's nothing in them!" I told her. And she scoffed, "It's Braille, you bonehead!"

9

He Loves Himself
Barry Much

AUGUST 27, 2001

I N THE SAN FRANCISCO GIANTS' CLUBHOUSE, EVERYBODY KNOWS the score: 24–1. ¶ There are 24 teammates, and there's Barry Bonds. ¶ There are 24 teammates who show up to pose for the team picture, and there's Bonds, who has blown it off for the last two years. ¶ There are 24 teammates who go out on the field before the game to stretch together, and there's Bonds, who usually stretches indoors with his own flex guy.

There are 24 teammates who get on the players' bus at the hotel to go to the park, and there's Bonds, who gets on the bus with the broadcasters, the trainers and the manager who coddles him.

There are 24 teammates who eat the clubhouse spread, and there's Bonds, whose nutritionist brings in special meals for him.

There are 24 teammates who deal with the Giants' publicity man, and there's Bonds, who has his own clubhouse-roving p.r. guy, a freelance artist named Steve Hoskins, who turned down George Will's request for an interview with Bonds because Hoskins had never heard of him.

There are 24 teammates who hang out with one another, play cards and bond, and there's Bonds, sequestered in the far corner of the clubhouse with his p.r. man, masseur, flex guy, weight trainer, three lockers, a reclining massage chair and a big-screen television that only he can see.

Last week, after Bonds hit his 51st home run in a 13–7 win over the Florida Marlins, most of the players stayed to celebrate the victory, and at least one was gone before the press arrived in the clubhouse: Bonds.

"That's Barry," says San Francisco second baseman Jeff Kent. "He doesn't answer questions. He palms everybody off on us, so we have to do his talking for him. But you get used to it. Barry does a lot of questionable things. But you get used to it. Sometimes it rubs the younger guys the wrong way, and sometimes it rubs the veterans the wrong way. You just hope he shows up for the game and performs. I've learned not to worry about it or think about it or analyze it. I was raised to be a team guy, and I am, but Barry's Barry. It took me two years to learn to live with it, but I learned."

If you get the feeling that Kent, who's in his fifth season with San Francisco, wouldn't spit on Bonds if Bonds were on fire, you might be right. Maybe it has something to do with last year, when Kent and Bonds were running neck and neck for the National League MVP award. The week before the award was to be announced, Bonds had a member of his entourage call the commissioner's office to try to find out who had won. We've got to know, said the stooge, because if he's not going to win, he can get out of town.

Perfect! No staying around to congratulate Kent. Or going to the press conference to shake his hand. Just, "If it ain't me, I'm outta here." The commissioner's office didn't know the results of the voting. Kent won.

Someday they'll be able to hold Bonds's funeral in a fitting room. When Bonds hit his 500th home run, in April, only one person came out of the dugout to greet him at the plate: the Giants' batgirl. Sitting in the stands, you could've caught a cold from the freeze he got. Teammates 24, Bonds 1.

Bonds isn't beloved by his teammates. He's not even beliked. He often doesn't run out grounders, doesn't run out flies. If a Giants pitcher gives up a monster home run over Bonds in leftfield, Bonds keeps his hands on his knees and merely swivels his head to watch the ball sail over the fence. He's an MTV diva, only with bigger earrings.

"On the field, we're fine," says Kent, "but off the field, I don't care about Barry and Barry doesn't care about me. [Pause.] Or anybody else."

Bonds will be a free agent after this season, and if he decides to sign elsewhere, will the Giants be devastated? Kent grimaces. "See: Seattle Mariners," he says, walking away.

Bonds is brilliant. He was the best player of the 1990s, and at 37 he's having his most magnificent season, on pace at week's end to break the single-season home run record of 70 and nearly lapping the league in slugging percentage, on-base percentage and walks. He should be the MVP.

But that doesn't mean you have to root for him.

Postscript: Because of this column and a few others, I've become the official clearinghouse for people's horrible encounters with Bonds. I collect them. They'd make Scrooge cringe. Yelling at make-up artists. Flipping off autograph seekers. Screaming at other players. Of course his karma has balanced out nicely. Nobody believes his numbers are clean. He's got more legal headaches than Judge Judy. And he's the most hated ballplayer since Ty Cobb. Couldn't happen to a nicer guy.

10

Strongest Dad
In the World

JUNE 20, 2005

I TRY TO BE A GOOD FATHER. GIVE MY KIDS MULLIGANS. WORK nights to pay for their text messaging. Take them to swimsuit shoots. ¶ But compared with Dick Hoyt, I suck. ¶ Eighty-five times he's pushed his disabled son, Rick, 26.2 miles in marathons. Eight times he's not only pushed him 26.2 miles in a wheelchair but also towed him 2.4 miles in a dinghy while swimming and pedaled him 112 miles in a seat on the handlebars—all in the same day.

Dick's also pulled him cross-country skiing, taken him on his back mountain climbing and once hauled him across the U.S. on a bike. Makes taking your son bowling look a little lame, right?

And what has Rick done for his father? Not much—except save his life.

This love story began in Winchester, Mass., 43 years ago, when Rick was strangled by the umbilical cord during birth, leaving him brain-damaged and unable to control his limbs.

"He'll be a vegetable the rest of his life," Dick says doctors told him and his wife, Judy, when Rick was nine months old. "Put him in an institution."

But the Hoyts weren't buying it. They noticed the way Rick's eyes followed them around the room. When Rick was 11 they took him to the engineering department at Tufts University and asked if there was anything to help the boy communicate. "No way," Dick says he was told. "There's nothing going on in his brain."

"Tell him a joke," Dick countered. They did. Rick laughed. Turns out a lot was going on in his brain.

Rigged up with a computer that allowed him to control the cursor by touching a switch with the side of his head, Rick was finally able to communicate. First words? "Go, Bruins!" And after a high school classmate was paralyzed in an accident and the school organized a charity run for him, Rick pecked out, "Dad, I want to do that."

Yeah, right. How was Dick, a self-described "porker" who never ran more than a mile at a time, going to push his son five miles? Still, he tried. "Then it was me who was handicapped," Dick says. "I was sore for two weeks."

That day changed Rick's life. "Dad," he typed, "when we were running, it felt like I wasn't disabled anymore!"

And that sentence changed Dick's life. He became obsessed with giving Rick that feeling as often as he could. He got into such hard-belly shape that he and Rick were ready to try the 1979 Boston Marathon.

"No way," Dick was told by a race official. The Hoyts weren't quite a single runner, and they weren't quite a wheelchair competitor. For a few years Dick and Rick just joined the massive field and ran anyway, then they found a way to get into the race officially: In 1983 they ran another marathon so fast they made the qualifying time for Boston the following year.

Then somebody said, "Hey, Dick, why not a triathlon?"

How's a guy who never learned to swim and hadn't ridden a bike since he was six going to haul his 110-pound kid through a triathlon? Still, Dick tried.

Now they've done 212 triathlons, including four grueling 15-hour Ironmans in Hawaii. It must be a buzzkill to be a 25-year-old stud getting passed by an old guy towing a grown man in a dinghy, don't you think?

Hey, Dick, why not see how you'd do on your own? "No way," he says. Dick does it purely for "the awesome feeling" he gets seeing Rick with a cantaloupe smile as they run, swim and ride together.

This year, at ages 65 and 43, Dick and Rick finished their 24th Boston Marathon, in 5,083rd place out of more than 20,000 starters. Their best time? Two hours, 40 minutes in 1992—only 35 minutes off the world record, which, in case you don't keep track of these things, happens to be held by a guy who was not pushing another man in a wheelchair at the time.

"No question about it," Rick types. "My dad is the Father of the Century."

And Dick got something else out of all this too. Two years ago he had a mild heart attack during a race. Doctors found that one of his arteries was 95% clogged. "If you hadn't been in such great shape," one doctor told him, "you probably would've died 15 years ago."

So, in a way, Dick and Rick saved each other's life.

Rick, who has his own apartment (he gets home care) and works in Boston, and Dick, retired from the military and living in Holland, Mass., always find ways to be together. They give speeches around the country and compete in some backbreaking race every weekend, including this Father's Day.

That night, Rick will buy his dad dinner, but the thing he really wants to give him is a gift he can never buy.

"The thing I'd most like," Rick types, "is that my dad sit in the chair and I push *him* once."

Postscript: This is another one that people seem to have taped up on their refrigerators or their desk lamps. Rep. John Duncan (R-Tenn.) liked it so much he read it into the Congressional Record. *Video of Team Hoyt on YouTube is now burning its way around the internet. People forward it to me with a note that says, "Dude, you've got to read this." And I write back, "Dude, I wrote it!" The Hoyts are still rolling, by the way. Last I checked, they'd entered 911 different events. They admit the number is more but they're too busy to update the total. Too busy. Ain't it great?*

11

Fairway Robbery

JUNE 24, 2002

YOU KNOW WHAT I'M SICK OF? PREPOSITION GOLF. ¶ I'M talking about all these courses with prepositions in their names—The Experience at Marina Meadows, or The Challenge at the Peaks of Del Frisco. And the more *e*'s in the name, the more it costs you. Play a round at The Linkes at Olde Harbour Centre, and you're in for $200, easy.

As if the names have anything to do with the courses. "Have you gents ever *enjoyed* The Tradition at Elk Crossing before?" the phony-grinned "director of golf" will ask you while he's dinging your AmEx for $175.

"No, pal, we haven't," you want to say. "And I'll bet a week's pay we don't *enjoy* any elk out there, either. Unless the Wal-Mart next door sent them over."

I just wish they'd call some of these courses what they really are. The Lakes at the Landfill. The Fumes of Toxic Acres. VISA Experience at Overmowed Pasture.

It's all so precious. You drive up to a Preposition, and 12 guys in matching plus fours descend on your car like Bombay street urchins, whisking your bag out of your trunk before you can get your shoes out. Next time

49

you see the bag, it's got a pewter tag that's slightly larger than an oxen yoke and can't be removed with an acetylene torch.

You get in a cart that's complete with a water mister, mango-scented towels, personal rake, Italian ball-marking coins, global positioning system and a video on which Arnold Palmer suddenly pops up, saying, "On this hole you'll want to hit a 220-yard high fade over the pond, but be sure to get it on the fourth level to give yourself a chance at a birdie." Yeah, Arnie, like if I hit a 220-yard shot over *agua*, I'm going to be pissed I'm not on the right green level.

But you don't get to play golf yet. First comes the 20-minute lecture from a "course host," who used to be just a marshal before Conglommo Golf bought the joint and started throwing prepositions around. He's always in plus fours and a headset and thinks he's Barney Fife. "Gentlemen, here at Bent Pine Ridge at Pelican Sanctuary we have some very strict guidelines for you to follow." One is, *Don't even think about taking the carts off the cement path, because if you do, you will be shot by one of the course hosts.* Which is another way of saying, "Enjoy your six-hour round, folks."

Then out comes another Plus Four who takes pictures of your group and will have them all laid out for you in a leatherette album when you make the turn. It'll be only $45 a photo, and why not have your first divot framed, too? "We really just want to play golf," you want to scream, "not buy time shares in the Swiss Alps!"

Every now and then the "mobile refreshment center" will drive up, and you'll have to pay $6 for a single "malted beverage," and the "mobile refreshment hostess" will look like you shot her kitten if she doesn't get to keep the $4 change.

The malted beverage will make you have to visit one of the "comfort stations" that are usually miles from the nearest "teeing ground." And there aren't just three teeing grounds anymore, there are six, so that the average chop feels like a florist if he doesn't play from the "bronze" tees, even though the course plays 2,000 yards longer than he can "enjoy."

Every tee shot is a 230-yard carry over absolutely off-limits "native grasslands," which means even if you see your $6 Titleist sitting in there, you can't step three feet in to get the ball. If you had this kind of native grasslands in your front yard, the neighbors would be leaving notes wondering if you'd like to borrow their Weed Whacker.

The front nine is longer than the March of Dimes, and at the turn a Martha Stewart picnic breaks out, in which you end up with an arugula sandwich, a bag of organic beet chips and a $4 iced tea in a bottle designed by I.M. Pei.

And you always end up shooting a radio station—a KOOL 105 or a WAVE 102—and lose four sleeves and have to tip $5 to each of the plus-four urchins who clean your clubs, which only hacks you off worse because you know you never hit any of your freaking shots on the club face anyway.

As you leave, it's everything you can do to keep from flooring your 1984 Taurus through the wooden security arm, across the 2nd and 11th fairways, spinning doughnuts on the 18th green and racing past the director of golf, screaming, "Enjoy that!"

12

White Like Me

FEBRUARY 4, 2002

LOOK HOW WHITE I AM. AM I LAME OR WHAT? CAN'T jump. Can't dance. Can't run. Can't dress. Can't hang. ¶ It's O.K. I know I'm a pathetic White Guy. I'm at peace with it. In fact I laugh about it all the time. I have to. Black athletes today love to make fun of us White Guys.

Last week, for instance, boxer Mike Tyson had a little fun with white reporter Mark Malinowski at Tyson's press conference–cage match with Lennox Lewis. Grabbing his crotch and using his best prison vocabulary, Tyson challenged Malinowski to fight and then accused him of being "scared like a little white p----" because he wouldn't. In American trash talk today that's three put-downs in a row. Little. White. And p----.

Now if a white heavyweight grabbed his crotch and called a black reporter a "little black p----," he'd be spending the rest of his days playing Parcheesi with Al Campanis and Dan Issel. Nobody, though, demanded that Tyson apologize to Malinowski, least of all Malinowski.

Not to worry, it's cool! Last season Toronto Raptors star Vince Carter came onto the court to discover he was being covered by the Minnesota

Timberwolves' Wally Szczerbiak. Carter turned to the Minnesota bench with a smile and said, according to Szczerbiak, "You better get this white guy off me, or I'm going to score 40." (Carter denies referring to Szczerbiak's race.)

Was Carter fined? Suspended? Ordered to spend six weeks in a white-sensitivity workshop? Nah. We're White Guys. What are we going to do, sue?

Sometimes we're not even White Guys. We're White Boys. In his book *Shaq Talks Back*, Shaquille O'Neal wrote, "If you get dunked on by a white boy, you got to come home to your friends and hear it."

Hilarious! Of course it wouldn't be nearly as funny if, say, David Stern wrote in his book, "If you get outnegotiated by a black boy, you got to go to the country club and hear it." He'd be taped naked to the hood of Jesse Jackson's car. Still, was Shaq rocked by scandal? Did principals pull the book out of school libraries? Nah. Because all us crackers know it's true! If we dunk on you, you *really* suck!

Besides, anytime you can slip in the phrase white boy these days, it's just damn funny. Now, if you called Jerry Rice a "black boy" or Ichiro Suzuki a "yellow boy" or Notah Begay a "red boy," you'd be begging spare change at a bus station inside a week. But it's fine. We're the last unprotected race, so bash away!

Some White Guys aren't sure it's all that amusing, like Denver Nuggets forward Raef LaFrentz. "When people call me 'white boy,' I take it as an insult," he says. "It's a negative racial term, just like the n word." However, Dallas Mavericks guard Steve Nash says he finds it funny when black guys tell him, "You're pretty good for a white boy."

"Besides," Nash says, "it's pretty accurate, right?"

See, we White Guys *know* we suck. We hear it all the time. When we hoop, we've got White Man's Disease. When we dance, we've got White Man's Overbite. When we jam, we're just Average White Band. We know if Larry Bird were black, he'd be, as Isiah Thomas said, "just another guy." We know we're supposed to giggle when Charles Barkley says, "See? This is what I hate about white people." He's right! We're all exactly the same!

When ESPN debuted its terrific new talk show, *Pardon the Interruption*, the preview ads promised it "wasn't pretty." To prove it, host Tony Kornheiser said, "We're old. We're fat. We're bald. And we're white." Then his partner Michael Wilbon, who is black, said, "And one of us is blind." Poor Tony.

He's got the big four strikes against him right there. Old. Fat. Bald. And white. Hey, the truth hurts.

We White Guys have faced it. We're wack at most everything. Basically the only thing we dominate now is stuff black people don't have the right clothes to try—lumberjack contests and luge. But we shred documents like nobody's damn business!

We're not mad. We've come to grips with it. Even when we do something good—like the three white firemen who raised the U.S. flag at ground zero—we understand you have to change two of the guys' race to nonwhite when you want to build the statue. Who wants three White Guys hanging around forever?

What, you thought White Guys had *feelings*?

13

Making Up for Lost Time

AUGUST 21, 2006

YOUR BLANK SCREEN MOCKS YOU AND THE TOWER OF unopened mail pulls at your coat, and you wonder why you didn't go into the insurance business. ¶ And you check in on your snoring 19-year-old son, home from college, and he's rounding noon and heading toward one and you wonder how you missed the typhoon that came through his room.

And so you trudge back to your desk and open a letter. And when you've finished, you go down, kiss your son on the forehead and wonder how you ever got so lucky.

Dear Mr. Reilly or whomever might take the time to read this:

I am not much of a writer, but since about 1996 I have wanted to nominate this kid for FACES IN THE CROWD.

I should have started with all the junior golf tournaments he won at ages six to 10. I should have sent in something when he was written up as a golf prodigy in our paper at age 12. I should have sent in something when he got two holes in one in the summer after eighth grade.

I should have nominated him for being a three-time state qualifier and hold-ing most all individual scoring records at his high school.

I should have sent in many of his wrestling accomplishments . . . but I'm having trouble remembering everything.

This young man was my very best friend. We were golfing partners for 16 years. You see, this young man was my son.

He was killed in a motorcycle accident.

So what I am doing to honor him is to nominate Cory Lemke for FACES IN THE CROWD.

Cory's real accomplishments were being the best friend a guy could ask for, the most loving and best son a father could ask for and a truly gentle and loving kid with the greatest smile in these United States.

I don't know how I will cope without him. I hurt so much, and I miss him so much, just to talk to or watch sports together. God, I loved that boy so much!!
Please accept this nomination!!
Mark Lemke—Cory's Father

You call him. He's a 51-year-old truck driver in Sheldon, Iowa. He's on the road four or five days a week, just him and his rig and his sorrow.

Even on the phone, you can tell he's one of those tough guys who's not used to fighting off tears. And you can hear that he's losing.

He tells you how he and Cory played golf together every day they could—"thousands of rounds," he says—kidded each other endlessly and then, when it got dark or cold, played video golf together or watched the Vikings or just shot the bull. How his son gave him 16 shots the last time they played and still took $20 off the old man.

He remembers telling the kid that night, July 7, as Cory left to go to a car show in Hull, "Get some sleep, buddy. You gotta play tomorrow." And later: the phone ringing and the sickening cry in his wife Maud's voice from the kitchen, moaning, "Is he dead?"

He didn't even wait to see what it was, he just sprinted to his car and floored it to Hull. But he couldn't get there fast enough because Cory was as good as dead the second he hit that van. "No brain activity at all," the doc-tor said. Great idea. *Let me test-drive your motorcycle.* No helmet. Kids.

The next morning they unplugged the respirator. On the way home he picked up his cell and played Cory's last message—"Got us a tee time Sunday over at Spencer," Cory says. "Let's leave at 7:30. Gonna kick your butt."

God, that Sunday morning came down hard on the big truck driver. He just sat in his chair, numb, like somebody'd cut off his arms. And Maud walked in, tears pooling in her eyes, holding out the car keys. "You better go," she whispered. "He'd want you to."

And he did. He pulled his two-ton heart out of that chair and mummy-walked through 18 holes, because buddies don't let each other down. And all the way he ached about all the things he never said or did for his son.

And later on he took out his pen and paper and fixed one of them.

Postscript: This is one of those columns that people come up to me, grab me by the shoulders and say, "That one made my cry!" And I always tell them, "You and me both." Honestly, this was the first time I ever cried writing one. I was on an airplane. I got to the part where his wife comes in with the keys and I just lost it. The depth of this man's grief just knifed me. I just started sobbing. Made the poor guy in 3B a little uncomfortable. But some good comes of everything. So many people have said, "I read that and then kissed my kid." And, "I called my son at college and told him how much I loved him." And, "I told all my kids to be careful—because if something were to happen to them, I'd be cut in half like Mark Lemke." And I know what they mean, because I did the same thing.

14

A Survivor's Tale

AUGUST 7, 2006

FIRST GUY TO THE DORM ALWAYS GETS THE BEST ROOM, right? So Dani Alon snagged the sweet second-floor room with the balcony. Building number 2, 31 Connollystrasse. Who was going to mess with Israel's fencing champ? ¶ Soon all the athletes were filing into their rooms—the shooters, the weightlifters, the wrestlers. Alon's event came early in the schedule and he won five of his foil bouts, beating a German, an Argentine, an Irishman, an Italian and a Czech. Life was beautiful at the Munich Olympics.

On the night of Sept. 4, 1972, the whole team went to see the play *Fiddler on the Roof.* At intermission the athletes were invited backstage, where a joyous team picture was taken. Alon was asleep at 4:30 a.m. when a big bang and a lot of shouting snapped him straight up in bed.

"What's that?" asked his 17-year-old roommate, fencer Yehuda Weisenstein.

"Probably some other team celebrating," Alon said. "Go back to sleep."

Twenty minutes later, machine-gun fire next door pierced the wall over Alon's bed. Three of his teammates—two shooters and a wrestler—burst into the room, ashen-faced.

Alon ran to the window in the front bedroom. Below, a man in a white hat was talking to two policemen. "We have killed two already," white hat said. "We have nine more inside. Get the Israeli government on the phone, or we kill everybody." Lying on the pavement, bleeding to death, was the wrestling coach, Moshe Weinberg.

Alon went back and peeked out the rear balcony door. On the balcony to the left, he could see a man with a ski mask and a machine gun. You've seen this man. He became the symbol of Black September, the Palestinian terrorist group that snuck into the Israeli compound in the Olympic Village and stormed buildings 1 and 3. But not 2. For whatever reason, the attackers had passed over number 2.

"What are we going to do?" Weisenstein whispered to Alon.

The shooters from the team had guns and would fire bullets into the head of white hat, then they'd run for it, Alon and his teammates decided. But what would that do but alert the other terrorists that they had missed a building?

The second plan was to creep down the stairs to the living room, go out the sliding glass doors, slip over the fence into the garden and sprint to safety. But they'd surely be spotted by the masked man on the balcony. It would mean some would die. Maybe all.

"We will run [and zig-zag], like slalom skiers," Alon told the others.

With their shoes in their hands, the five took a gulp and—"Wait!" said one of the shooters, mad-eyed. "I must brush my teeth!" And he turned to do just that, before they shook some sense into him.

The stairs were wooden, every creak a possible death sentence. The athletes slid the door open and rushed out. "As I jumped the fence, I was looking at the man in the mask, and he was looking at me," Alon remembers. "For some reason, he didn't shoot. He never shot."

Within hours, the nine Israeli hostages were dead, slaughtered at the airport in a futile rescue attempt featuring, ironically, German police snipers who turned out to be merely weekend competitive shooters.

The next day Alon had the grisly task of going through his dead teammates' rooms and collecting their things. "There were dolls and games everywhere that they had bought to bring back to their families," he remembers. "That was the saddest thing—cleaning all the blood off the toys."

Alon stopped fencing after that. Every new building terrified him. "I always think, Who here wants to murder me?" he says. Nightmares grew long and his temper short. He served in the Israeli air force and loaded bombs on jets during the Yom Kippur wars. And never would he speak of what had happened.

Thirty years later, on a routine business trip to Munich, he took a cab to 31 Connollystrasse. He stood in front of building number 2, watching the residents go in and out, and sobbed.

Finally, the release of Steven Spielberg's brilliant film on the massacre— *Munich*—last year moved him to speak. "Watching it was like déjà vu," he says.

The old fencer is 61 now, and Israel is at war again, and he is sick to death of living by the sword. One of the Black September attackers, Jamal Al-Gashey, is still alive. And if he met him?

"I'd forgive him," Alon says. "He was so young. He was a soldier. I have been a soldier too. We have to make peace. All this bloodshed only leads to more bloodshed."

This weekend Alon will be in Phoenix, opening another international athletic event—the 2006 Maccabi Games.

He will stay in a hotel.

15

Matador in FootJoys

APRIL 15, 2002

WHAT A LOSER PHIL MICKELSON IS. THE CHAMP chump. Gagger Vance. Yeah, so he skis double-black-diamond slopes. And is licensed to fly jets. And cashes more sports book winners than any boiler room full of 1-900 experts. But he has never won a major, and it just pisses you off. He may be 0 for 38 in majors, but he has finished second twice and third three times, and even got beat by a guy who decided to play a 227-yard par-3 in one. And he's ranked No. 2 in the world behind possibly the greatest golfer who's ever lived, but he has never won the Masters, and that just chaps you.

True, he's the one who signs autographs 10 minutes past forever. He's the one with the manners of Jeeves and the charm of Bond, the one who looks more people in the eye than an optometrist. Once, in an all-out monsoon, he stopped the courtesy car he was riding in with his caddie and his wife, ran out in the rain, popped the trunk, got out his golf umbrella and gave it to a homeless guy slumped on a corner. But he has never won the U.S. Open, so screw him.

O.K., he's the guy who unfailingly shows up to face the nastiest questions—all the ones about what a loser he is for beating 154 guys but not 155. He gives his unblinking answers from the heart, even though he knows that they can and will be used against him later. *How bad do you want this Masters, Phil?* "Desperately," he answers. But does it happen? No. So we trot out "desperately" like a mirror to remind him of how he has failed himself.

Oh, he has won golf tournaments. Won 20 times on the PGA Tour. But none of them were the four tournaments some golf writer dreamily referred to as the "grand slam" on a slow column day, so he has failed all of us.

So what if he's a witch who does things to a golf ball that would have had him burned at the stake 300 years ago? So what if he's more fun to watch than demolition derby? So what if he had his layup gene removed at birth, which means he's the matador in FootJoys that golf so badly needs? He has never won the British Open, so he's lamer than Lawrence Welk.

Yeah, the dude's cooler than a penguin's freezer. Plays baccarat in Vegas. Slam-dunked a ball off a tramp at halftime of a Phoenix Suns game. One time he landed a Cessna twin engine with the instruments out. The three other people in the plane practically chewed off their armrests while Mickelson never got a hair out of place. But he has never won the PGA, so he's pure Alpo.

Everything about him torques you off. He has more money than Peru. He married a Suns dancer so gorgeous she'd make a bishop bite his hat, and they have two gorgeous kids, so after 9/11 he just dropped everything to focus on them—and you said he must be yellow.

He's Indiana Jones, the guy who would rather walk around the building's ledge than take the hallway. He loves the juice, needs the action and doesn't care what it costs him. "If I try to just hit fairways with irons, hit the middle of greens, it's no fun," Mickelson says. And so, as at Bay Hill three weeks ago, he'd rather try to punch-cut a choke-down four-iron 180 yards off bark, under limbs and over *agua* than chip out, because the only thing worse than losing is being bored.

So he tries the tightrope with no net, and sometimes his Titleists go gurgle-gurgle, and you rip him a new one, forgetting you had already ripped all the Paycheck Petes who go for the top 10 instead of trying to win.

You don't care that he's the only player out there who will stomp on Tiger's tail, who has punked him four times at groin-shrinkage time. Or that he's one of the few who doesn't suck up to Eldrick, either: He was one of only three players who turned down Tiger's invitation to the Williams World Challenge this year. You only care that he *isn't* Tiger, and that's flat unforgivable.

That he plays golf the way he wants and lives life the way he wants doesn't mean jack. In your book he's a wimp and a wuss until the day he wins a Big One. And on that miraculous Sunday, when the waste suddenly turns to the wonder, what will you say?

My man, Phil!

Postscript: For a kind, talented and funny guy, Phil Mickelson takes more crap than many Port-a-Potties. I've never been able to figure it out. Some people don't like his smile, or his body, or his wife, or his kids running out to hug him. They make up these ridiculous gambling and paternity suit rumors that are never proven and yet will never die. In the clubhouse, the other players call him Carnac because "he has all the answers." But that's not the Mickelson I know. The Mickelson I know is giving and real. He signs autographs for at least 15 minutes every tournament day; he even did it after he committed hari-kari at the U.S. Open at Winged Foot in 2006. One of the best people with the worst reps I've ever covered.

16

Blind Justice

MAY 24, 2004

H EY, CONGRATULATIONS, JAYSON WILLIAMS. ¶ LOOKS like you won't be going to the clink for shooting and killing that limousine driver. All the jury nailed you for was covering up something the jury said wasn't a crime. Neat trick, huh? ¶ You beat the most serious charges. Unless they retry you for the reckless manslaughter thing (the jury was deadlocked) you might only do some house arrest. And since you live in a 31,000-square-foot mansion on a 65-acre lot with two par-3 golf holes, a skeet range and an ATV track—paid for courtesy of the New Jersey Nets—that ain't exactly Leavenworth.

But before you go on with your life, some of us just want to let you know a few things about the man you shot dead and then tried to tar as a suicide.

See, that's the funny thing. Gus Christofi was about as far from suicide that day as a man could be. The day before you blasted him with your shotgun, his sister agreed to cosign a loan for him. Gus was so pumped. He was going to own his first house. At age 55.

Gus's life really didn't begin until about 10 years ago, when he finally beat alcoholism and heroin addiction. He went to a New Jersey rehab center called Freedom House for 18 months and emerged such a changed man that the place hired him as a counselor. Recovering addicts could count on Gus to take the phone call, jump in his beat-up old Plymouth and come over with enough coffee and patience and love to get them through a wicked night.

You should've seen the funeral, Jayson. It was packed. Hundreds of people, many of whom Gus's relatives didn't even know. "I can't even tell you how many people came up to me and said, 'Your uncle saved my life,' " says Anthony Christofi Jr., Gus's nephew. "Or they said, 'Your uncle saved my boy's life.' It was amazing."

How's that for irony? You, a guy whose blood-alcohol level was still over the legal limit eight hours after the shooting, killed a guy who thought he was finally safe from booze. Boy, was he wrong.

Really, life was just about as good as it had ever been for Gus that night. He was sober, reunited with his family and doing great at the limo company. In fact, he was so well-liked there that when the job came up to drive your party from a Globetrotters game to a restaurant, the owner surprised Gus with the trip, seeing as how Gus was such a huge sports fan.

Gus even bought one of those little disposable cameras to take a few pictures. Of course, maybe it wasn't such a Kodak moment when you—as people later testified—made fun of Gus, swore at him, called him a "stoolie" and a "fed," and, when Gus got up to leave the restaurant, told him, "Sit back down and get your shine box, kid." Then you said, "I'm only kidding with you, man." Hilarious.

Gus must have really felt clammy, though, when you got the gun down from the cabinet. Gus hated guns, had hated them since he was a kid and his dad would invite him to go hunting. You can't shoot those rabbits, Dad, he pleaded. You just can't.

Gus would've hated hanging with you, Jayson, since you once allegedly shot your own rottweiler in the head, shot out the tires of a security truck at the Meadowlands and accidentally shot close to New York Jets receiver Wayne Chrebet. Do you realize how many times you mentioned guns in your autobiography? Twenty-five empty shells were also found in your master bedroom, where you kept six guns, four of them loaded.

Maybe, around three that morning, you were only clowning with Gus—

pointing the gun at him as if to say, You again?—and maybe you weren't. But it was for damn sure pointed at Gus when it went off, turning the early hours of Valentine's Day good and red.

The jury called it an "accident," but Gus's nephew Anthony wants to know exactly what the *accident* was. "When Williams got drunk?" Anthony asks. "When he got the gun out of the cabinet? When it went off? To me, if Williams [shoots] a hole in his floor or his ceiling, that's an accident. If the hole is in my uncle's chest, that's reckless."

You ought to know that you left a pretty big hole in Gus's family, too, Jayson. The little kids still cry when they think about their uncle. Gus's niece Maria El Hadidi has nightmares about his blood-soaked shirt. And his relatives all want to spit when they remember some of the things said by the jurors, like the woman who announced, "He didn't have the look of a cold-blooded killer. I didn't see it in his eyes." You know you're in good shape when the prosecutors aren't exactly a Dream Team and the jurors are calling you by your first name and looking at eyes, not evidence, right?

But you know what really makes the family push away their supper plates? This: As Gus lay there bleeding, some witnesses said, the first thing you hollered was, "Oh, my God! My life is over!"

Wrong life, pal.

Postscript: Amazingly, a jury acquitted Williams on the aggravated manslaughter charges, but was deadlocked on reckless manslaughter. He was convicted on four obstruction of justice charges, and the family's wrongful death lawsuit against him was settled out of court. In April of 2006, an appeals court found he can be retried on the reckless manslaughter charge. He made one minor-league basketball comeback, which failed, and has had two business ventures flop. My hope is he goes broke and has to start driving a limo.

17

The Fat of the Land

SEPTEMBER 22, 2003

I S YOUR LITTLE LEAGUER SO FAT HIS BLOOD TYPE IS CHEE-TOS? Do the other kids wait for your Cub Scout to jump in the pool so they can ride the wave? Is it difficult for your six-year-old to play Hide and Seek anymore? ¶ *I see you, Amber! At both ends of the Buick!*

You're not alone. Americans have the fattest kids on earth. Over the last 20 years the number of overweight children in this country has doubled. Soon, if that trend continues, one of every three kids will be obese. I live near an elementary school and see it every day. Chubby little girls are now singing this rope-skipping rhyme:

Georgia, Texas
North Carolina!
I think I'm suff-ring
Acute angina!

WE USED to play Kick the Can every summer night. Now kids play Sit on Your Can, or a game more like Mother May I Finish Off the Double-Stuff

Oreos? "Generation Y," says U.S. surgeon general Richard H. Carmona, "is turning into Generation XL."

We only have each other to blame.

It's you, Mr. Dad, pumping your bike madly while you let your triple-chinned five-year-old lie in the back of his little vinyl bike caboose. He's back there on his cellphone, gorging on marshmallow bunnies. Let him pedal himself!

It's you, Mrs. Elementary School P.E. Instructor, letting policy wonks talk you into replacing sports that actually make a kid sweat—dodgeball, kickball, tag—with "activities" like competitive cup-stacking. Hey, nothing burns off fries like competitive cup-stacking. Can we let them do it in recliners?

It's you, Mr. School Board Member, cutting gym classes to supposedly focus on "literacy." Or reducing gym to one or two times a week. Do you realize about half the states require only a year of high school P.E. or less? Wonderful. Now we've got kids who not only can spell myocardial infarction but also will have one by their 30th birthday.

It's you, Mrs. U.S. Senator, spending hundreds of billions of dollars to check grandmothers for shoe bombs while letting funding for schools shrink to the size of Dick Cheney's heart. Meanwhile, our kids blow up like Macy's floats. It's all part of the No Child Left Behind Except the Ones We Couldn't Get with the Forklift Act.

You want a threat to America? According to the Centers for Disease Control, one in three kids born in 2000 will contract type 2 diabetes—and potentially the heart disease, blindness, asthma, sleep apnea, gall bladder disease and depression that may come with it—because they are obese. This could be the first generation in American history to live *fewer* years than the one that came before it.

At least there's one person who wants to do something about it, and you won't believe who it is—LeBron James. The Cleveland Cavaliers rookie is fast-breaking a campaign, sponsored by Nike, to get kids off the PlayStation and back on the playground. He's visiting 47 schools in seven cities and donating sports equipment, getting courts and school yards resurfaced, and paying for instructors who think kids ought to play something other than Capture the Flab. It took a 19-year-old to say, "Uh, I don't mean to say anything, but your first-grader just got mistaken for a tollbooth."

If a kid can do something about it, why can't we? Let's all of us—every parent—make a vow to. . . .

• Stop jumping up and driving the kids three blocks to their friends' house. Let them take that cobweb-covered contraption in the garage. It's called a bike.

• Watch what your kids are jamming down their throats. When I was a kid, a fast-food soda was 12 ounces. Now it's 32. In the last 20 years hamburgers have grown by 23%. And so have our children. Thanks, McDonald's. You supersized *us*.

• Stop treating the kid like the Little Prince. "You wouldn't believe the signed excuses kids bring in to get out of gym," says Rich Wheeler, who teaches seventh-grade P.E. in La Cañada, Calif. "'My kid has a sore thumb.' . . . 'She's got a bruise.' . . . 'He was up late.' Parents are escape artists for their kids!"

• Pull fast-food carts and candy machines and exclusive-deal soda contracts out of the schools. One third of all public high schools sell fast food. Meanwhile, fewer and fewer schools teach home ec anymore, so kids have no idea what a healthy meal is. We've raised an entire generation that thinks ketchup packets are a food group.

• Turn off the cathode-ray tubes once in a while. The average kid spends *5½ hours* per day in front of a TV, a video-game monitor or a computer. Our kids have the strongest thumbs in the world. It's the rest of their bodies that jiggle like a San Andreas Jell-O factory.

We've got to do something—and quick. Out my window the kids are starting another round of Hot Potato.

Only they've got forks.

Postscript: It's only getting worse. Now schools are banning "tag" and other chase games on the playground because of "liability and self-esteem issues." Oh, no! Alexis is it! Summon the school psychiatrist!

18

Saved by the Deep

JANUARY 10, 2005

W HEN WARREN AND JULIE LAVENDER SURFACED
from their first-ever certified scuba dive on the
day after Christmas, they pulled off their masks,
looked at each other and said, "That sucked." ¶
Then Warren threw up. ¶ The dive had sucked because the water was
choppy on the surface and the current was hellaciously strong at the bottom
and, for some reason, the fish were all hiding in crevices. The Lavenders
happily climbed into the dive boat for the half-hour trip back to the beach,
where glorious Alka-Seltzer awaited.

On the way Julie noticed something weird in the water. "Somebody's wallet," she said, pointing at it. Then came a chair. Then a coconut tree.

Then Warren noticed something worse—a horrified look on the captain's
face. He spun around to see that the beach wasn't there anymore. "That's
when we knew something was very, very wrong," Warren remembers. "That
beach had to be 150 meters wide, and it was just . . . gone." So were the
docks. Waves were crashing straight into the hotels, some of which caved in
like sandcastles.

The Lavenders had unknowingly scuba-dived through a tsunami, which was now hammering their vacation spot, the resort town of Beruwala on the western coast of Sri Lanka, gobbling up homes and boats and people, pulling them into the Indian Ocean and then flinging them back at the town again and again, killing hundreds.

Suddenly, it all made sense to the novice divers, the way they'd had to fight the torrential current at the bottom. "It was like a hurricane underwater," is how Warren describes it. Twenty meters below the surface, his mask was ripped off. It was all they could do to hold on to coral to avoid being sucked away. "We were hanging parallel to the ocean floor," Julie says. Warren is 6' 4", 280, but Julie is only 5'3". "I was terrified Julie would lose her grip and be swept away forever," he recalls. "I remember thinking, Gee, I could really learn to hate this sport."

They eventually made it to the guide rope and climbed to the sunny surface, still oblivious to the fact that they'd survived a tsunami that had been moving at up to 500 mph on its way to mauling the coastlines of Indonesia, Malaysia, Thailand, India, Sri Lanka and Somalia, moving entire islands and killing more than 140,000 people in one of the worst natural disasters of our time.

As the boat neared the dive center, Warren says, "everything that the tidal wave had wrecked going ashore was now in the wave coming back at us. The dive instructor told the captain to turn the boat and outrun it, but I said, 'Screw that! Get us on shore!' Because with all the debris flying around in the water, I didn't think we'd survive."

Somehow the baby-faced captain steered the boat through the whirling chaos. He saw a house balcony that had been ripped away and decided to use it as a makeshift dock. Turned out it was the balcony from the dive instructor's guest house. She watched, stunned, as the house collapsed, her new Sea-Doo lit out to sea and footlong angel fish flopped on the lawn.

The Lavenders jumped from the boat to the balcony, then ran in bare feet over smashed glass and brick for higher ground. When they hit the street, the couple saw two policemen running toward them, followed by hundreds of wild-eyed locals. Another wave was coming. The Lavenders ducked into a sturdy three-story concrete building and made it to the top floor as the water rearranged the lobby.

Later, they tried to walk back to their hotel but couldn't find it. Half a kilometer from the shore they passed boats marooned on sidewalks. The Lavenders spent the night on the cement floor of a hilltop home that the owner had opened to the stranded. The next day Warren found the now unemployed dive boat captain wandering the streets, picked the guy up, hugged him and gushed, "You saved our lives!" Then he handed him every rupee in his pocket.

Two days after the tsunami the Lavenders paid a man triple the usual rate to drive them to the capital city of Colombo for their flight back to Kuwait City, where the Canadian couple are schoolteachers. As they drove, only emergency and relief vehicles passed them going the other way. The driver wept.

"It seemed so unfair that we could simply buy our way out of a situation," Warren e-mailed to friends later, "and so many others have no choice but to stay."

Looking back, they realize how preposterously lucky they were to just that week have taken up a sport that wound up saving their lives. "If we hadn't been diving," says Julie, "we'd have been lying on that beach."

"Who would've thought," concludes Warren, "that we were in the safest place of all? Underwater."

Postscript: The Lavenders are intrepid. They returned to Sri Lanka on the exact same day a year later to dive the same spot with the same company. As they walked up to the dive shop, the staff ran up and hugged and kissed them. Since they were separated by the tsunami, the staff didn't know if they'd lived or died. It was a nerve-racking dive, Warren reports, but uneventful, except for a trigger fish who decided to take a bite out of his fin.

19

Excuse Me for Asking

JULY 8, 2002

I T WAS A SIMPLE, STRAIGHTFORWARD QUESTION FOR CHICAGO Cubs bomber Sammy Sosa. ¶ "You've said if baseball tests for steroids, you want to be first in line, right?" I asked him last Thursday at his Wrigley Field locker.

"Yes," Sosa replied.

"Well, why wait?" I said.

"What?"

I wrote down the name and phone number of LabCorp, which has a diagnostic test lab in Elmhurst, Ill., 30 minutes from Wrigley. I told him what LabCorp had told me: If any person wants to be tested for steroids, all he has to do is have his physician give a written order and bring in a blood or urine sample. The lab could have the results back within 10 days.

Sosa looked at the piece of paper as if it were a dead rat.

"Why wait to see what the players' association will do?" I continued. "Why not step up right now and be tested? You show everybody you're clean. It'll lift a cloud off you and a cloud off the game. It'll show the fans that all these great numbers you're putting up are real."

Sosa's neck veins started to bulge.

I tried to tell him how important I thought this was. How attendance is headed for the cesspool. A former MVP told SI that 50% of the players are on steroids. The fans are starting to look at every home run record the way people look at Ted Koppel's hair. And there's the threat of a strike. Something good has to happen. What could be more positive than the game's leading home run hitter's proving himself cleaner than Drew Carey's fork?

Sosa looked at me as if I were covered in leeches.

"Why are you telling me to do this?" he said. "You don't tell me what to do."

I tried to explain that I wasn't *telling* him to do it, I was just wondering if he didn't think it would be a good move for him and the game.

"You're not my father!" he said, starting to yell. "Why do you tell me what to do? Are you trying to get me in trouble?"

I asked how he could get in trouble if he wasn't doing anything wrong.

"I don't need to go nowhere," he growled. "I'll wait for the players' association to decide what to do. If they make that decision [to test], I will be first in line."

But didn't he think a star stepping forward now, without being told to be tested. . . .

"This interview is over!" He started looking around for security. "Over, motherf-----!"

(Note to young sportswriters: Always make your steroid question your *last* question.)

Plenty of people doubt Sosa is on steroids. He has never missed more than six games in any of the last five seasons. Most nukeheads come apart like Tinkertoy houses.

A whole lot more wonder: Here's a guy who went nine years without ever hitting more than 40 home runs. In the last four seasons he's hit 66, 63, 50 and 64. Here's a guy who was once a skinny, 165-pound, jet-footed Texas Ranger. Now he's a bulky, 230-pound Mr. Olympus.

"This was because of my tooth," he had said earlier in the interview. "When I first came to Texas [in 1989], I had a bad wisdom tooth. The doctor discovered this, and he fixed it. After that, I start to eat much better."

What'd he eat, Fort Worth?

Sosa also explained that the extra muscle and added girth came from feverish weightlifting, not a feverish pharmacist.

"I have a gym in my house [in the Dominican Republic]," he said. "I work out every day, seven days a week. Sometimes at two or three in the morning."

He said the media's suspicions have hurt him. "They think everybody is guilty," he said. "They judge me, but they don't know me."

That's about when I offered up my brilliant public relations maneuver of having himself tested. Soon we were discussing my relationship with my mother.

Maybe Sosa feels he would undermine his union's bargaining power if he had himself tested. But when I asked him if that's why he didn't want to do it, he again mentioned, rather crisply, "You're not my father."

No, but if I were, I'd tell him to get tested. And I'd say it to Barry Bonds and anybody else who says he cares about the game. If they've got nothing to hide, why wait?

True, it would take some large *cojones*. Of course, if these players are on steroids, they lost those a long time ago.

Postscript: Every now and then, you wake up to find yourself in the tumble-dry cycle of life and this column put me in it for weeks. Fine by me. I stick to my original story: I actually thought Sosa would jump at the chance to prove his numbers real, the players' union be damned. But he freaked out. Does an innocent man do that? His reaction just made people want to look harder. Once drug testing came to baseball—weak as it was— Sosa shrunk like a cashmere swimsuit. He was run out of Chicago—where he made more enemies than Bartman—flopped in Baltimore, and didn't even play in 2006. He was not especially missed. Says a former Cub teammate, Sosa was "the worst teammate you could have."

20

Revving Up the Grapes

MAY 30, 2005

WE NASCAR FANS WILL GOBBLE UP ENTIRE Wal-Marts full of crap as long as it ties us to the sport we love—like talking bottle openers, driver-faced wall clocks and that home decorating essential, *Star Wars Episode III* Pepsi Jeff Gordon replica car hoods. ¶ But NASCAR wine?

Richard Childress, the longtime team owner whom the late, great Dale Earnhardt once raced for, has started a winery. No, seriously. One of the biggest names in NASCAR is bottling Chardonnay, Merlot and Cabernet Sauvignon. He's even going to make special-edition wines commemorating his team's wins.

Now, I think you'll find this little wine amusing. Notice the subtle hints of oak, butter and Pennzoil.

Do those words—*NASCAR wine*—go together? Isn't that like debutante wrestling?

The mind reels. How is NASCAR wine served? When you're ready to open a bottle, do four guys come running up, jack up your chair, yank your head back, pull your chin down, stick the end of one of those long gas cans in your mouth and pour it into you? All in 14 seconds?

Can't you just see it? You're at a restaurant that serves Childress wines, and the sommelier comes up in a hat, headphones and fireproof suit. He pours you just a taste for your approval. You swirl, sip and nod yes. And the guy hollers, "Get 'er done!"

Don't know if you've noticed, Richard, but we NASCAR fans are not generally seen reading *Wine Spectator* during time trials. We enjoy Pabst on our Frosted Flakes.

Merle, Daytona's on, so why doncha bring over a bag a pork rinds, maybe some fried Twinkies, and what about a nice bottle of Pinot Grigio to go with it?

In fact, until now there had only been one NASCAR whine: "These restrictor plates are killin' racin'! "

Really, how good would your wine have to be to please our palates? *Now this is the good stuff! It's been aging ever since Talladega.*

Hey, Richard, they better not find out about this in Darlington. They'll think you're French! They'll storm your garage with shovels and torches! My Lord, they nearly stone Jeff Gordon to death just for combing his hair!

Childress ain't scared. He's got the Fast Track Wine Club, and at his online store you can buy Finish Line gift baskets 'cause wine and stock cars both rely on good finishes.

But isn't Childress turning his back on NASCAR's roots? After all, this is a sport that began with moonshiners outrunning cops on the back roads of the Carolina hills, right? Now a NASCAR icon is selling unassuming bottles of Cabernet?

Put it this way, you think Richard Petty would've ever won Daytona, stood on top of his car and taken a sip of Syrah to celebrate? He'd sooner stand in front of the world and admit he needs a pill to get sexually aroused. (Oops. Sorry, Mark Martin.)

The Childress winery is on 65 acres north of Charlotte, with a faux Tuscan villa and a gift shop. The other night they entertained a pack of sportswriters and sportscasters. Childress even had three NASCAR rides out front, including the Intimidator's ol' black number 3. They've started having jazz concerts there, too. Somewhere, Billy Carter weeps.

In fact, there's a tour this Saturday that stops at Richard Childress Racing headquarters, the Childress winery and then the Dale Earnhardt Tribute Center down the road in Kannapolis. Tipsy NASCAR fans at Dale's memorial? They'll hug his bronze statue so hard you'll need a tow chain to get 'em off!

But wouldn't you love to tour that winery? "We run a very streamlined operation here at Childress," Lurleen, your tour guide, would say. "Notice that the mechanics working on the engine have their shoes and socks off and are stomping grapes at the same time. In this way, we can pass the savings on to you!"

You'd be standing at the tasting bar when two guys in overalls started arguing in the back room. *"Dammit, Luther! I told you 100 times! The Chardonnay goes in the blue barrel and the antifreeze in the green!"*

(Spit.)

Actually, I had a glass of the Childress Merlot the other night, and I have to admit—it was pretty good. The vintner at Childress, Mark Friszolowski, says winning some wine competitions is "key" to the label's success now. If he does, you think he'll talk to the press the way Childress's drivers do?

I'm not sure what happened in barrel 3. I think Jimmy mighta cut me or I mighta cut Jimmy, but she poured smoother'n a gravy sandwich after that, and I just wanna thank my Fruit of the Loom grape-pickin' team, my Listerine spit squad and, acourse, God.

And wouldn't it be wonderful if then Friszolowski started to drive off but suddenly veered onto the front lawn of the American Wine Society headquarters and started spinning donuts?

Postscript: It got worse. After the wine, NASCAR came out with its own cologne. Hell, ain't that what STP's for?

21

What, Me Panic?

NOVEMBER 24, 2003

S O, WHAT WOULD YOU SAY, TREMBLING AT THE EDGE of an open airplane door at 13,500 feet with a videographer waiting on a ledge outside the plane and 10 world-class jumpers harrumphing for you to get out of their way, and then the 225-pound brute you're attached to hollers in your ear, *"Are you ready to skydive?"*

"No, I'm not ready to skydive!" you want to say. "I'm about to suffer a premature deployment in my boxers and jettison my lunch here! Every other flight I've ever been on, they wouldn't let us off the plane until the jetway was within two inches of the door, and you want me to step out into the bottomless blue sky? I'd sooner floss crocodiles, thanks."

But how do you tell the U.S. Army Parachute Team—the legendary freaking Golden Knights—*that*?

How do you explain that everybody you've talked to and everything you've read and everything you've feared since you agreed to do this has knocked on the inside of your eyelids as you tried to sleep and screeched, *Don't do it, you dumpster brain!*

"You'll hardly be able to breathe at that altitude," my family said. "You could pass out. Or get knocked unconscious by a bird."

"I've heard that guys break their sternums on their chins when the parachute opens," my golf buddy said. "*If* it opens."

"Do you have a death wish?" my agent said.

Even the man I was trusting my life to, the man I was attached to by strap and hook and faith, my 42-year-old tandem master, Sgt. 1st Class Billy Van-Soelen, was no help. On the way up he kept slapping his wrist altimeter and holding it up to his ear, as if the damn thing wasn't working.

Very funny, Billy.

And when I worried aloud about how much protection the headgear was going to give me in a crash (seeing that it resembled Gerald Ford's leather football helmet), Billy replied, "Oh, no help at all. But it'll keep the skull and brains together for the investigators."

Hilarious.

These poor guys had been answering all my paranoid questions for two days. We pull the chute at 5,500 feet and, no, nobody's ever seen a bird higher than 5,000. Yes, you'll be able to breathe. No, the opening of the chute won't hurt—"It'll be as soft as huggin' a fat lady," Billy said. And yes, those *are* Army medics in that truck next to the landing zone, but it's just procedure.

Besides, they said, you're with the Army's Golden Knights, one of the greatest skydiving teams in the world, winners of 16 national and world championships, and they've never had a fatality in 3,000 tandem jumps.

"O.K.," I panted, as we climbed higher over Fort Bragg, N.C., and I grew whiter than Edgar Winter, "I trust you guys, but what about the pilot? What if he gets knocked out? There's only one pilot on this plane! We'd all be dead!"

And that's when the commander of the Golden Knights, Lieut. Col. Paul MacNamara, leaned in and said simply, "Rick, we'd just jump."

Oh, right.

And so, as we duckwalked to the door in that freezing fuselage and Billy perched us on the doorsill of death and popped the question, "Are you ready to jump?" I said what you would have said, which was, "No!"

And Billy jumped anyway. Taking you-know-who with him.

A friendly piece of advice for those of you planning to jump at an altitude the Chicago-Moline commuter plane never reaches: Do not leave your mouth open. Every drip of saliva you ever had or will consider having will be blown dry instantly. You will be more dry-mouthed than Dennis Rodman in confession.

But you can't help it. Because everybody's falling at the same speed, you lose the sense of falling and gain the sense of flying. Your mouth has to flop open to scream with numb-founded delight. You *are* Clark Kent.

We free-fell 8,500 feet, about the equivalent of jumping off Half Dome. We free-fell for 60 seconds, which is longer than it takes to order, receive and pay for a Whopper combo meal. We laughed, screamed and spun 720s, all at 120 mph. I fell like an octopus from a cliff, arms and legs flailing madly. And behind me poor Billy was trying to keep us from flipping upside down like a fat Wallenda.

I don't know how it is in our nation's incarceration facilities, but it's the most fun *I've* ever had with a man clamped on my back.

And somewhere between flashing the Wu-Tang sign at the video camera and hugging the fat lady, I realized that skydiving with the Golden Knights is not a death wish at all. It's a life wish.

Still, I had one small thing to discuss with Billy after we came to our sweet stand-up landing.

"Billy!" I asked, laughing and peeling the billowing chute off my head. "Didn't you hear me say, 'No!'"

"Ohhhh!" Billy grinned. "I thought you said, 'Go!'"

Love that lug.

Postscript: That was amazing. That was unforgettable. That was thrilling. But it's kind of like getting married. It's great fun, but you'd really like to do it just once. Next time I want to hug a fat lady, I'll call Aretha Franklin.

22

Picking Up Butch

MARCH 10, 2003

THE BEST COLLEGE TRADITION IS NOT DOTTING THE *I* at Ohio State. It's not stealing the goat from Navy. Or waving the wheat at Kansas. ¶ It's Picking Up Butch at Middlebury (Vt.) College. ¶ For 42 years Middlebury freshman athletes have been Picking Up Butch for football and basketball games. It's a sign-up sheet thing. Carry the ball bags. Gather all the towels. Pick Up Butch.

Basketball players, men and women, do it during football season. Football players do it during basketball season. Two hours before each home game, two freshmen grab whatever car they can get and drive a mile off campus to the tiny house where 56-year-old Butch Varno lives with his 73-year-old mother, Helen, who never got her driver's license. And they literally Pick Up Butch, 5' 3" and 170 pounds, right off his bed.

They put him in his wheelchair and push him out of the house, or one guy hauls him in a fireman's carry. They pile him into the car, cram the wheelchair into the trunk, take him to the game and roll him to his spot in the mezzanine for football games or at the end of the bench for basketball.

82

Butch always smiles and says the same thing from the bottom of his heart: "CP just sucks." Cerebral palsy. While his fondest dream has always been to play basketball, it'll never happen. There is little that he can physically do for himself.

"At first, you're a little nervous; you're like, I don't know," says freshman wide receiver Ryan Armstrong. "But the older guys say, 'We did it when we were freshmen. Now you go get him. It's tradition.' So me and my buddy got him the first week. He's pretty heavy. We bumped his head a couple of times getting him into the car. He's like, 'Hey! Be careful!' But he loves getting out so much that afterward you feel good. It's fun to put a smile like that on somebody's face."

And the kids don't just Pick Up Butch. They also Keep Butch Company. Take Butch to the Bathroom. Feed Butch. "He always likes a hot dog and a Coke," says 6' 8" Clark Read, 19, a power forward. "It's kind of weird at first, sticking a hot dog in his mouth. The trick is to throw out the last bite so he doesn't get your fingers."

Thanks to 42 years of freshmen, Butch hardly ever misses a Middlebury game. Not that he hasn't been late.

"One day this year, the two guys were calling me on their cell," says Armstrong, "and they're going, 'We can't find Butch!' And I'm like, 'You lost Butch? How can you lose Butch?' Turns out they just couldn't find his house."

Nobody at Middlebury remembers quite how Picking Up Butch got started, but Butch does. It was 1961. He was 14, and his grandmother, a housekeeper at the dorms, wheeled him to a football game. It started snowing halfway through, and afterward she couldn't push him all the way back home. A student named Roger Ralph asked them if they needed a ride. Ever since then, Butch has been buried in the middle of Middlebury sports.

Sometimes he gives the basketball team a pregame speech, which is usually, "I love you guys." He holds the game ball during warmups and at halftime until the refs need it. He is held upright for the national anthem. Once in a while, just before tip-off, they put him in the middle of the players' huddle, where they all touch his head and holler, "One, two, three, together!" When the action gets tense, the freshmen hold his hands to keep them from flailing. After the games some of the players come back to the court and help him shuffle a few steps for exercise, until he collapses back in his chair, exhausted. Then it's home again, Butch chirping all the way.

And it's not just the athletes at Middlebury who attend to him. Butch is a campus project. Students come by the house and help him nearly every day. Over the years they taught him to read, and then last year they helped him get his GED. Somebody got him a graduation cap and gown to wear at the party they threw in his honor. During his thank-you speech, Butch wept.

"These kids care what happens to me," Butch says. "They don't have to, but they do. I don't know where I'd be without them. Probably in an institution."

But that's not the question. The question is, Where would they be without Butch?

"It makes you think," says Armstrong. "We're all young athletes. Going to a game or playing in a game, we take it for granted. But then you go Pick Up Butch, and I don't know, it makes you feel blessed."

Now comes the worst time of the year—the months between the end of the basketball season, last week, and the start of football in August. "It stinks," Butch says. He sits at home lonely day after day, watching nothing but Boston Red Sox games on TV, waiting for the calendar pages to turn to the days when he can be one, two, three, together again with the students he loves.

On that day the door will swing open, and standing there, young and strong, will be two freshmen. And, really, just seeing them is what Picking Up Butch is all about.

Postscript: Nothing's changed at Middlebury. The freshman still pick up Butch, and he's always waiting. The only difference now is that they're carrying a semifamous person. ESPN picked up on this column, did a feature on it, and won an Emmy. That's about the third they've won following up on one of my columns. Do I get a card? A thank you? A free plate of wings at ESPN Zone? Nope.

23

Spittin' Image

MARCH 18, 2002

I S THERE ANYTHING MORE COLORFUL THAN SPRING TRAINING? The lush green grass? The rich honey infield? The cancerous white lesions forming inside the players' tobacco-caked lips? ¶ Hey, kids! Time to start imitating your favorite major leaguer by cramming tobacco in your mouth, spitting brown streams on your uniform and giving yourself 50 times the chance to get oral cancer as kids who grow up not chewing!

Everybody sing, *Take me out to the graveyard. . . .*

It's so funny, it's sick. A player can't smoke on the field or in the dugout, yet he can chew or dip during the game, even though using spit tobacco for 30 minutes provides the same amount of nicotine as four cigarettes. Can you imagine every player who chews or dips having four cigarettes sticking out of his mouth instead?

The spit tobacco industry likes to call its products smokeless tobacco. It wants us to hear "smokeless" and think "harmless." But half of the people who get cancer from using smokeless tobacco die within five years of being diagnosed.

85

And it's not just baseball. Golfers on the PGA Tour are giving themselves fat lips. David Duval likes to put in a big pinch after a birdie. Rodeo riders will forget their horse before their Skoal. Girl athletes are loading up, too. They pack it in their armpits and their vaginas. They also poke little pinholes between their toes and pack it in there. "In 30 seconds," says Neil Romano of the National Spit Tobacco Education Program (NSTEP), "the rush hits their head." And no unsightly prom dress stains!

Spit tobacco is banned on the college and minor league levels of baseball, but in the majors it's *Welcome to the big leagues, Rook! Let's get you started on a nice big hole in your lip!* The players' association says any attempt by owners to control tobacco use would be a collective bargaining issue. They will defend to the death their members' right to die.

Of 2,000 minor leaguers examined last year by dentists retained by NSTEP, 300 had lesions inside their mouths, including 21 that appeared cancerous or precancerous. NSTEP also says that one in 10 high school boys is using spit tobacco. I did when I was a kid, too. Nearly everybody on my high school baseball team chewed. We'd sit in the cafeteria, filling up Big Gulp cups with our great expectorations. We bet a kid named Bullet Bob 50 bucks he wouldn't drink a full cup. He did it. Made like a bullet heading for the bathroom, too.

When you find out what chew can do to your face, it'll make you want to hurl. Former major league outfielder Bill Tuttle chewed until he lost his teeth, his taste buds, his right cheekbone, his hearing and, finally, his life.

Umpire Doug Harvey worked the bigs with a cheek full of chew for 31 years. He retired with a lump in his throat—not from emotion but from the chaw. He had 60 radiation treatments, dropped from 205 pounds to 145 and fed himself cans of Ensure through a straw-sized hole in his breast bone just to stay alive. Recovered, he's now told 156,070 school kids to stay off spit tobacco.

People who've been through both say quitting spit tobacco is twice as hard as quitting cigarettes. Ask Arizona Diamondbacks righthander Curt Schilling, co-MVP of last year's World Series. Four years ago doctors removed a precancerous lesion on the inside of his lower lip, and he can't quit dipping. His New Year's resolution was to quit. He lasted three days. His father died of lung cancer and his wife just spent a year battling it, and he *still* can't quit. "It's so unbelievably hard," says Schilling, who has tried sunflower seeds, gum, nicotine patches, hypnosis and counseling. "I've got to quit—I want to see my kids grow up, and I want them to see me with a full face—but I haven't been able to."

These are big, tough guys getting whipped by a little tin can. Schilling's teammate Greg Colbrunn can't stop either. "I've tried," he says. "I wish I'd never started." Raves teammate Brian Anderson, also a dipper, "It's dirty, it's filthy, and your breath reeks." *Hey, where'd all the groupies go?*

Ads for spit tobacco are everywhere, including in this magazine. The players' association allows its members to use spit tobacco in front of millions of kids. You've heard of National Smoke Out Day. Somebody needs to start a National Chew Out Day. Anybody dipping in front of kids gets chewed out but good.

Then again, maybe Bullet Bob hit on the best way of all to quit. You spit it, you chug it.

Postscript: Guess whose full-page ad ran next to my column the very next week? Copenhagen chewing tobacco.

24

Out of Touch with My Feminine Side

APRIL 8, 2002

YOU THINK IT'S HARD COACHING IN THE FINAL FOUR? You think it's tough handling 280-pound seniors, freshmen with agents, athletic directors with pockets full of pink slips? ¶ Please. Try coaching seventh-grade girls. After working with boys for 11 years, I helped coach my daughter Rae's school basketball team this winter. I learned something about seventh-grade girls: They're usually in the bathroom.

In one tight spot I was looking around madly for my best defensive guard to send in. "Where is she?" I yelled.

"In the bathroom, crying," our little guard in the blue rectangular glasses said. "Her friends kicked her out of their group today."

Worse, when one girl ran to the bathroom crying, three others automatically followed to console her, followed by three others to console *them*, followed by three others who didn't really want to go but were sucked in by seventh-grade-girl gravitational pull. This would always leave just me and the girl in the blue rectangular glasses, who would slurp on her Dum-Dum and shrug.

Students at Rae's small school are required to go out for at least one sport a year, and 11 girls came out for basketball. But you never had the idea the game was more important in their lives than, say, Chap Stick.

For instance we had a forward who never stopped adjusting her butterfly hair clips, even during our full-court press. Before the opening tip-off of our first game, she came back from the center-court captains' meeting and announced, "O.K., the ref said whoever wins the tip thingy gets to go toward that basket."

Well, that *would* be an interesting rule.

Another difference between boys and girls: Girls have many questions. Our team meetings were sometimes longer than our practices. Apparently girls use team meetings as a chance to process feelings, whereas boys use team meetings as a chance to give each other wedgies.

During our first meeting we had long, emotional deliberations over what our huddle cheer would be and whether we should wear matching bracelets. Then one of our best dribblers stood up, took a deep breath and said, "I have an announcement. I am *not* going to bring the ball up this year, because last year Sherry got yelled at by everybody because she didn't pass them the ball, and I don't want to get yelled at." *As if!*

During one game our best rebounder slammed the ball down and stomped off the court. "Everybody's yelling my name, and I'm sick of it!" she said, and ran to the bathroom—followed by the mandatory nine other girls. I looked at the little guard in the blue rectangular glasses, who popped her Dum-Dum out of her mouth and said, "Don't worry, Coach. She's having her period."

You think Red Auerbach ever had to deal with this stuff?

Coaching girls was fun. It was rewarding. It was awkward. When they came off the court, it was difficult to know how to give them their "good job" pat. On the. . . . Nope. On the. . . . Nope. I always ended up just tapping them lightly on the top of the head. But not so I messed up their butterfly hair clips.

One thing about our team: We were always polite. One time my tallest and gentlest player tried to block a shot and accidentally hit the shooter on top of the head. Our player covered her mouth in horror with both hands, enabling the other girl to drop in a layup. "I thought I hurt her!" our player explained. I believe that started my facial tic.

We lost worse than Michael Dukakis. We got creamed our first eight games, losing one 23–2 and another 19–1. Yet the girls were over it the second the games ended. (Quite often, in fact, they were over it in the third quarter.) Afterward they headed to the one place they loved to be together—the bathroom.

Finally, in our ninth game, all heaven broke loose. For the first time we hit the cutter for a layup. Our shooting guard hit three running 15-footers. We hadn't even hit a 15-foot *pass* to that point. We came from behind and won 16–15 in a shootout, capped by the little guard in the blue rectangular glasses setting the most beautiful pick to free up the player who made the winning layup.

In all my years of coaching, I never felt more giddy than after that win. In the delirious celebration, I grabbed the shoulders of the little girl in the blue rectangular glasses and yelled, "That was the greatest pick I've ever seen!"

And she screamed, "What's a pick?"

Postscript: I don't know of a single girl on that team who went on to play basketball after middle school, though plenty went on to other sports. I see them now and again. One day I was getting some pictures developed at Rite Aid when the young woman behind the counter said, "Don't I know you?" We rummaged through each other's lives until it suddenly hit her. She shrieked, "You coached us in basketball!" It was the girl with the blue rectangle glasses, much taller now and with Yoko Ono glasses. She said she writes poetry these days for an underground goth magazine. I wonder if the whole staff follows her into the bathroom.

25

Ain't It Grand!

APRIL 16, 2001

A GRAYBEARD AND A WOMAN IN A LARGE RED VISOR were under the old oak tree at Augusta National Golf Club on Sunday afternoon, hoping to say hello to their hero, Tiger Woods, before the biggest round of his life. Suddenly, the clubhouse door burst open like a bad Western, and two security guards came barreling out, hollering, "Make a hole!"

Behind them strode Woods, with a look in his eyes that could have wilted titanium. He blew past the fans, not seeing the graybeard stick out his hand or hearing the woman in the visor say, "Good luck, Tiger!" They were a little disappointed, but no less in love with him. They were Nike chairman Phil Knight and Tiger's mother, Tida.

Hey, the man who's paying him $100 million and his own mother be damned—Tiger had things to do, and he went straight from that clubhouse door and did them, namely, making all our jaw muscles lose their grip and knocking off the unthinkable Grand Slam. O.K., you say it isn't the Grand Slam. But why whine about what it isn't? Why not wallow for a while in what it is?

Woods's Sweet Sweep is the most amazing feat we've seen in sports since 1920, when Babe Ruth hit more home runs than every American League team except his New York Yankees. Woods's Mod Quad is the single greatest achievement in golf history, and I don't want to hear another word about Bobby Jones in 1930. You go over to Haggis-on-Bumford and beat three sheep and two guys named Nigel in the British Amateur, you ain't within 1,000 kilometers of winning a fourth major in a row in 2001.

And don't give me any of that "the competition isn't as good now" drivel. Do you realize that David Duval's 14-under-par 274 would've won 59 of the 65 Masters and put him in a playoff in two others? Duval, Phil Mickelson and Ernie Els are all part of the Unlucky Sperm Club, born in the time of the man-eating, trophy-swallowing Cablinasian. They might as well begin studying to be CPAs. They have no chance. They'll never have a chance. What's worse is they now realize that every time they think Woods is slipping, it's only because he's up nights building something even better in the garage.

Example: This year there was the so-called Tiger Slump. He didn't win a tournament in January, in February and on into March. NBC's Johnny Miller kept referring to the "awful" shots Tiger was hitting. *Golf World* magazine ran a WHAT'S WRONG WITH TIGER? cover. But what Woods was doing was playing the Masters thousands of miles from the course.

"The West Coast, Florida, everything was geared to this," says Woods's coach, Butch Harmon. Even during tournament rounds Woods was working on shots that he would need only at Augusta. The big sweeping draw. The high, soft arm shots with no spin. The skip-and-spin chips.

How many did he use last week? "All of 'em," Woods said after finishing 16 under par. The big sweeping draw set up three birdies on number 13. The soft shots led the tournament in greens hit in regulation. The skip-and-spinners saved pars all week, including a crucial one on number 9 on Sunday.

Of course, you knew it was over on Saturday night, when Mickelson was about to be lowered into a lion's den wearing a hamburger suit. "I want this desperately," he said. "I want to be part of the history of the game." When we asked Woods if he was thinking of history that night, he only glared and said, "I'm thinking about my swing."

Now one man in the world can put his feet up on a coffee table that has all four major trophies on it. (There's a downside, too: A meteor hits his house, and golf as we know it is extinct.) So, what do we call this run of four straight majors? "To me," said Tiger's father, Earl, on Sunday, "it's like when a scientist discovers a star. He discovers it, he gets his name on it. Nobody's ever done this before, so Tiger should get his name on it."

A star is born: the Tiger Slam.

About five minutes after the Tiger Slam was a reality, google-eyed fans were coming up to his parents and congratulating them on the marvel they'd begot 25 years and three months before. The two of them had tears in their eyes and, though they have long since split, looked warmly at each other. Earl said, "I guess that *was* one lucky night, huh?"

For all of us.

Postscript: 'Tis a privilege to be alive and covering golf when Tiger is playing it. Must be like the guy who got to unlock the Sistine Chapel every morning for Michelangelo. Or the woman who swept the office while Lennon and McCartney wrote songs. And while Tiger may be a very tough "get" (as we say in the business), he is dedicated to his craft, fun when he gets the chance, and absolutely aware of what he means to the world. This man is arguably the most famous person on the planet, and yet, have you ever heard of him acting a fool, even once? In a bar, in traffic, at a movie? Never! He was raised impeccably in a house full of love and discipline. And that's why it was so sad for all of us when the following column had to be written. . . .

26

Pops' Last Lesson

MAY 15, 2006

I SUPPOSE WE COULD CELEBRATE THE LIFE OF EARL WOODS WITH a whiskey and ginger ale, which he loved. Or with jazz, which he loved. Or with a long drag on a cigarette, which he also loved too much, seeing as how smoking probably figured in his death last week at 74.

Or we could do it with tears, since with Earl there was always more crying than on the first day of kindergarten. Every time I saw him get up in front of a crowd to talk about Tiger, he'd wind up bawling. And every time, Tiger would hop up, grab the mike and go, "That's my Pops. I love him."

I suppose we could remember Earl as perhaps the most famous black man in America who is celebrated solely for his fatherhood. In sports, all we hear about is the black father who runs, but Earl was *constantly* there, *famously* there, *lovingly* there.

Hell, Earl couldn't leave the kid's side. He never left him with a babysitter. Wound up quitting his job for the kid, mortgaged the house twice, took out home equity loans. He couldn't bear to punish Tiger—that was his wife's job. Earl was hopelessly in love with the boy he called the chosen one.

94

You wondered what Earl's other kids thought of that—the chosen one. Because those three kids from his first marriage—Earl Jr., 50; Kevin, 48; and daughter Royce, 47—were not the chosen ones. They hardly knew him. A career Green Beret, he'd be gone for six months to a year at a time. "I wasn't around," he once told me. "I'd come back, and I'd find three totally different children."

Maybe Earl didn't know how to be a father the first time around. He was the youngest of six kids, and both his parents were dead by the time he was 13. He learned to be alone. But when he married Kultida, a Thai secretary, and got a mulligan for fatherhood at 42, he made the most of it.

Earl was fun to play with—gave me a lesson once, too—and even more fun in the bar afterward. And Tiger loved his burly playmate from the start. Even as a toddler, he had his Pops' phone number at the office memorized, so he could call and beg to play together after Earl got off work. Earl had 1,000 crazy games to play on the course. He needed to. Tiger was beating him by the time he was 11.

But it killed Earl to be called "the dad who built the greatest golfer ever." No, he was trying to build a kid who would be kind and happy and responsible. He gets an A+ for that. But much trickier still: He kept his Mozart from burning out.

Never once did he tell Tiger to practice. Never once told him to try harder. He and Tida would withhold golf if his homework wasn't done. Golf was the dessert Tiger got when he ate all his vegetables.

Together, father and son started a fund of trust. Tiger trusted his dad when Earl tried all his psychological training on him—dropping his golf bag as Tiger swung, calling like a crow on his backswing, rolling stray balls at his putter. And Earl trusted Tiger, who would put his pop four feet in front of him at clinics, have him hold his hands up like goal posts and hit full flop shots between them.

You think Earl did all this to get rich? Then why didn't he ever leave that little house in Cypress, Calif., the one he was living in when Tiger was born? No, Earl did it because golf's Stevie Wonder fell into his big lap. He did it for the three kids' childhoods he missed. And maybe he did it to make up for all the father-son days he missed when his own dad died.

And when Tiger hit his mid-20s and started to pull away—moved away from that little house all the way to Florida—Earl nodded proudly, but secretly ached. "It's sad in a way," Earl was quoted as saying. "This is what I've prepared for. Still, it leaves a hole because he's not there."

Now, Tiger must know exactly how he felt.

But more than all else, the thing Earl will be remembered for is his hugs. He did for hugs what Mrs. Fields did for cookies.

Remember the one he gave the triumphant Tiger coming off 18 at the 1997 Masters? That hug always chokes me up. Earl swallowed him in his huge arms and reminded us that this baby-faced, ice-blooded hit man was still somebody's little boy. From then on, those hugs became the one place this new god in spikes knew he could go to hide from the cameras and the pressure, the one place he knew he could feel loved and wanted and safe. Bet Tiger could use one right now.

And *that's* the best way to celebrate Earl Woods's life, by finding your kids right now—no matter how old—and giving them one of those great, smothering, lungbuster Earl Specials. See if you can squeeze the Skittles out of them.

Because all kids need to be reminded that they don't have to be Tiger Woods to be the chosen one.

27

Extreme Measures

MAY 19, 2003

IN 25 YEARS I'VE BEEN TO AT LEAST 1,000 PRESS CONFERENCES. World Series, Super Bowls, prizefights—huge rooms full of tough guys. But the most gripping press conference, the most unforgettable one, was last Thursday in a little room in Grand Junction, Colo., starring a guy as skinny as a two-iron.

That was when 27-year-old adventurer Aron Ralston described for the world how he had saved his life by cutting off his lower right arm with a dull pocketknife.

For five days Ralston's arm was pinned by an 800-pound boulder—after he'd lowered himself off it, the boulder had shifted onto his arm—in a forbidding three-foot-wide crevice in the remote Bluejohn Canyon in southeastern Utah. He tried everything to move the boulder, throwing his body at it, chipping away at it. The thing didn't budge.

On the third day, out of food and water and ideas, he stared at his cheap multiuse tool, the kind you get free with a $15 flashlight, and realized what he had to do. He used a pair of cycling shorts for a tourniquet, picked up the knife, took a deep breath and began sawing into his own skin.

The blade was too dull to even do that. "Wouldn't even cut my arm hairs," he said.

Still, for two more days, he kept at it--through skin, muscle and agony. As he spoke, his parents, Donna and Larry, sitting on either side of him, wept quietly. Donna held Aron's left hand under the table. Hardened members of the media, people who'd covered wars, were crying, but Aron didn't cry. He told his story like a man describing how he had fixed his lawnmower.

But imagine it. How do you keep slicing into yourself against unthinkable pain, when you know it's you inflicting that pain? "I felt pain," he said with a half smile. "I coped. I moved on." Then he stopped cutting. He had to. He couldn't get through the bone.

Now, even for a Carnegie Mellon honors grad, a former mechanical engineer for Intel, a man who has climbed solo 45 peaks of at least 14,000 feet, all in winter, often after midnight, usually without oxygen canisters, GPS or radio, this seemed a problem he couldn't solve. "I needed a bone saw."

Alternating between depression and visions of family members, friends and dreams of "tall, tasty margaritas," getting a "kind of peace" from the idea of death and yet willing himself on, a revelation suddenly came to him: "It occurred to me that if I could break my bones up at the wrist, where they were trapped, I could be freed."

It *occurred* to you? It *occurred* to you that if you snapped the bones of *your own arm*, this would be a *solution*?

Sorry, but if it's me, I'm dead. Bring on the wolves and the vultures. Let the winds spread my remains over the sandstone. In fact I'm pretty sure I don't even saw into my arm. I weep when removing a Garfield Band-Aid.

But not Aron Ralston. He found a way to live. "All the desires, joys and euphorias of a future life came rushing into me," he said. "Maybe this is how I handled the pain. I was so happy to be taking action."

It took him most of the morning, but—and how often do you get to write this sentence?—he was finally able to break the wrist bones in half. Yes, he did. Using torque and the strength he had left, the man purposely broke two bones in his already flayed arm. As he described that, everyone in the room forgot to blink, scribble, breathe.

Though he declined to describe what he had to do next, there is only one thing Ralston could've done—and a hospital official later explained this: He would've had to stretch his body away from that trapped hand to separate the broken ends of those bones. That would be the only way to make a path for the pocketknife to pass through.

Who's hungry?

That done, "it took about an hour," he said, to finish the amputation. Amazing. The man sawed off a body part and timed himself.

Finally free, the mountain-shop worker from Aspen crawled through that narrow, winding stretch of canyon, rappelled 60 feet down a cliff and hiked about six miles, all with one arm and one profusely bleeding stump, until he met what had to be two horrified Dutch hikers.

Ralston may never play concert piano again (he minored in performance piano composition at Carnegie Mellon), but he vows to keep exploring every inch of the West, as did the great John Wesley Powell, for whom Lake Powell is named—the great one-armed explorer, John Wesley Powell.

They call Ralston an extreme athlete, but the courage and will he displayed over those five days is not extreme, it's legendary. Don't care who you meet, you'll never find anybody tougher than this guy. After the press conference, back in his hospital room, he said, "I wish I could've been funnier."

Yeah, Aron. Next time, can you do something to liven it up?

Postscript: Nothing can still the unquenchable adventurer's heart inside Aron Ralston. He continues to climb all kinds of hairy stuff, usually alone, often at night, in the winter. He kids that he's an even better climber now, since he can attach a kind of ice-axe to his severed limb. He's a wonderful motivational speaker too. The world knows his story by heart now and it never gets old. In fact I went on Letterman and we spent most of the time talking about Ralston. Aron called me once and said his favorite account written about his ordeal was mine. But I disagree. The best is his own riveting book Between a Rock and a Hard Place. *(Don't read while eating.)*

28

Getting By on $14.6 Mil

NOVEMBER 15, 2004

O N A TEAM OF THE MOST SELFISH, GREEDY, SPOILED to the Spleen, Multimillionaire Athletes You'd Most Like to See Thrown to a Dieting Lion list, Latrell Sprewell would have to be the coach and captain. ¶ He's the Minnesota Timberwolves guard who choked his coach when he was with Golden State. ("It's not like he was losing air or anything," he told *60 Minutes*.) He's the one who brandished a two-by-four during a run-in with Warriors teammate Jerome Kersey at a practice and then reportedly threatened to get a gun. He's the guy whose pit bull bit off his 4-year-old daughter Page's ear and mauled her face, but he didn't want the dog to be put down. "Stuff happens," he shrugged.

Now Spree has topped his own remarkable self. He'll be paid $14.6 million this season, but last week he was talking to reporters about how disgusted he is that he doesn't have a contract for next season. *Why not help the T-Wolves win the NBA title this season and then see what happens?* he was asked.

And Spree said—are you ready for it?—Spree said, "Why would I want to help them win a title? They're not doing anything for me. I'm at risk. I have a lot of risk here. I got my family to feed. Anything could happen."

On three, let's all hurl at once!

Whose family is this guy feeding, Brigham Young's? According to U.S. Department of Agriculture calculations, he should be able to feed his wife, Candace, and six kids for $19,237 this year. Even if you take out taxes and agent fees—which leaves him about $8.3 million—he could feed not only his family, but also 431 other families of eight. Actually, through the World Vision relief program, he could feed 8.3 million people for one day. Or a village of 400 for nearly 57 years. Or Bill Parcells for two weeks.

He could still feed his family, three times a day every day for a year, the following: shark-fin soup ($100 a bowl in Hong Kong), beluga caviar ($920 for 8 ounces), Kobe beef ($49 a pound), preserved black winter truffles ($175 worth would be enough) and a box of the world's best chocolates (by Pascal Caffet, 14 pieces for $90) and still have almost $7 million left.

You know, for snacks.

Of course, kids don't want that crap. They want McDonald's. Fine. He can get them McDonald's. In fact, at the low-end price of $466,000 apiece, he can get each of his kids a McDonald's *franchise*, and 11 for himself.

Or forget his family. Spree could buy every fan at Target Center a pizza and a large Coke (cost: about $10) at every home game this year and still have dough left over.

Not that he cares about fans. By asking "Why would I want to help them win a title?" Sprewell spits in the eye of every Timberwolves fan. (If the NBA ever dies, we'll carve that quote on its tombstone.) Why win? Uh, because they're paying you the gross national product of a small nation? Because fans making half of 1% of what you make scrimp for months to see you play one time?

Spree can't relate. Spree doesn't have time to. Spree is busy tending to his huge yacht. Spree is busy driving his fleet of cars, including a custom-designed Lamborghini Diablo, a Rolls-Royce Phantom and a $300,000 Maybach, the one with a champagne cooler in the armrest. Spree is busy being pissed about the three-year, $21 million extension the Wolves offered him. "Insulting," Spree said.

Oh, it's insulting all right.

Shame on Latrell Sprewell. Shame on somebody so self-absorbed, so out of touch that he could say something so grotesquely selfish. And not just once, twice. Asked the next day if he regretted playing the "feed my family" card knowing that thousands in the Twin Cities are out of work and facing a bitter winter, Spree said—are you ready for it?—Spree said, "That's where *I* can be if something happens to me."

Can't we *please* throw this man a telethon?

No, you know where Spree could be without his God-given gifts? Standing in line at an Emergency FoodShelf outside Minneapolis with Michael Larson, an injured house painter living off Social Security, who gets $93 in food stamps a month. "If you can't feed your family on $8 million a year," says Larson wryly, "you're not budgeting properly."

Says Marc Ratner of FoodShelf, "I wish Mr. Sprewell could come here for a day. We have people who have to decide, every month, whether they should buy food or heat."

And Sprewell has the gall to talk about risk?

Spree, the only risk you face is running into an out-of-work piano mover late at night who has a wife and kids to feed but really has nothing to feed them—except maybe you.

But don't worry. When he chokes you, it's not like you'll be losing air or anything.

Postscript: A man of principle, Spreewell turned down that insulting $21 million extension by the T-Wolves, then got offers from Dallas and San Antonio, among others, but rejected them all. His phone never rang after the '05–06 season, so he's still sitting it out, and it looks like he'll never play another NBA game. What I'm hoping is that he winds up on a street corner somewhere, holding a tattered cardboard sign that reads, HAVE FAMILY TO FEED.

29

The Silent Treatment

NOVEMBER 22, 2004

ALMOST NOBODY YELLS FOR MY FAVORITE FOOTBALL team. Their coaches never give them a single encouraging word. Their cheerleaders rarely make a peep. That's because my favorite football team is California School for the Deaf at Riverside, which is 9–1 and plays like a light-rail train. The Cubs are fast, noiseless, and you definitely don't want to get hit by them.

Only when they celebrate do they get noisy. CSDR won the San Joaquin League title last week for the first time in the school's 51-year history, and the players partied by slamming into one another, waving their hands like Al Jolson and turning the bass up on 50 Cent one crank past WINDOWS SHATTER and dancing madly to the vibrations.

"Teams really hate to lose to us because they think we're a handicapped team," signs coach Len Gonzales, who is deaf too, as is his coaching staff. "But we're not handicapped. We just can't hear."

They sure put up some loud scores. Last Friday CSDR thumped Twin Pines High from Banning, Calif., 34–8. It was so bad, Pines asked for a running clock in the fourth quarter. Said their coach, Jim Bridgman, without irony, "They do all their talking on the field." Uh, Coach? They don't do their talking anywhere.

Oh, well, that's not the dumbest thing anybody said that day. The dumbest thing was said by me, seeing the big bass drum CSDR uses to send instructions in warmups and asking, "Do you have a band?"

No, but they do have cheerleaders, who dance perfect routines on the sidelines to music only they can hear, while their crowd applauds with jazz hands. Hell, last season in Hawaii they won a competition in which CSDR was the only deaf school entered. "The good thing about being a group of deaf cheerleaders," says their coach, Stacy Hausman, "is that if the music cuts out, we just keep going."

There are advantages to being a deaf football team too. The receivers don't hear footsteps. There are no coaches screaming. And you don't have to listen to local sports-talk yokels rip you when you lose.

Oh, and there's this: When CSDR quarterback Mark Korn got creamed near the sideline in the first quarter, the Twin Pines defender came up jawing, "All day, baby! All day!" Korn just flipped the ball to the ref without a glance. Damn. Nothing deflates a trash talker like a deaf ear.

Up in the stands Korn's deaf mother, Wendy, was talking to another mom, who hears. "Oh, I hate hearing those terrible hits," the mom signed to Mrs. Korn. "I get so worried they're going to get hurt." Mrs. Korn's face fell like a bad soufflé. "You can *hear* the tackles?" she signed back. "I really didn't want to hear that."

Not to worry, Mrs. Korn, the Cubs deliver a lot more spleen-shakers than they get. "Everybody comes in doubting us," signs tight end Joey Weir, "but we're in the playoffs and they're not."

Actually, teams come in with a lot of questions. How do the Cubs handle snap counts? (Everybody watches the ball and goes on a tap from Korn to his center.) How do they audible? (They don't.) How do they hear the whistle? (They don't.) They've learned to stop when everybody else stops, but that can be trouble. One game this year Korn stopped on a rollout near the end zone because he saw his receiver stop. But the receiver had stopped because he was out of room. Korn got crushed and coughed up the ball, which was returned for a touchdown.

Some things you just have to learn for yourself. At halftime last Friday two kids sneaked into the little gym the CSDR players use to regroup and stared goggle-eyed as the Cubs signed and encouraged one another wordlessly. "See! I told ya!" the one kid whispered to the other. "They ain't sayin' nothin'! "

A few players tried hearing schools, but they knew they were home when they hit CSDR, the only all-deaf high school in Southern California. "I was first-string in summer camp my freshman year at one [hearing school]," signs running back Alberto Martinez, who rushed for 198 yards against Twin Pines and 319 the game before. "Then the coach shoved me aside because they couldn't talk to me. But I knew I'd make it somewhere."

The Cubs play for more than their school's colors. "I have deaf friends all over the state who are pulling for us," signs Weir.

They'll need it. This weekend Weir and his Riverside Brothers, as they call each other, will try to become the first CSDR team in any sport to win a playoff game. And as they pounded that drum and whooped their shrill coyote whoops and slammed their hands on tables in that tiny echoing gym after Friday's victory, I put my fingers in my ears and secretly hoped they would.

Assistant coach Keith Adams saw me, smiled and signed, "When you're done with this story, you'll be deaf too."

As I looked around and saw all the lung-crusher hugs and Lotto grins, I thought, That doesn't sound so bad at all.

Postscript: The Cubs won their league again in 2005 and Adams, who took over the top job that season, was honored by the NFL as the High School Coach of the Year for Southern California. They put a 68–0 pounding on Lakeside and beat Twin Pines 50–0 the next week. So they're still making teams whimper; it's just that they can't hear it.

30

The Ceremonial First Sales Pitch

MARCH 13, 2006

I FEEL SORRY FOR CERTAIN PEOPLE. LEON SPINKS'S ORTHODONTIST. Bode Miller's agent. Anybody in a ham-eating contest with James Gandolfini. ¶ But nobody has it worse than the poor souls in marketing for some major league baseball teams. ¶ Thanks to owners with the financial acumen of Mike Tyson, baseball has no salary cap, which means only about 10 teams out of 30 have a chance to win a championship. They know it. We know it. Tibetan monks know it.

So the marketing guys have to come up with a slogan that will lure fans to the park without flat-out deceiving them. I mean, it's not like the Kansas City Royals can put up billboards that read FOLLOW US TO THE WORLD SERIES!

In the world of advertising, this is considered a very tough sell. Like pitching Asian chickens or fur sinks or vacation time-shares in Kabul.

Still, they continue to amaze with their ability to find something good about their teams. Take a look at this year's batch of marketing slogans.

AMERICAN LEAGUE

TAMPA BAY DEVIL RAYS
Coming Soon! Major League Baseball!

DETROIT TIGERS
We Guarantee We'll Get More Wins Than the Lions!

BALTIMORE ORIOLES
Steroid-free Since February!

KANSAS CITY ROYALS
Usually Not Mathematically Eliminated from the Playoffs until May!

CLEVELAND INDIANS
This Is Our Year (and If Not This Year Certainly Three Years from Now!
Or the Year after That!)!

NEW YORK YANKEES
Home of the Most Generous, Wonderful, Caring, Dynamic—Did We
Mention Handsome?—Team Owner in America.

TORONTO BLUE JAYS
Not Just Voyeuristic Sex Anymore!

MINNESOTA TWINS
We Have Absolutely No Chance, but We'll Almost Certainly Kick the Royals' Ass!

LOS ANGELES ANGELS
of Anaheim, Bakersfield, Barstow, Fullerton, San Diego, Tijuana—Proud to
Be Your Hometown Team!

SEATTLE MARINERS
O.K., So We'll Continue to Suck, But at Least You Won't Get Wet!

TEXAS RANGERS
If You Can Throw the Ball over the Plate, We'll Sign You Up!

NATIONAL LEAGUE

ATLANTA BRAVES
Your One-stop Bridesmaid Center!

FLORIDA MARLINS
Root for the Uniforms That Won Two World Series!

NEW YORK METS
Come Sit in Anna Benson's Butt Heat!

PHILADELPHIA PHILLIES
Now Embarking on Our 75th Five-Year Rebuilding Plan!

MILWAUKEE BREWERS
Steadfastly Refusing to Participate in That Whole Buying-Spoiled-Superstars-Just-to-Win Thing!

CHICAGO CUBS
Ironically Hip Since 1908!

CINCINNATI REDS
Bet on Us!

PITTSBURGH PIRATES
Ben Roethlisberger Once Watched a Few Innings Here!

ST. LOUIS CARDINALS
The Best Team in Baseball, at Least Until Early in September!

ARIZONA DIAMONDBACKS
Once Again Featuring Exciting Between-inning Highlights of Our 2001 World Championship Season!

COLORADO ROCKIES
True, We Will Lose Like the French Army, But at This Altitude the Beer Goes to Your Brain Really Fast!

WASHINGTON NATIONALS
A Dick Cheney Shotgun-Free Zone!

Postscript: The 2006 World Series inspired two new slogans. For the Tigers: Now signing pitchers who can field! *And for the Cardinals:* Yes, it was a fluke, but wasn't the parade fun?

31

Monster Mash

AUGUST 25, 2003

I HAD SIX CARS IN FRONT OF ME THE OTHER DAY. NOT ONE OF THEM moving. And I was running out of time. So . . . I just ran right over them. ¶ Up their trunks, over their roofs and down their hoods. Smooshed them. Left them flatter than Kate Moss holding a three-day-old beer. ¶ Enjoyed it so much I turned around and did it again, cackling like Vincent Price.

Was I jailed for that? Arrested? Even tsk-tsked? No. I was praised, slapped on the back and offered a pinch of Copenhagen.

That's because I was not on the street. I was in an arena. And I wasn't driving my car. I was driving a five-ton, 1,400-horsepower, 10-foot-tall, eardrum-ruining, groin-tingling Bigfoot, the mother of all monster trucks.

You may think only those married to their cousins feel this way, but I'm a monster fan of monster trucks. I *own* Bigfoot videos, including ones that show a Bigfoot purposely crashing through a Winnebago, a Bigfoot crushing an entire new-car showroom, two Bigfoots pulling a 1979 Chrysler K-car from each end until it rips in half. Honestly, can you have more fun without using some form of lard?

Before a recent monster-truck show, I got a shot at crushing cars with one of the five Bigfoots competing around the country. My instructor was the immortal Bigfoot driver Dan Runte—a small man with monster marbles, a man who once jumped a Bigfoot over a 727. He missed the plane by a good 94 feet, which is better than some airline pilots have done.

Dan showed me the 66-inch-tall tires (they're two inches taller than Ian Woosnam!), the plexiglass floor (you can see what you're crushing!) and, in case anything went wrong, the remote engine kill switch that he would hold at the ready while I drove ("works up to three quarters of a mile!" Dan said proudly).

As a man with two teenage sons, I can see how such a device could come in very handy.

Older teenage son: All right, you gun it while I lie on the roof of the car firing bottle rockets outta my butt!

Younger teenage son: Hey, it won't start!

Other oddities included the steering wheel located in the center of the cab, no doors (you climb into the cab through the chassis) and no rearview mirror. Bigfoot never looks back!

I asked Dan if he'd ever crushed something he wasn't supposed to. "Well," he said, kicking the dirt, "it's just that the crowd really likes carnage. So, one time, I ran over a storage shed full of popcorn. Hell, I've crushed cars I woulda liked to drive home!" What would you give for one day with a Bigfoot inside a Wal-Mart?

After exhaustive safety instruction that lasted 10 minutes, Dan turned me loose with one of the most destructive vehicles on earth. And no insurance forms to sign! The arena was set up for the show: two dirt ramps facing each other with six beat-up cars set door-handle-to-door-handle between them. I flipped the toggle ignition. Over the engine noise and the chattering of my teeth, Dan yelled in my ear, "Now, 'member, if you flip, undo your chest belt first, otherwise you'll hang yourself! O.K., have fun!"

Thanks!

Suddenly wishing I was back home watching my videos, I nervously lined up Bigfoot in front of one of the ramps. I swallowed hard, jammed it into first and took off. I must've been going 75 mph when I went flying up the ramp and landed on top of those poor cars. Thrown around in the cab like a loose

St. Christopher statue, I forgot to look down through the plexiglass to see the carnage. Damn!

Still, it was glorious. Dan climbed up into the cab and said, "Good! I think you almost got it to 15 [mph]. Try it one more time, only *gun* it!"

Cocky now, I lined up again and floored it. Bigfoot jumped from under me like a goosed Clydesdale. I went sailing off the ramp, didn't touch down until my front tires hit the *fourth* car (a three-car improvement) and became terrified that I was going to flip over forward. Then, just as suddenly, Bigfoot rocked back, and when the rear tires landed, the front flew straight up again. Luckily, I was looking down through the plexiglass when the truck cleaved the bejesus out of a 1981 Bonneville's hood.

Only problem was, I hadn't taken my big foot off Bigfoot's accelerator. I was heading straight for the arena wall. Luckily, my cat-quick professional driver instincts stopped the truck just in time. Well, that and Dan's throwing the kill switch.

He climbed in again and with a huge grin said, "I think you almost got it to 20 [mph] that time!"

After the show—Dan won the competition on points, as usual—I went to the pits to savor those last sweet smells of burnt methanol. The 66-inch tires were yanked off Bigfoot and replaced with normal-sized tires so the truck could fit back inside a trailer. It was deflating, like going backstage and seeing Dolly Parton removing falsies.

Still, as Bigfoot's trailer drove off, I said what was in my heart: "Next time, the Yankee Stadium parking lot!"

Postscript: I'd like to borrow Bigfoot again, just so I could run over my ex-wife's divorce lawyer and then look through the plexiglass floor to see his reaction. I'm guessing: surprise.

32

Heaven on Earth

H E WAS A UPS TRUCK OF A MAN, 6' 4", MAYBE 250 pounds, 55 years old, with a chin you could use to crack open coconuts. ¶ He waited until the end of my little speech and then stood there in front of the podium, his eyes rimmed red with tears. No words would come to his mouth. He must have stood there for a full minute, trying to use all his muscles to force up a single sentence: "My daughter is dying."

He wept, then went on. "We just found out. Brain tumor. She's got a year to live. If she's lucky." He gave a huge sigh. "She *lives* for sports, you know? Would you write her a note? I don't know. Just something to cheer her up?"

I wrote something. It wasn't that inspiring. I told him how sorry I was. He thanked me and walked off. I felt helpless.

Now, after thinking about it, I wished I'd written her this. . . .

If I had only next year to live, I'd do whatever it took to see, one last time, Michael Vick's happy feet, Allen Iverson's XL heart and Ichiro's bionic arm throwing out some poor slob at third who didn't even think he'd have to slide.

I'd chase goose bumps coast to coast. I'd make sure I saw Tiger Woods windmill a driver. I'd go to the Kentucky Derby paddock and watch the parade of thoroughbreds, dropping my Starbucks when I see how huge they are. I'd beg, cheat and bribe my way onto the Super Bowl field, so I could be there when the F-18s polish off the national anthem with a flyover that turns your spine into marmalade.

I'd go to Fenway and sit above the Green Monster, see Mia Hamm before she starts having tiny Olympians and go to a UCLA game to shake the 93-year-old hand of the wisest man in the land, John Wooden.

I'd see the Palio in Siena, hotwire a Ferrari and drive the Amalfi coast road, and see how long I could sprint behind Lance Armstrong as he melted another Alp.

I'd read *Ball Four* a few dozen times more, watch *Slap Shot* again, listen to Vin Scully call one last game on my transistor while I hooked up a steady I.V. of Dodger Dogs.

I'd get to Augusta and watch the par-3 tournament on the prettiest swatch of golf in the world. And on Sunday I'd watch the last group go through Amen Corner and then whip the seven-iron out of my pants leg and play number 12 right quick. So you go to jail. When they hear your story, you'll be out by 9 p.m.

I'd want a few laughs, so I'd go to Logan Airport the day after the Boston Marathon and watch the poor runners walk backward up staircases because their calves are so sore. I'd sit with the Cameron Crazies to see them dangle a Big Mac in front of a visiting Jabba the Center. I'd pay $10,000 to enter the World Series of Poker just to sit next to Amarillo Slim and hear his hilarious whoppers.

I know what I'd *stop* doing. I'd stop wasting time worrying about my 401(k) or what the Madman and Coach think on SportsBlab 1090 or NFL receivers who make cell calls to their egos.

I'd try to become part of sports as it weaves through the fabric of life. I'd go an hour late to the starting line at the Iditarod just to hear the sorrowful howling of the sled dogs left behind. I'd see if John Madden would let me hitch a ride. I'd walk into physics class, sign out my kid and his buddies and go play Wiffle ball. Now *that's* physics.

I'd write some letters, not caring if I got a response. I'd thank Derek Jeter for playing so hard, Pete Sampras for playing so well and Kevin Garnett for never showing up in the sports section, which my daughter reads, with two Girl Scouts and a bottle of X.

I'd find Bill Buckner and forgive him, Steve Bartman and hug him, Rasheed Wallace and slap him.

I'd blow off the annual jersey exchange that pro sports has become and get to where the passion is—the colleges, the high schools, the jayvee basketball game.

I'd go to Midnight Yell Practice at Texas A&M with the 30,000 other wackos who like to be hoarse for kickoff. I'd call Bobby Bowden on his listed phone number and talk trick plays. I'd go to Senior Day at Kansas' Allen Fieldhouse, where the floor gets covered with carnations and the jerseys with tears.

I'd catch the milk run on Ajax, at Vail, in powder you could lose Doug Flutie in. I'd hit the best tailgate in America—a Kansas City Chiefs game— and try to become the first man to drown in Gates Bar-B-Que sauce. I'd play 72 at Oregon's Bandon Dunes, where the cliffs and the waves and the Scotch make you want to chain yourself to the starter's hut on check-out day.

I'd relish friends and catch up on bliss and bake in all the tastes I've acquired. I'd wallow and dawdle and completely ignore my cholesterol. I'd spend my last year reminding myself why I loved it all so much in the first 45.

And I'd die happy, knowing it was going to take the embalmers two hours to bend the grin off my face.

Postscript: Small world. Turns out the woman was the wife of a math teacher at my kids' high school. I never met her but everybody said she was fun and lovely. She lived another three years.

33

Looks Aren't Everything

MAY 28, 2001

I'M GOING TO BRING AN NBA LEGEND INTO THE ROOM, AND I want you to close your eyes while I describe him. ¶ Compared with the rest of today's superstars, he's small—mostly heart and scabs—but as tough as a '48 pickup. In his prime he was a wind-up toy who never stopped moving without the ball, busting through picks and elbows and knees as though he was trying to break the world record for bruises. He'd go 48 minutes most every game, usually nursing more injuries than an *ER* episode. He was a Nintendo-type scorer with a gorgeous jumper who considered being knocked to the floor part of his follow-through.

You're thinking Jerry West, right?

Wrong.

This guy was electric. He could carry an offense, a team, a city by himself. One night he would torch an opponent for 50 points and the next decide to beat the opposition with assists. He was unpredictable, unguardable and unforgettable. He had moves that could make your pupils dilate. He was the idol of millions around the world, one of the three greatest players of his day.

You're thinking Michael Jordan, right?

115

Wrong.

This guy seemed to be appreciated only by the fans who saw him night after night. He was shy with the press, yet honest as a Sunday confessional. He dressed the same every day and was mocked for it. He was the same man whether in front of the camera or in the line at the deli. He stayed true to his high school friends. He was a family man whose first move after he left the locker room was to sweep up his two small kids. He never let the fame or the money or the trophies change him.

You're thinking John Stockton, right?

Wrong.

This guy had the 100,000-watt smile of a lotto winner. He had the joy of the game in his blood, and he knew how to spread it. He would hug his coach only slightly less than he hugged his mom, which was constantly. He had the courage to dive into the crowd at least once a game, and the sense of humor to hug the fan who caught him. He had the game to win the shiniest awards, yet the humility to share credit with everybody else in the room.

You're thinking Magic Johnson, right?

Wrong.

Now open your eyes and look at him.

He's Allen Iverson.

That changes everything, doesn't it? Now you see the cornrows and the tattoos and the pierce-holes dripping gold, and they bug you, right? You think *thug* and *rapper* and *criminal*. SI put the NBA's soon-to-be MVP on the cover of its April 23 issue, posed as himself, nearly naked, hip-hop to his heart, and suddenly you're mad. West and Jordan and Stockton and Magic, they're welcome on your coffee table, but not this guy. We're up to our clavicles in hate mail.

"Christ!" wrote a subscriber in Tucson. "Don't you have enough tattooed, body-pierced, earring- [and] necklace-wearing, corn-rowed freaks on the inside [of the magazine] that you have to put them on the cover?"

"The cover with Allen Iverson made me sick to my stomach," read one e-mail. "I feel the magazine has sent a poor message to young readers."

From Richardson, Texas: "Those preening idiots barely belong to the human race."

Montgomery, Ala.: "Iverson is just another reason why our country is in such bad shape."

Adams, N.Y.: "His angry young oppressed black-man image is b------. . . . I am white and not prejudiced, but I do not feel sorry for Allen Iverson."

Another e-mail: "[The] stare, tattoos and pants to the waist showing his jockstrap sum up the reason I have not watched an NBA game in years."

San Diego: "The picture of Allen Iverson is revolting."

Lindon, Utah: "I object to this grotesque and irreverent picture."

Hundreds of people were obsessed by what's on the outside of the man, not the inside. Not a word about will and loyalty and effort. Not a word of praise for a young superstar who has stuck with one team, one woman his whole career. You see him, but you don't see him.

And he lives with this crap every freaking day.

I'm canceling *their* subscriptions.

Postscript: I get it. It's not easy to be an Iverson fan. The gangsta rap lyrics. The disdain for practice. More ice than Kodiak, Alaska. But if there's one NBA player I'd pay twice the ticket price to watch, it's Iverson, who gives every ounce of himself every night. As I write this, by the way, he's still leading the league in scoring but has finally punched his ticket out of Philly.

34

No Ordinary Joe

JULY 7, 2003

WHY IN CREATION DID JOE DELANEY JUMP into that pit full of water that day? ¶ Why in the world would the AFC's best young running back try to save three drowning boys when he himself couldn't swim? ¶ Nobody—not his wife, not his mother—had ever seen him so much as dog-paddle. A year and a half earlier, when he went to the Pro Bowl in Hawaii as the AFC's starting halfback and Rookie of the Year, he never set even a pinkie toe in the ocean or the pool. "Never had," says his wife, Carolyn, who'd known Joe since they were both seven. "In all my years, I never had seen him swim."

So why? Why did the 24-year-old Kansas City Chief try to save three boys he didn't know with a skill he didn't have?

He'd been sitting in the cool shade of a tree on a tar-bubbling afternoon at Chennault Park, a public recreation area in Monroe, La., when he heard voices calling, "Help! Help!" He popped up like a Bobo doll and sprinted toward the pit.

What made Delaney that kind of person? Why did he mow that lonely woman's lawn when he was back home in Haughton, La., rich as he was? Why did he check in on that old man every day he was in town? Why did he show up on the Haughton streets one day with a bag full of new shoes and clothes for kids whose names he'd never heard?

Why could he never think of anything that he wanted for himself? Why didn't he even make a Christmas list? The man never cashed a paycheck in his life. He would throw his checks on top of the TV for his wife. "Don't you want *nothing* for yourself?" Carolyn would ask Joe.

"Nah," he'd say. "You just take care of you and the girls."

"Nothing?"

"Well, if you could give me a little pocket change for the week, I'd appreciate it."

Why didn't he ask somebody else to help those three kids that day? After all, there were hundreds of people at the park, and not another soul dived into that pit. Nobody but Delaney, one guy who *shouldn't* have.

The boys in that pit were struggling to stay afloat. They were two brothers—Harry and LeMarkits Holland, 11 and 10, respectively—and a cousin, Lancer Perkins, 11. Of course, LeMarkits was always with Harry. He idolized his big brother. A water park adjacent to Chennault was staging a big promotion with free admission that day, and the boys had wandered over to the pit and waded into the water. Like Delaney, they couldn't swim.

So much of it doesn't make sense. Why hadn't the pit—a huge rain-filled hole that was left after the dirt had been dug out and used to build a water slide—been fenced off from the public? Who knew that four feet from the edge of the water the hole dropped off like a cliff to about 20 feet deep?

LeMarkits has said that he remembers the water filling his lungs, the sensation of being pulled to the cold bottom, when all of a sudden a huge hand grabbed his shoulder and heaved him out of the deep water. Delaney dived for the other two boys, sinking below the surface. Folks along the bank waited for him to come up, but he never did. Harry and Lancer drowned with him.

As much as you might hope that LeMarkits has done something with the gift Delaney gave him, so far he hasn't. In an interview with the *Philadelphia Daily News* two years ago, LeMarkits said he has been tortured by the thought that he got to live and Harry didn't. He said he made his mom sell Harry's bike, bed and toys. He even burned Harry's clothes, as if fire could burn his brother from his heart. But it never did. Thirty years old now, LeMarkits got out of jail in May after serving time for distribution of cocaine. There's still time for him to do something wonderful with the life Delaney gave him. After all, Delaney was doing wonderful things with the one he gave up.

He was buried on the Fourth of July, 20 years ago. A telegram from President Reagan was read at the memorial service. The Presidential Citizens Medal was awarded posthumously. Three thousand people came to his funeral. A park in Haughton was named after him. No Chiefs player has worn number 37 since. The 37 Forever Foundation, a nonprofit group in Kansas City, honors him to this day by providing free swimming lessons to inner-city kids.

"I wish they'd had that for Joe and me when we were kids," Carolyn says glumly. She thinks of her Joe every day. She can't help it. Their three daughters and four grandkids remind her of him constantly. There is a pause. "I never thought we wouldn't grow old together."

She's only been on two dates since Joe died. Twenty years, two dates. "Why should I?" she says. "I just keep comparing them to Joe, and they can't stand up. Nobody in the world is like my Joe."

Anyway, the point is, next time you're reading the sports section and you're about half-sick of DUIs and beaten wives, put it down for a second and remember Joe Delaney, who, in that splinter of a moment, when a hero was needed, didn't stop to ask why.

35

Giving Seattle the Needle

FEBRUARY 6, 2006

O KAY, SEATTLE, GRAB A GRANDE, SKINNY, NO-FOAM, half-caf Espresso Macchiato and let me explain why the Pittsburgh Steelers are going to grind you up like a Sumatra blend in Super Bowl XL. ¶ You suck at sports. ¶ You always have. You make nice motherboards, but you're dweebier than Frasier Crane's wine club. You've had the big three pro sports for 30 years now—almost 40 for the NBA—and you have one lousy championship to show for it. *Uno*. The 1978 Seattle SuperSonics. My God, you people have fewer parades than Venice.

What's amazing is, you do college sports even worse. In the 70 years that a mythical national championship has been awarded in college football, the University of Washington has one half of one title: in 1991 (with Miami). Zippo in basketball, baseball, track or field. O.K., the Huskies are good at crew (three women's titles, one men's). Wonderful. Somewhere, three salmon cheer.

Your most famous athlete is a horse, Seattle Slew. Your most famous athletic moment was Bo Jackson's turning the Boz's chest into a welcome mat on *Monday Night Football*. Your greatest contribution to sports was the Wave, the fan-participation stunt that screams to the world, "We have no idea what the score is!"

And do you know why you stink, Seattle? Because . . .

1. You're too damn nice.

Look at your Seahawks. Your MVP halfback, Shaun Alexander, teaches kids chess. Your scariest player is named Pork Chop. My God, last week, you offered valet parking service to reporters at Seahawks headquarters. (Seattle fans: If you see valet parking at Detroit's Ford Field this week, they're trying to steal your car.)

Nearly every five-dollar-steak-tough athlete who comes to Seattle leaves— Gary Payton and Randy Johnson for instance. Consider Seattle's two favorite athletes—Steve Largent and Fred Couples. Those guys wouldn't complain if somebody extinguished a Cohiba in their ears. Your sportswriters are more forgiving than Hillary Clinton. If they covered Jeffrey Dahmer, they'd refer to him as "a people person."

You Seattle fans don't just accept mediocrity. You crave it. You support your boys come hell or low water. You show up at the rate of three million a year for the Mariners, who never fail to let you down. Even the stadium sounds cuddly: Safeco Field. You pack the house for the underachieving SuperSonics, led by the NBA's nicest loser, Ray Allen. Your Seahawks went 21 years without a playoff win, and the fans didn't so much as clear their throats. Everybody just goes, "Well, that was fun. Let's kayak!" Hey, you can't spell Seattle without *settle*.

The whole town is 100% June Cleaver. I once walked into Nordstrom, the Seattle-based department store, and sheepishly asked if I could bring back a shirt I'd bought a month before in another town. The clerk said, "Sir, this is Nordstrom. You could wear it for 10 years, throw up on it and roll down a mountain in it and we'd take it back." Ask that at Neiman Marcus and they call security.

It ain't happening. Walruses don't do triple Salchows, and Seattle teams don't win titles.

2. You're too damn geeky.

Your owner, Microsoft cofounder Paul Allen, looks like the kid in high school who always got taped to the goalposts. If Allen wins, will he call all his friends from band camp? Throw his slide rule into the air? Plot his joy on a scatter chart?

Look, your average Seahawks fan drives a Prius. Your average Steelers fan drives a Ford Excursion, which has Priuses in its tire treads. Seahawks fans own poodles. Steelers fans eat them.

3. You're too damn wet.

Seattle is a great place if you happen to be mold. It just rained 27 straight days and it wasn't even a record. Seattle is basically a lot of guys waiting for a bus with rain starting to seep into their socks. Most kids are seven years old before they realize the umbrella is not an extension of the right arm. No wonder most great athletes leave. Ken Griffey Jr. left, basically saying, "I want my kid to be able to play outside once in a while."

In short, you people are too damn peaceful and happy in your Emerald City. You ever know anybody from Pittsburgh? You want this Super Bowl. Pittsburgh *needs* it. You're going to get smoked like a platter of smelt.

(But do you mind if we come live there?)

Postscript: Seattle was really torqued off about this one. Of course, getting hate mail from Seattle is like having your refrigerator raided by Kate Moss. One guy e-mailed me and ended it with, "And I want you to know, I purposely wrote this in a difficult-to-read font!" Oooh, six-point calligraphy. Scary.

36

On His Last Leg

JUNE 4, 2001

THE SUPREME COURT IS EXPECTED TO HAND DOWN its decision on *PGA Tour, Inc.* v. *Casey Martin* any day now, so I want to update you on how Martin and his cart are ruining the game of golf. ¶ I caddied for Martin two weeks ago at the Richmond Open on the Buy.com tour and found out the cart is a *huge* competitive advantage for him. For instance, when he's in the cart, the pain in his diseased right leg stops for *minutes* at a time. Of course, when he's standing, the pain comes back. And, of course, it's worse on uphill lies and sidehill lies, and when he gets down to read putts.

True, the cart is no help when he'd like to practice but can't, because standing too long makes his leg throb like a bass drum. Or when he'd like to work out. Or run. Or bike. The cart doesn't help him sleep, either, which he does in two-hour chunks some nights, mostly between swallows of Advil. He's up to eight or 12 tablets a day.

O.K., the cart doesn't help him when some ol' boy comes up to his table, slaps him on the leg and says, "Howzit goin'?" and Martin looks as if he might faint from the pain. And the cart doesn't stop all the camera crews and gawkers and busybodies from coming up to him during a round so they can chastise him or tell him he's their hero. In Richmond a kid with a prosthesis limped up to Martin to shake his hand. That might've been a little distracting, because Martin's doctors tell him that they'll probably be fitting him for one of those down the road.

And I noticed he doesn't embrace the cart for the cheating boondoggle that it is. "I hate the cart," Martin said. "I hate playing golf in it. I hate being the center of attention. People don't come to see me play golf. They come to see me limp."

He showed me his leg in his room one night. I asked to see it, actually. He stood up, took off his pants and then the two nylon restraining stockings on his right leg that are supposed to keep down the swelling. What was underneath looked like a baseball bat somebody had used to hit a thousand rocks.

"Watch the blood drain into it," he said. Over the next two minutes that bony stick of a leg started turning purple and globby and marbled right in front of my eyes, bloating to twice its diameter. Grotesque pools of blood gathered in his hip, knee, ankle. He let me run my hand gingerly along his shin, which felt like a long, fat sandwich bag filled with spaghetti and meatballs. It was fascinating, except I felt dizzy.

And he plays golf with that leg—six days some weeks. But that's no reason to give him the cart, right? Hasn't Martin ruined the fundamental nature of golf? Every day now, don't we see disabled pros tearing up the tours? O.K., no other disabled person has even come close to being good enough, but you just know that hordes of cripples who can break 70 are coming soon, right?

In truth, Martin hasn't broken 70 much lately, either. He lost his card on the PGA Tour after last year, and he has made only four cuts in eight tries in his return to the bush leagues this year. The limp gets worse every month. Yet he's never withdrawn from a tournament.

Maybe he should've bowed out in Richmond. He was playing pretty well in the first round until he got to 17, where he suddenly started swinging like Richard Nixon and limping back to his cart like Chester. "Something tweaked in my leg," he whispered. Three-hundred-yard drives were now 200. He bogeyed that hole and the next, and wound up missing the cut by two shots.

Still, we must protect the sanctity of the game! So don't give in, Supreme Court.

When the ruling comes down against Martin, don't go soft, Tour commissioner Tim Finchem. Don't grandfather him in—as so many pros, including Jack Nicklaus, have suggested—for however long he has until the leg snaps. And, hey, Tiger Woods, don't speak up for your old Stanford teammate, because you haven't so far. Besides, that leg might miraculously heal itself, and Martin would suddenly jump up and finish within 20 shots of you.

Ladies and gentlemen of golf, this is no time for weakness. After all, we've got a game to think of.

Postscript: Martin finally won his Supreme Court case and was allowed to play PGA Tour events in a golf cart. As far as anybody could tell, golf itself did not collapse, nor did the world implode, nor was the Tour flooded with one-legged scratch golfers. Martin and his pain and his optimism beat on hopelessly that year, week in and week out, but he'd already lost his Tour card by the time the court ruled. He's now the head golf coach at Oregon. May his dreams be full of very long runs.

37

Not Your Typical
Tearjerker

JUNE 18, 2001

I THINK IT WAS JUST AFTER THE FIRECRACKER HIT ME AND JUST before I was teargassed last Saturday night that I knew this was a very bad column idea. Still, here it is.

8:30 p.m. (MDT)—Sitting in a cozy press box at Pepsi Center in Denver during Game 7 of the Stanley Cup finals, I'm thinking, After the Colorado Avalanche wins this game there will be a riot, because these days there's almost always a riot after a team wins a championship. But wouldn't it be interesting to be *inside* a fans' riot for once? See how one gets started? Besides, it's either that or try to get a column out of Mrs. Ray Bourque.

8:47—I walk about 10 blocks from Pepsi Center, to 16th and Wynkoop, where 60 Denver police officers are donning riot gear, nearly the exact same equipment that Patrick Roy is wearing: helmet with visor, and chest, shoulder, shin and arm pads. Plus two cans of fogger mace, a nightstick, a gas mask, plastic flex-cuffs, metal handcuffs, a .45 SIG Sauer pistol and bullets. The cops know the riot is coming. The Army-Navy stores in town had nearly sold out of gas masks the day before. It's clear: When the game is over, the game will begin.

9:15—On a huge outdoor TV screen at 19th and Blake, Ray Bourque triumphantly hoists the Cup. A man on a Harley, watching, revs his engine menacingly. The crowd of 18,000 starts emptying out of Pepsi Center. Let the stupidity begin.

9:22—One block away, at Coors Field, the Colorado Rockies—St. Louis Cardinals game ends, sending 47,000 fans, many of them plastered, onto Blake Street. Uh-oh.

9:31—At 15th and Larimer, maybe 1,000 happy people are sardined into one rollicking intersection, doing the usual all-American things: passing humans above their heads and chanting for women to remove their tops.

10:02—Three energetic youths start a little fire out of a newspaper, a T-shirt and a skateboard. Everybody starts jumping as if they were on pogo sticks. Somebody tosses in a pack of Black Cat firecrackers. Somebody jumps through the flames. Then many jump through them. Now a man stands in the middle of them, and his pants catch on fire. Now we're having fun.

10:07—There seem to be a lot of energetic youths in gas masks around. I don't remember seeing *them* at the game. Many cops are around too, some on horseback. Five or six energetic youths get too close to the cops and get maced. Two get cuffed. Somebody is shooting bottle rockets, and one hits me in the butt. As we say in sports, we are all taking it to another level.

10:14—The cops march in, force back the crowd, stamp out the fire and box off the intersection. I notice many of the fans take off their Avalanche jerseys and cover their faces. I do not have an Avalanche jersey. I finger my tie nervously.

10:24—A cop on a bullhorn says, calmly, "This is your third warning to clear the streets." I did not hear the first two, but I notice nobody is clearing the streets. Many energetic youths are chanting, "F--- the police!" very sincerely. Suddenly a cop lobs a silver, smoking tear gas canister 10 feet from me. I flee, sprinting like an energetic youth myself. Another canister whistles by my ear and lands 20 feet to the right. I zig in a new direction and nearly get trampled. I zag. A canister lands smack in front of me and before I can rezig, I have run through the cloud. Have you ever stuck an entire serving of wasabi up your nose? Then stuck a spoonful of horseradish in each eye? Then gargled with chili peppers? Me neither, but it *can't* be as bad as tear gas. I cover my mouth and nose with my tie, but it's much, much too late.

10:26—Retching and running, I make it into a 7-Eleven, lurch for the beverage coolers, yank out a bottle of water and pour it in my eyes, down my throat and, sideways, in my nose. Then a second bottle. A third. When I can finally see, I notice my reflection in the cooler door. I am a mucusy, snarling, coughing, spitting, panting, soaking maniac standing in a puddle of water. In other words, not much different from many other 7-Eleven customers.

In the end 700 cops will be called in, 60 people will be arrested and seven police vehicles will be damaged, but the TV reports will label the soiree "tame. "And I will have learned three things about sports riots: 1) They have *nothing* to do with sports; 2) they should be scheduled, like the games themselves, because the yahoos who start them *want* to start them; and 3) they are not fun to be inside.

I should've interviewed Mrs. Ray Bourque. There still would've been crying, just much less of it by me.

Postscript: As I write this, Colorado's beloved Avalanche is in last place, causing even more tears.

38

Fatal Distractions

JANUARY 29, 2001

SEE, IF YOU'RE THE BALTIMORE RAVENS, THE KEY TO THE Super Bowl is making sure your unblockable star linebacker, Ray Lewis, doesn't have any distractions that might affect his play. You'd hate to have distractions. ¶ You'd hate to have anybody bring up the two men he and his pals left bleeding on a street corner in Atlanta after last year's Super Bowl. You'd hate to have anybody mention the two men—one a hairstylist whose fiancée had a baby on the way, the other an artist who sent money to help out his grandma—who were left dying from knife wounds as Lewis and his pals sped away in his rented 40-foot Lincoln Navigator limo. Because on Sunday, while the media are making Lewis into a god, it would be really unfair to bring up Richard Lollar and Shorty Baker, right?

You don't remember Richard and Shorty? They're the two guys nobody killed, according to a Fulton County jury. Lewis, who was charged with murder and aggravated assault, pleaded guilty to a misdemeanor charge of obstructing justice and walked away. The other two defendants, Lewis's friends Reginald Oakley and Joseph Sweeting, were acquitted of murder and aggravated assault charges. There have been no more arrests, and no detectives are looking to make any.

Let's hope the two dead men won't cross Lewis's mind on Sunday, but there's a woman in Decatur, Ga., who won't be able to help thinking of them. Her name is Kellye Smith, and she was Lollar's fiancée. Every time she looks at her 10-month-old daughter, India, she thinks of Lollar, because India looks just like him. India was born five weeks after her father was murdered. "I still don't understand it," said Smith, 31, last week. "I believe Ray Lewis played a definite part in Richard's death."

It had been such a great Super Sunday, too. Smith and Lollar had spent the day together, going to Lamaze class and then to dinner at an Outback Steakhouse. But being eight months pregnant, Smith was too tired to go party with Lollar's pals visiting from Akron. No problem. He'd kiss her when he got in and then make her his special cheese, egg and biscuit breakfast in the morning.

So Lollar, 24, once Akron's Barber of the Year, went to pick up his 5' 2" buddy Jacinth (Shorty) Baker, 21, for a night on the town. Baker was a stitch, loved to wear sweet clothes, liked to draw cartoons, but he needed a little cheering up. Both his parents had died within the past year and a half.

Nobody seems to be sure what happened at four the next morning at Buckhead's $100 cover Cobalt Lounge, but we know Lewis's group and the Akron group crossed paths, and a fight ensued out on the street. Next thing you knew Baker was stabbed three times and Lollar five, twice in the heart. Lollar was dead within 90 seconds; Baker died on the way to the hospital.

Atlanta police found Baker's, Oakley's and Sweeting's blood in Lewis's limo and Oakley's and Sweeting's blood in the lobby rest room of a nearby Holiday Inn, where the fleeing limo stopped immediately after the stabbings. Police never found the clothes that Lewis wore that night. And wasn't it a coincidence that Sweeting had bought three knives the day before the Super Bowl at a sporting goods store while Lewis was making an appearance there? Lewis even testified that Sweeting told him in the Holiday Inn lobby, "Every time they hit me, I hit them," and that Sweeting held a knife in his hand as he said that.

None of it meant a thing in court. Lewis copped to the misdemeanor, testified for the prosecution and walked straight into the NFL Defensive Player of the Year award. The families of Lollar and Baker walked straight into a hole in their lives that sure doesn't feel misdemeanor. "To tell you the truth," Lollar's aunt Thomasaina Threatt said between sobs last week, "I wish Ray Lewis were dead."

"Ray Lewis can sit there and smile, the big comeback kid," says Lollar's cousin Charita Hale, who says she will take candles to that Buckhead street corner on Jan. 31 to mark the first anniversary of the murders. "His family will always see him, but we'll never be able to see Richard again."

"I keep wishing," says Smith, "that Richard would've been able to see India once. Just *once*."

When Lewis left the courtroom last June, a free man, his attorney Ed Garland said his client wanted to talk to the families of the dead men. But according to Hale, Smith and Threatt, he never has.

Good thing. It'd be an awful distraction.

Postscript: It was a shock to see the Ravens linebacker on the cover of SI recently, praying, and the headline: The Gospel According to Ray Lewis. *The story says he got religion and has really changed. He was lucky. He got the chance.*

39

Corrupting Our Utes

AUGUST 11, 2003

THANK GOD FOR THE NCAA. WITHOUT IT, COLLEGE sports would have more thugs than a Snoop Dogg video. ¶ Last week, for instance, the NCAA brought notorious Utah coach Rick Majerus and his outlaw basketball program to justice. Just look at what the NCAA nailed this cretin on:

•Unashamedly purchasing a dinner in 1994 for his player Keith Van Horn at a Salt Lake City deli. At 3 a.m., no less! So what if Van Horn's father had died that night? Or that Majerus was the one who had to tell him? Or that Van Horn wanted Majerus to stay with him until his 8 a.m. flight home? This ain't *Dr. Phil!*

"I guess I should've reached over as he was getting on the plane and said, 'Hey, you owe me $9.90 for the ham and eggs,' " Majerus says.

Do you see? Do you see the attitude?

•Brazenly buying a bagel for a player. Who cares if the player was upset about his brother's recent suicide attempt and had come to Majerus to talk? "I could've talked to the kid in my office, I guess," Majerus says. "But if you go get a bagel, it kind of relaxes a kid. It's not coach-player anymore. It's two guys talkin'."

Bah! It's one guy cheating, and, in truth, Majerus got lucky. The report never states what *kind* of bagel Majerus bought the kid. For instance, an "everything" bagel is a considerably larger offense in the eyes of the NCAA. And don't even get me started on the ramifications of lox.

•Twice—*twice!*—allowing assistants to buy groceries for players who didn't have enough money to eat: $20-$30 for a player whose meal plan hadn't begun yet and $20 for a prospect who hadn't yet received his scholarship. "I just felt sorry for those guys," Majerus says. "Maybe because I was that kid once, you know? No money, no friends, and you haven't eaten for two days."

Sentimental hogwash!

Majerus just doesn't get it. Take the pizza. In one instance he bought himself and a player a pizza pie at a Salt Lake eatery. So what if seeing Majerus not eating pizza is like seeing Carmen Electra in a nun's habit? Buying the pie was still wrong. And it doesn't matter that according to NCAA rules, Majerus would've committed no infraction had that very same pizza been a) delivered, b) sent up by room service, c) carried back to his room or d) served at home.

In fact a coach can serve his players catered lobster and caviar in his home if he wants, at least on occasion. (True, Majerus doesn't *have* a home. He lives in a hotel room year-round. Is that the NCAA's fault?) But when you wantonly *go* to a known pizza joint, mister, you're just *begging* for it.

And I don't want to hear how clean the Utah program has been either, or how, under Majerus, the Utes have had four Academic All-Americas in the last five years, more than any other Division I basketball program. Clyde Barrow used to floss. So what?

And so what if the NCAA didn't find any hidden cars or substitute test takers? What about the *massive* slush-fund payments? The worst example was Majerus's giving the players $10 each to go see *Remember the Titans.* Ten bucks? The discount theater in question charged $5 for a ticket. That left-over $5 could've gone toward all kinds of temptations—drugs, alcohol, Junior Mints.

There was more: letting a player send a housing application in a FedEx envelope when the NCAA rule specifically states that only transcripts or standardized test scores can be included; serving milk and cookies made by Majerus's 76-year-old mother, or by Utes basketball fans, or by an athletic department secretary, at film meetings. Sure, milk and cookies sounds small, but how long is it before we're talking about the harder stuff, like pie and coffee?

There were other violations: practices going over the allotted four hours a day; Majerus watching 15 minutes of a pickup game he wasn't supposed to see and another 10 minutes of informal dribbling and dunking. You let that stuff go unchecked, and pretty soon you've got frogs falling from the clouds.

It's not an easy job, picking nits this tiny, but nobody is up to the task like the NCAA. Take the time the organization told Aaron Adair, a third baseman at Oklahoma, that the book he'd written about surviving brain cancer meant his amateur career was over. Or the work the NCAA is selflessly doing today, like making Colorado receiver Jeremy Bloom curtail his world-class skiing career and kill his modeling because they would somehow make him a professional football player. (Now, when the NCAA uses its athletes in TV ads to promote itself during the Final Four, that's just good marketing.)

I support the small-mindedness of the NCAA. In fact, my hope is that someday the NCAA will get so small—so microscopic—that it will slide down the holes in its shower drain and be gone for good.

Postscript: The NCAA gives me a facial tic. It's constantly trying to shoot the rabbits while the elephants stomp all over them. Go into a locker room of any major college football team after the game and you'll see more diamonds than at a Tiffany's sale. Reggie Bush may have received a rent-free house and yet USC has faced no penalty. Quarterback Troy Smith of Ohio State admitted accepting $500 and missed two games. But buy somebody a bagel, mister, and you're busted!

40

Heart and Seoul

FEBRUARY 27, 2006

O LYMPIC MEDALS CAN LEAD TO RICHES, FAME OR A new girlfriend. They can lead to a job, a life or an appearance on the *Today* show. But Toby Dawson hopes his leads to something else—his birth parents. ¶ Left on the front stoop of a police station as a toddler and then placed in an orphanage in Seoul, Toby was adopted at age three by two Vail ski instructors, Deb and Mike Dawson. They had him skiing by four. He was beating them down the mountain by nine.

In those days he never thought about being the only Asian kid in powder-white Vail. Never wondered who his blood parents might be. Never wanted to know, even though his brother, K.C.—also adopted—flew to Seoul 10 years ago and met his. Toby hated hearing about that meeting. The man in Korea wanted K.C. to call him father. Nuh-uh. No way.

Whether it was fear of the unknown or love of his adopted parents, Dawson showed no curiosity about the subject. Didn't ever go by his Korean middle name—Soo Chul. Complained when his parents dragged him to Korean Heritage Camp. Didn't want to be anything other than "a blond-haired, blue-eyed regular American kid," he says. "All I cared about was skiing."

Problem was, Toby (Awesome) Dawson got too good. Started winning World Cup events in the freestyle moguls. Pretty soon the planet started noticing him. And people sure as hell noticed he wasn't blond-haired and blue-eyed.

I'm your father, Koreans e-mailed. *I'm your mother. I'm your cousin.*

And Dawson's response was always the same: Get bent. "I think he was blocking it out," says Deb. "Which was too bad. Because his dream was the Olympics, but mine was that the Olympics would be how he'd find his parents."

Then something happened. Asked to return to the Korean Heritage Camp he so hated as a kid, he went and discovered something within himself. Suddenly he wanted to know who he was. "There was such a buzz with the kids there," he recalls. "A lot of them had already found their birth parents. Some of the stories were amazing."

One of the stories he heard was my daughter's.

We adopted Rae at four months, and she was the anti-Toby. She thought constantly about her birth mother, who *had* to be a princess. Or a movie star.

So when she was 11, we flew to Seoul, even though we were told that her birth mother would not meet with us. Unwed, she'd sneaked away at 16 to have the baby, and only her sister knew. She was married now, with three kids, and she dared not be discovered. And yet—the interpreter told us—not a day went by that she didn't think of Rae.

Finally, she agreed to 30 stolen minutes, in a coffee shop two hours from her home. We waited three hours. Rae looked heartsick. Finally, a cellphone rang. She'd meet us in the alley. And suddenly, there she was, tiny and white-faced. She climbed into our van. She looked at everybody but Rae. She said she had 10 minutes.

"Rae," I said, "if you have any questions for your birth mother, ask them now." Rae took out a folded piece of paper we didn't know she had.

Question 1. *Why did you give me up?* "Great shame," the woman told the interpreter, never looking at Rae. Two: *Where's my father?* "Don't know." Finally, a shocker. Three: *When you had me, did you get to hold me?*

The birth mother hung her head. No.

And that's when the interpreter said, "Well, you can *now*."

That broke the woman. She wheeled on Rae and swallowed her in her arms and kisses and sobs. Maybe the only people crying harder in that van were my wife and I. She wouldn't let Rae go. Finally, she had to. We haven't seen her since. Rae was beaming. "It feels like it fixed a little hole in my heart," she said.

So when Toby Dawson shredded the Turin freestyle course last week, beating his more ballyhooed teammate, Jeremy Bloom, and winning a stunning bronze, his picture ran in nearly every South Korean newspaper and on every TV station. Somewhere, maybe his birth mother has read his story and seen him for the first time in more than 25 years, shouting, "Oh, my God! That's my son!"

Only now, at last, Dawson is open to a meeting. "I think it'd be cool," he says. "I'd like to be friends."

He's got lots of possibilities. Since winning the medal, Dawson seems to have more long-lost parents than a PowerBall winner. But so far, nobody's agreed to a blood test.

I hope somebody does. I hope Dawson makes it over this one last mogul. Because an Olympic medal can fix a lot of things, but not little holes in the heart.

Postscript: One year after this column ran, Toby Dawson was reunited in Seoul with his biological father, a 53-year-old bus driver named Kim Jae Su, who cried as the two embraced. DNA tests confirmed that Kim was the dad; he said his wife (from whom he is now divorced) had lost Toby in a market in Busan when he was three. Kim said he futilely searched the city's orphanages for his son but never gave up. Dawson, whose Korean name is Bong Seok, also met his biological younger brother, 24-year-old Kim Hyun Cheol. When Toby first saw his father, he hugged him and said, in Korean, "I've been waiting a long time, Father."

As for Rae, she still has not heard from her birth mother, but she plans to write and sing a song that goes No. 1 all over the world in hopes that her birth mom will reach out to her once again.

41

Read My Lips!

JANUARY 14, 2002

F OR GOOD TIMES, THERE'S NOTHING LIKE INVITING A
car full of lip-readers over to watch Sunday's NFL games.
¶ Lipreading is a feverish topic in the NFL these days.
Coaches are covering their mouths when they send in
plays because they're suspicious that thieves are watching. The coaches
look like they had onions for lunch or just graduated from the Istanbul
Spy Institute. "We hear rumors all the time about [opposing] coaches
hiring guys to read our lips," says Cardinals offensive coordinator Rich
Olson.

It's no rumor, pal. "Our guy keeps a pair of binoculars on their signal-
callers every game," says Broncos coach Mike Shanahan. "With any luck, we
have their defensive signals figured out by halftime. Sometimes, by the end
of the first quarter."

Giants coach Jim Fassel thinks it's all lip service. "If someone is that
smart," Fassel grouses, "he should be curing cancer, not coaching football."

To check it out, I hired three lip-readers, all women, all football fans and
all either hearing impaired or profoundly deaf, to come by the house last

weekend. Nice people. They didn't even complain when my younger son tried to sign *good morning*, but wound up signing *screw you* instead.

The first game was the Colts' easy win over the Broncos, and the one guy who should've covered his mouth was not a coach but a player, Indianapolis quarterback Peyton Manning. He's Dudley Do-Right in public, but on the field Manning seems to have the vocabulary of a dyspeptic carnival employee. The lip-readers counted nine televised *f---s*, many *dammits*, and, once, just for variety's sake, a *f-----' dammit*!

In the first quarter, after a replay had overturned an apparent touchdown pass to wide receiver Marvin Harrison, Manning was seen to say, disgustedly, "Why'd they show the f-----' replay?" When a running back short-armed his screen pass, he yelled, "F-----' get in there!"

After the game, when our correspondent went to the locker room and told Manning the lip-readers had nailed him, Manning took the stringer's cellphone and called me.

"They got me, huh?" he said, dejectedly.

"Nine times," I said.

"Man, I don't like to use that kind of language. I hate for the kids to see that stuff. But you forget the camera is on you, you know? It just pops out. Nine times? My mother is going to call and reprimand me for that."

Lip-readers are more fun than naked Jell-O fights. One time an unidentified Colts fan went up to the Broncos' ubiquitous Barrel Man and said, apparently, "Hey, we can get you some pants!" Now that's the new American spirit shining through.

(For kicks, we watched a replay of the Rose Bowl game. The camera zeroed in on a gorgeous blonde who smiled and appeared to say something vaguely sexy to her friend. Turns out, the lip-reader says, it was, "Is there something gross on my face?" Sometimes life's better without a sound track.)

The next game was the Jets' 24–22 win over the Raiders, in which we found out Oakland coach Jon Gruden has a mouth he shouldn't kiss his mother with. He also has one that's easier to read than a stop sign. Most of the time he made no effort to cover his lips, which meant the lip-readers could read what plays he was sending in. Once, they read him saying, "Left side, 290, radical," and it went for a left-side touchdown pass to tight end Roland Williams. When our correspondent asked Williams after the game if that was, indeed, the name of the play, Williams's eyes got big, and he said, "Where'd you *get* that?"

It is a very odd feeling to have three hearing-impaired women telling you what play the Raiders will run next. If Fassel didn't believe it before, you think he does now?

Even when Gruden tried to cover his mouth, he did it two inches too low and with his play card, so that an entire side of plays could be read easily by any schlub with a TV set and a zoom button. Hey, nobody said football coaches were Mensa members.

All in all, despite the rampant profanity, I decided there are three major advantages for hearing-impaired NFL fans:

a) They have access to a part of the game that's unknown to most of us.

b) They gain a new appreciation for its verbal intensity.

c) They never have to listen to Jerry Glanville.

42

The Real
New York Giants

MARCH 25, 2002

T ALK ABOUT A REBUILDING YEAR. THE NEW YORK CITY Fire Department football team starts its National Public Safety League season next week missing seven starters, 12 alums and two coaches. But the firemen are playing. Hell, yes, they're playing. ¶ Says cornerback Mike Heffernan, whose brother John was among the Bravest who died in the collapse of the World Trade Center towers, "Somebody said to me, 'Probably not going to be a team this season, huh, Mike?' I told him, 'We'll have a team if we only have 10 guys. We're playing.' "

Most of the guys on the team have a nasty case of the WTC cough, which is what you get from digging week after week, up to 18 hours a day, and inhaling dust, smoke, glass particles, asbestos and, indeed, microscopic remains of their fallen comrades. But the guys are playing. "Damn right," says fullback Tom Narducci. "It's tradition."

But how? Forget about replacing the players. How do you replace the *men*? How does starting cornerback Danny Foley replace the starting cornerback on the other side—his brother, Tommy?

142

Last season, if it wasn't Danny pulling Tommy out of the pile, it was Tommy pulling Danny out. "That was the most fun I ever had playing football," says Danny, 28, the younger of the two by four years. "We both played high school and college, so we never got to see each other play. On this team, we were always together."

After 10 straight days of digging through the rubble, it was Danny who found Tommy. One last time, Danny pulled Tommy out of the pile. "When we found him," says Danny, "it was kind of a relief. I promised my mom I wasn't coming home without Tommy—and I didn't. But a lot of families had nobody to bury."

Play football? How will they even get a play off? They lost their No. 1 and 1A quarterbacks, Paddy Lyons and Tom Cullen. It was Lyons who came into the game last May against the Orange County (Calif.) Lawmen and rescued his teammates. They trailed 14–0, but he led them to a 28–21 win. He was good at that kind of thing. He was with Squad 252, along with cornerback Tarel Coleman, and his friends believe those two rescued a lot of people that day before the steel-and-concrete sky collapsed on them.

How do you replace tight end Keith Glascoe, who was so good only a bum shoulder kept him off the New York Jets' roster in the early '90s? Or big lineman Bronko Pearsall, who insisted on singing *Wild Rover* after every game, win or lose?

Who's going to kick now that Billy Johnston is gone? Everybody called him Liam because he looked so bloody Irish. He was automatic on extra points, which was a luxury. Hell, there were years when the Bravest had to go for two after every touchdown just because they didn't have a kicker. Then they found Johnston.

They found Johnston again three weeks into the digging. Heffernan was there, and he helped carry his teammate out.

Even if you can replace the players who were lost, how do you replace all the other guys who made the team so damn much fun? Tommy Haskell was the tight ends coach and wrote the team newsletter. Mike Cawley set up the after-game beer parties. Danny Suhr, the first fireman to die that day, was the treasurer. Offensive coordinator Mike Stackpole lost his brother, Tim. Linebacker Zach Fletcher lost his twin brother, Andre.

How do you go on when so many guys are dead that you can't even retire their jerseys because you wouldn't have enough left to dress the team? How do you play a game draped in sorrow like that?

Came the first team meeting, and the club didn't get anywhere near its usual 60 guys. It got 120. All the lineup holes were patched. Guys who had retired signed up again. Guys who'd been asked 10 times said yes on the 11th. You cry together at enough funerals, you figure you can bleed together on a football field, too. One thing about firemen, they don't let each other fight battles alone.

Talk about a comeback year. "You've got to understand," says the team's president, Neil Walsh. "We all go to each other's weddings, christenings, graduations. I broke your brother in, and your dad broke me in, and I carried your son out of the pile. We're all brothers."

Not long ago a third-grade teacher found the team's water boy—Walsh's son Ryan—sobbing uncontrollably in the boys' bathroom. "To him, all those guys were his uncles," says Walsh. "He couldn't handle losing them all in one day."

Some holes are easier to patch than others.

Postscript: The team never got so much attention as it did that first season after 9/11. Their annual rivalry with the NYPD team was held at Giants Stadium no less, with the cops winning, 10–0. The next season, they won the National Public Safety Football League championship, beating the Los Angeles Police Department in the finals. An absolutely great bunch of guys to drink beer with.

43

Golden Retriever

SEPTEMBER 19, 2005

W E DESPISE TENNIS PROS. ❡ THEY DON'T SPEAK to us. They don't look at us. They don't acknowledge us. We mean slightly less to them than mealworm excrement. ❡ And yet, how could Roger Federer have won without us? Or Kim Clijsters? In fact, without us, how could the 2005 U.S. Open have been held at all?

We are ball persons. We fetch their balls, their towels, their water and ice. We stand in the punishing sun and shade them with umbrellas, as if each of them were the infant prince of Siam.

And yet do they thank us? Do they offer us high knuckles? Do they tip? No, they do not. We are their appendix—they don't notice us until we bother them.

I know. I was one of the 250 ball persons at the Open, even though I was 30 years older, a foot taller and three ephedra slower than just about everyone else.

Still, wasn't I there for you, Meghann Shaughnessy, on court 9 in your doubles victory? Didn't I bounce the balls perfectly to you, except for the one off your ankle? Didn't I stand perfectly still between serves, apart from that one time when I thought you'd already hit two? You bet your spanky pants I did! And yet when I approached you afterward and asked for your evaluation of my work, you said, "You were out there? *Today*?"

Your partner, Nadia Petrova, might remember me. I'm the one who chased a ball that wound up in the mitts of a middle-aged woman in the stands. She wouldn't throw the damn thing back. "Ma'am, please!" I mouthed. And she snipped, "We're supposed to be able to keep them this year!"

"Only on the Arthur Ashe court," I snipped back.

That's when I realized Petrova was staring AK-47 holes in me, waiting for me to return to my spot before her next serve. Oops.

My mentor, 27-year-old ball person Thinh Dinh, consoled me afterward with the Question Game. We'd stand in the plaza between matches, in our totally cool Polo blue-and-white ball-person uniforms. People would ask questions, and Thinh would politely jerk them around.

Q: Do you guys get paid?

Thinh: Yes, we're paid on commission. Twenty-five cents a ball. (Real answer: Ball persons get $9 an hour.)

Q: Do you go to school for this?

Thinh: Yes, we go to Ball Person University. It's in upstate New York. (Real answer: Ball persons get a week of training just before the Open.)

I liked the Question Game so much I tried it.

Q: What's the worst part of the job?

Me: Shaving the fuzz off the balls. It gets everywhere.

Real answer: Trying to gather all the balls that are hailing on you from your five ball-person teammates while trying to get the player his stupid towel to wipe his sweat off even though he just wiped the sweat off last point, and then sprinting back to your spot, all in 14 seconds. ("And don't block the sponsor signage!" everyone reminded me.)

Andre Agassi is a pill about the service. "He's nice, but he's very, very particular," says lawyer Gary Spitz, who, at 41, has been ball-personing for 26 years. Pete Sampras didn't like anybody throwing balls behind him. Jeff Tarango gets mad if the ball is bounced to him. He wants it thrown in the air. *Sorr-eee.*

But the unanimous choice for the pro the ball people would most love to throw under the number 7 train? Conchita Martinez, the Nurse Racket of tennis. "She's rude," Spitz says. "She's all 'Gimme the ball now! No, not *this* ball! *That* ball!' She even hits balls at you! When the kids misbehave around here, we make them do one of her matches."

Italy's Giorgio Galimberti ain't no field of daisies, either. I was his chair valet for one set when he suddenly yelled out, "Ice!" Ice? I had no idea. I brought him a little Dixie cup full of ice. "No, no! Ice! For my leg-a!"

For his *leg-a*? I floundered around for maybe 20 seconds. Suddenly a teammate rushed me a bag of ice, which I was about to hand to him when time ran out. Galimberti waved the bag away with something that sounded like, "Idiot-a!" and limped back on the court. And one set later he retired with leg cramps. Oops.

Afterward, still in uniform, I gingerly approached him in the press area and said, "Do you know me?"

He braced as if I were going to present him with paternity papers. "No."

"I was one of your ball persons tonight," I said. "You don't remember me?"

"No, I don't notice you," he said. "But to be honest, I never worry about the ball boys in New York because they're so good. Very quick. They're always ready for you."

We love tennis pros.

Postscript: In 2006, a women's pro tournament in Madrid used male models as ball boys. And the players hardly seemed to notice, except to say they weren't very good. "I don't think they really know what they have to do on the court because they are too busy watching the players," Elena Dementieva complained. Oh. My. God. Tennis players could have Jesus and his 12 apostles working a match and the only thing they'd say is, "They were a little slow in the corners."

44

Petra Shines On

PETRA NEMCOVA WAS DROWNING THE DAY AFTER Christmas, 2004. One hundred feet inland. Naked. Hanging from a roof. Crazy place to drown, on a roof, but there it was. "I was being sucked down into the water," she says. "Each time, for two or three minutes. I realized, I'm going now. It's over. This is how I die. I let it go. I stopped fighting, and it was pure bliss."

In a way, death would have been a relief. When the tsunami hit the beach of Phuket, Thailand, it swept the 25-year-old Czech supermodel and her boyfriend, British photographer Simon Atlee, out to sea. But then it sucked them back in and deposited them in all the debris it had raked up—metal posts and doors and cars. And one of these things slammed hard into Nemcova, shattering her pelvis, ripping her swimsuit off and tearing the love of her life away forever.

A supermodel lives out of her day planner, but, she says, "Simon taught me to live in the moment. He said, 'Any two days off in a row? That's the weekend! We celebrate!' " And they did, taking time to be together all over the world—from Cape Town to Miami to Vermont. Finally, Nemcova had

148

brought Simon to her favorite place, Phuket. But now she was watching him die while he screamed her name, not to be seen again until he was identified in a morgue by DNA testing 69 days later.

She grabbed hold of a floating bungalow roof, but the debris smashed her body over and over. The pain was blinding. And that's when the water overcame her. "I stopped fighting," she says. "And as soon as I let go, I saw the blue sky again. "

She careened toward a palm tree and grabbed it. She held on for eight hours that you just can't imagine—repeatedly fainting from the pain and dehydration (the hot sun scorching the gashes in her body, the waves pushing her under trash again and again), seeing nobody but hearing screams. Finally, two Thai men pulled her out, got her on a floating car door and paddled her to the hospital.

And that's when it got worse. "I was in such pain, even the morphine would only last for an hour and a half," says Nemcova. And it wasn't black water drowning her now, it was her grief over Atlee. What could she grab hold of?

Finally, on New Year's Eve, her doctor shook her out of it. "You must not drift into sorrow!" he said. "You must not dwell on the pain and the grief! Think of anything! Anything!"

She thought of a beautiful flower, and felt better. She thought of sunshine, and felt better. Within a day the pain diminished. As the months went by, she began to experience as much beauty as pain. Soon, she saw the duality of all things.

Take the tsunami. "It was horrifying, but it also brought so much love," she says. "It brought so many people together. The world is a more unified place now. People reached out from all over the world. People are helping each other. There's more sense of connection now."

She sees it in herself, too. "I used to think, All these models worrying about this wrinkle or that tiny ounce of fat. Why am I doing this? What's the meaning?" But now she sees it. A percentage of her income goes to the foundation she started for orphaned Thai children: the Happy Hearts Fund. Nemcova has one of those, too, now—a happy heart. But, yeah, she has flashbacks. She'll be at some shoot, posing on some beach, and suddenly she will be flung back there, into hell. *Simon's face. The palm tree. The screams.*

She has gone back many times to Thailand, to the place of her torment, and seen that nothing is the same. The hotel was rebuilt. She can't find the tree she'd clung to. "The landscape seems all new." And isn't her landscape all new too? Six months before that wave hit, Simon made Petra a book of all the things he loved about her. After he died, she and it were inseparable. Not anymore. She put it in a safe. "I have to move on," she whispers.

She knows that, sometimes, letting go is what saves you.

Postscript: Last we checked, Nemcova was getting on with her life, dating pop singer/songwriter James Blunt. Her Happy Hearts Fund had raised more than $1.5 million.

45

Jack Nicholson's Diary

JULY 26, 2004

NEW YEAR'S DAY, 2005

DEAR DIARY, I THINK I'M GOIN' FREAKIN' NUTS, MAN. I don't make movies anymore. I don't shower. I don't shave. I just stare into this laptop and write to you. ¶ It's been almost six months since we traded the greatest player on earth for three guys who can't play dead in a *Quincy* episode. Right now Staples Center is about as exciting as an acid reflux seminar. You talk about *Heartburn*.

What did they do to my beautiful Lakers? Who the *hell*'s idea was it to hand the franchise over to a guy who, as I write this, is *still* on trial 30 games into the season? And why the hell is Kato Kaelin testifying day after day?

Because the stupid trial goes every day, Kobe can't fly back and forth to play, which means we're getting beat like rented mules. By the freakin' Nuggets no less!

It's not just the losing and the half-filled seats. The *buzz* is gone. I used to see people from the industry at games, you know? Chris Rock, Adam Sandler, Cameron Diaz. You know who was on celebrity row with me last night? Florence Henderson, Urkel, and that "I'm spicy!" guy from the Burger King ads.

Is this as good as it gets?

Lakers floor seats used to go for $1,500. Now they're $27.50 with a chalupa and a Slava Medvedenko bobblehead thrown in. I had some guy sitting next to me last night who said he got his ticket with two Slurpee proof-of-purchase seals. All night the schmo is going, "Jack, you know what your problem is? You can't *handle* the truth!!!"

Maybe he's right. This Lamar Odom guy we got plays defense the way Kathleen Turner diets. Brian Grant couldn't score on Lil' Kim. Shaq's gone. Karl Malone's gone. Derek Fisher signed with Golden State. Did you ever think you'd see that? A Laker signin' with freakin' Golden State! Worse, Gary Payton's still here.

I'm tellin' you, I haven't seen ball this bad since we shot the hoops scene in *Cuckoo's Nest*.

And if you think I'm bad, you ought to see the owner, Jerry Buss. He used to be all tan and teeth. But ever since he fired a coach with nine rings and traded a center with three, he looks like a guy whose Viagra just ran out. He used to always have hot-and-cold-running starlets on each arm. Now you see him with two 53-year-old housewives from Oxnard. You'd think they'd at least take their curlers out.

Turns out Buss never meant to make the Shaq trade. He says he was floating on his yacht off Italy the week it went down. He called Mitch Kupchak, his G.M., and said, "I really want to go younger this year." Mitch thought he meant players. Jerry was talking about *dates*.

Now he can't get a coach to stay at any price. Rudy Tomjanovich took one look at his starting lineup—featuring Kareem Rush and Luke Walton—and ran like Roman Polanski's nanny. We're on our fourth coach this season: the little-known *third* Van Gundy brother, Vern.

The only one more depressed than me is Jeannie Buss, Jerry's daughter. Not only did Daddy cut loose her sweetie, Phil Jackson, but now she has to market this cadaver. This is a team that's had two losing seasons since 1977. They've never had to *sell* tickets before. She has no clue.

Check out the team's marketing slogans so far:

That was Zen, this is now!

Hey, you can still come see the banners!

Park where celebs used to park!

Halftimes blow now too. I mean, I can understand budget cutbacks, but I can't get into these damn Laker Boys. I used to always sneak back to that "private room" at halftime, too, and hang with McEnroe and Springsteen and whoever the coolest people were in the building that night. No more. I checked in there last night and it was just Ryan Seacrest playing solitaire.

Somethin's gotta give here. I'm losing my freakin' noodle. I was here for Magic, Kareem, Worthy. I never thought I'd have to sit through Slowtime.

They're sayin' Staples could be a tomb for five or six years. Buss is stuck. We had to pay Kobe $20 million a year to stay, and we've got to pay Payton and these three nobodies a combined $31 million this year, so we've got less room under the cap than Ben Wallace in a skully.

Six years? I can't do six years of this, man! I'm losing my grip! I think I got a facial tic! I hear voices!

Sometimes, when I'm at my very darkest, and life doesn't seem worth living, I think about—I swear to God I do—going to a *Clippers* game.

And that's why I sit at this stupid laptop, hour after hour! You know what they say, right?

All work and no play makes Jack a dull boy. All work and no play makes Jack a dull boy. All work and no play makes Jack a dull . . .

Postscript: I was told Nicholson loved this one. I've known him for years. One time, I was riding in a limo with him when he called two different women and made a date for the exact same time and place. I said, "Jack, you just messed up. You've got two girls coming to the same hotel!" And he said, with that famous arched eyebrow, "I like an audience."

46

Flying in the Face of Reason

FEBRUARY 19, 2001

O NE THING ABOUT LIFE AND THE BIG 12 BASKETBALL
season: They go on. And so it was that 10 days after one
of the three private planes used by the Oklahoma State
team crashed, killing 10, including two players, the Cowboys had to fly again—on three private planes.

At the Stillwater airport they waded through all the dread cries of, "We'll
pray for you!" and "Call the *second* you land!" They talked down the fear in
their hearts and the lunch in their stomachs, de-iced their nerves, tried to
ignore the minicams on the tarmac and took their seats next to 10 ghosts.
"Me," said an Oklahoma State student who was watching, "I'd have to be
sedated."

Assistant coach Kyle Keller looked as if he was. Slit-eyed, he'd hardly
slept since the night of Jan. 27, when coach Eddie Sutton had switched him
out of the doomed plane for the flight home from Colorado and sat Keller's
cousin, freshman point guard Nate Fleming, in his place. Sutton wanted
Keller on the faster jet instead of the turboprop so Keller could get back to
Stillwater a half hour earlier and start grading film. Now Fleming was gone.

"I don't go 10 seconds without thinking about it," said Keller, who had to pull over on the interstate between funerals last week and sob for 20 minutes. "Someday, I'm hoping God explains this all to me."

The guy sitting behind him now, broadcaster Tom Dirato, knew the feeling. Sutton had switched Dirato from the turboprop to the jet, so he and his aching back wouldn't have to sit so long, and put junior guard Danny Lawson in Dirato's place. Now Lawson is in a grave in Detroit. "I go from grief to relief," said Dirato, who will undergo counseling starting this week. "I'm 56. Danny was 21. He had his whole life in front of him."

As the cabin door closed, 7-foot freshman center Jack Marlow was thinking the same thing. He'd always hated to fly, but when the crash killed his road roomie, Lawson, his fear doubled. Sutton had asked the players if they wanted to take the 55-minute flight or the eight-hour bus ride to Lincoln for their game against Nebraska, and Big Jack had yelped, "Bus sounds great, Coach!" But he was the only one. So as the Lear engine revved, he stuck his Choctaw mandala in the window, kissed it once, bowed his huge head and started praying.

Two planes back, 280-pound center Jason Keep clamped assistant coach Sean Sutton's hand so tight it went numb. Not that Sean, Eddie's son, wanted Keep to let go. Every time he closes his eyes, he imagines the inside of that turboprop, beelining nose-first for a Colorado pasture. "I can't stop seeing them," said Sutton, whose best friend, director of basketball operations Pat Noyes, died in the wreckage. "Did they know they were going to die? Were they screaming? Panicking? I have nightmares about it."

Last to buckle in was Eddie Sutton, the 64-year-old coaching legend who had to call the 10 wives and mothers and fathers and girlfriends that night and tell them their men weren't coming home. Sutton said he carries no guilt over having changed the seating arrangement. "We've switched 100 times, every trip, for 100 reasons," he said. But those calls, those funerals, those what-ifs have added 10 years to his face. His friends worry about him. Bill Clinton called to check on him. "Eddie's in denial," said Patsy, his wife. "He's had to be so strong for everyone else, he hasn't been able to grieve."

Well, my God, where would you start? With Will Hancock, the sports information assistant who loved Beethoven, his soccer-coach wife and his two-month-old baby? Or student manager Jared Weiberg, who was making his last scheduled road trip of the season? Or radio engineer Kendall Durfey, who with his wife had just adopted a little girl whose parents had died? Or trainer Brian Luinstra, who had two kids under three? Or the two pilots, Denver Mills and Bjorn Fahlstrom? Who has that many tears?

Now the jet engines shudder, and now the planes lurch, and now it's wheels up. And now, for the first time in his life, star point guard Maurice Baker's hands drip with sweat on a flight. And now Dirato remembers that his dead colleague, play-by-play man Bill Teegins, had a commercial ticket home from Denver before a spot opened up on the turboprop. Talk about luck: Turns out the commercial flight was canceled because of the bad weather.

This time, of course, nothing happened, not a bump. All three planes made it safely to Lincoln, where the Cowboys lost to Nebraska 78–75 in overtime.

The newspaper said they had trouble rebounding.

Postscript: I could've written 10 pages on that trip. The sorrow was thick. And if they could ever get the tragedy off their minds for even five minutes, something would happen to remind them. We landed in Lincoln and got in vans to go to the team's lucky Italian restaurant, but we got lost. After 45 minutes of looking for it, Sutton was a little miffed. "What's going on?" he barked when the vans stopped by the side of the road. Turns out the only guy who knew how to get there was Pat Noyes, and he was dead.

47

Late Hit from
A Con Artist

MARCH 8, 2004

YOU KNOW WHO YOU ARE. ¶ YOU KNOW WHAT YOU DID. ¶ You ripped off a down-on-his-luck, Alzheimer's-spun Hall of Fame football player. ¶ You went to Philadelphia Eagles great Pete Pihos's house, made nice with the ex-wife he lives with and took nearly every piece of football memorabilia he had, leaving Pete and Donna with $30,000 in bogus checks and a stack of bills they still can't pay.

You had to know—once you saw that emptiness in Pete's 80-year-old eyes—that the only reason they were selling his stuff was to pay for his care. Maybe you didn't know that Donna is also staring into the teeth of a $6,000 dental bill for Pete and that prescriptions run $625 a month, all on a high school librarian's salary. But you knew you were digging them a nice, deep hole.

You said you were a New York pediatrician, "Dr. James Hart," and you were starting a "museum." A month ago you went to their home in Winston-Salem, N.C., and took Pete's last two jerseys—ones he wore in Pro Bowls during the 1950s. You took his original leather pads. You took a near-priceless football that was signed by 25 Hall of Famers, including Night Train

Lane and Bulldog Turner. Yeah, you took all that, and you took their hope too.

Hey, it's what you do. You look for Hall of Famers who are either punch-drunk or suffering from dementia or Alzheimer's. You contacted Ernie Stautner, the Pittsburgh Steelers great who has Alzheimer's, about paying him to sign autographs and to buy memorabilia. Calling yourself "Dr. James Hart," you spoke to his wife, Jill, who agreed to a meeting in Dallas but not at their home and only if you paid in cash. You never came.

You also set up a meeting with Baltimore Colts great John Mackey, who cannot remember what he had for breakfast today. This time you said you were "Dr. James Hart," psychologist. But you never showed, leaving Mackey and his wife, Sylvia, waiting at a Baltimore hotel for three hours.

Which NFL legend will you try to steal from next? Jim Ringo, the Green Bay Packers center? Steve Van Buren, the Eagles' coal train of a halfback? John Henry Johnson, the Steelers' workhorse? They've all got Alzheimer's. Otto Graham had it, too, and Tom Fears died from it. The AMA hasn't quite proved the link between all those years of taking forearms to the head and Alzheimer's, but you know. And you're using it to line your pockets.

For Pihos, it started up a few years ago. "What are we going to do tonight?" he'd ask Donna 10 to 20 times a day. She'd find frozen TV dinners in his closet. He'd pull Advils out of his pocket and say, "What are these for?"

So now the bull of a man who served two years under Gen. George Patton, who was all-NFL at wideout and defensive end, spends his days playing solitaire, looking out the window and waiting for Donna to come home. He can't read or write much anymore, soon won't be able to drive and may start wandering away.

It's not like Donna wanted to sell the stuff. She ached at having to do it. After all, Pete himself can't remember specifics about his great career, doesn't remember how many NFL titles he won (two), can't recall his coaches. For Donna those jerseys, those pads, that ball were the last means by which she could hang on to the old Pete—the man Pete himself has forgotten.

Donna still shakes with anger over what you did. She doesn't sleep some nights. And she has no idea what she'll do about taking care of Pete.

Anyway, you better fence the stuff soon. Hall of Famer Ron Mix, an attorney who also runs the Hall of Fame Players Association, says the organization is offering a $5,000 reward (619-688-9630) for information leading to your "arrest, conviction and, if possible, hanging."

The cash might soon go to a collector in Richmond, Jeff Whitmore, who told me this all smelled like the work of a memorabilia dealer from upstate New York with a reputation for skipping out on payments. "He's a real sick puppy," says Whitmore.

Then there's this: When you blew off Mackey at that Baltimore hotel that day, you left an address when you made your "Dr. Hart" reservation. The clerk gave that address to Sylvia Mackey. SI researchers linked it to a man with a different name—the same name provided by Whitmore.

Sylvia remembers working with that man at a memorabilia show in 2002. She describes him almost word-for-word the way Donna described you: good-looking, 25-ish, "too young to be a doctor," she says. And Sylvia remembers the man's wife, who also shows up as living at that same address.

So either the man and "Dr. Hart" are the same person, or it's a very crowded house in upstate New York. I called the numbers that the man and the so-called doctor had given to the players' wives, and they were either disconnected or the calls went unreturned.

Doesn't matter. Detectives should collar you posthaste. And how do you think juries will take to your ripping off a football legend who can't remember his glory days?

Maybe it's a good thing these men think like toddlers now. This way, the wickedness of what you've done can never sink in.

See you at the hanging.

Postscript: This story got so much better. A memorabilia dealer named Jeff Whitmore read the column and thought: "This smells like the work of Shawn Stevens," a 26-year-old autograph dealer from New York who's ripped off more people than three-card monte. An SI reporter named Luis Llosa and I linked "Dr. Hart" to Stevens via an address "Hart" left at a Baltimore hotel. Then a dealer named Mike Hauser found a photo of Stevens and e-mailed it to Donna Pihos, who yelped, "That's him!" Bingo. Stevens was convicted of state and federal charges including grand theft, forgery and transporting stolen property across state lines. He served a year and a half in various penal institutions, where I hope some of the larger residents gave him some very special memories.

48

Choking Up at the Plate

MARCH 28, 2005

DEAR MARK McGWIRE, ¶ I'VE KNOWN YOU—WHAT?— 19 years, since you broke into the majors. You were always a big man with big hands that hugged the little people and a big heart that made you cry at corny movies. ¶ But last week in Washington, D.C., in front of a congressional committee, you looked small and weak. You were the Incredible Shrinking Man up there. They say getting off steroids will do that to your body. Can it do that to your morals, too?

It's hard to get used to this new you. I remember when you had the courage of 10 men. And always talked about "karma." And refused millions from McDonald's because you didn't eat Big Macs. And started a foundation and gave $3 million to help abused kids. What happened to caring about kids, Mac? Did that disappear like your 17-inch forearms?

I know, I know. You don't want to talk about the past. You said that almost every time a committee member asked you a question. You'd swallow a little more of your pride and then choke out, "I'm not here to talk about the past."

But I am. Remember? Seven years ago? Number 62?

Against a blinding glare, you thrilled us with your power and humility. Fans held up signs—HIT IT HERE, MARK—at *football* games. Columnists said you were helping the country heal from Monicagate. Even President Clinton said, "I'm sorry," for cheating.

Imagine that.

You went on to hit a pupil-popping 70 home runs in 1998 and became a god to high school athletes around the country. And then the steroid possibilities started sinking in a little. You had admitted using androstenedione, the steroidlike supplement now banned by baseball. Your younger brother, Jay, a bodybuilder you occasionally lived with, had once been hooked on steroids.

Then you walked away from the game in 2001, just as this steroid thing was starting to blow up. Suddenly, you didn't see anybody, talk to anybody, show up anywhere. It was as if you knew the other shoe was going to drop on your head. You were right.

This year, in his book *Juiced*, former teammate Jose Canseco wrote that he personally injected you with steroids. Then the New York *Daily News*, citing FBI informants, linked you to a confessed steroid dealer who allegedly shot you up with the drugs.

And there you were last Thursday, with Rep. William Lacy Clay (D., Mo.) asking, "Can we look at children with a straight face and tell them that great players like you play the game with honesty and integrity?"

You looked like a cat with a mouthful of feathers when you muttered, "I'm not here to talk about the past."

If it weren't so pathetic, it would've been funny. It was as if, like a cartoon lightbulb, a giant asterisk popped up over your head. If I were in St. Louis, I'd be thinking up a new name for that stretch of I-70 the state named after you. The Integrity Bypass, maybe?

The Mark McGwire I remember would've never turtled. That father, Donald Hooton, who testified earlier on Thursday that he believed steroids drove his 17-year-old son to kill himself, was right when he said, "Players that are guilty of taking steroids are not only cheaters—you are cowards."

And then you had the gall to tell Congress you'll do "everything in my power" to get the message out that "steroids are bad. Don't do 'em." Yeah, that ought to really fly with the teens.

Mr. McGwire, how do you know steroids are bad?

I'm not here to talk about the past, Billy.

I feel sorry for you, Mac. There are no bars, no ankle bracelet, yet you're a prisoner just the same. You broke baseball's coolest record and you can't talk about it. Maybe *that's* karma.

I know you. It's got to be sitting in your stomach like a bowl of razor blades. Last Thursday you kept insisting you could "turn this into a positive." O.K., you want to do something positive? Be that big man again. *Tell the truth.*

If you didn't juice, tell us. If you did, tell us. Americans forgive everything but lies. We need to know. The family of the late Roger Maris needs to know. The guys on the home run list you passed like hitchhikers need to know—Carl Yastrzemski (182 pounds), Stan Musial (175), Ernie Banks (180). And teenage boys like my 17-year-old son, Jake, need to know.

He used to be so skinny that you could fax him places. But he's been lifting the last six weeks. Hardly misses a day. A couple of his friends, though, are taking creatine and blowing up like a California governor. He wants to know why I won't let him take the supplement. Creatine messes with your kidneys and sends you on a slip 'n' slide toward steroids, I tell him, and steroids could send you to your funeral. But it would be nice if he could hear it from you, Mac.

In '98, when you tied Maris with your 61st, the late, great Cardinals announcer Jack Buck said, "Pardon me while I stand and applaud."

Well, right now, pardon us while we sit and cringe.

Postscript: This one hurt to write. I always respected McGwire. He was one of the few baseball players I ever met who read books. He was smart, caring and actually interested in the world outside baseball. But real journalism—as opposed to the I-can't-rip-him-he-plays-in-my-golf-tournament kind perpetrated by certain ESPN anchors —can't protect friends when they screw up. His Hall of Fame candidacy is here now and anytime one of his apologists wants to talk about his amazing home run numbers, I say, "We're not here to talk about the past."

49

Giving It Up for Zo

DECEMBER 15, 2003

WHAT KIND OF PERSON WOULD DO THAT? ¶ WHAT kind of sports-addled bratwurst brain would give away one of his kidneys to a multimillionaire superstar athlete? Somebody he's never even *met*? ¶ Does he think the player will sign his bedpan? Has he always wanted to get an organ into the NBA?

What insanity would cause more than 600 people to offer one of their kidneys to Alonzo Mourning, the New Jersey Nets center who was forced into retirement on Nov. 24 after doctors told him that his kidney disease was not only career-ending but also life-threatening if he couldn't find a matching donor?

Well, a 5' 2", 30-year-old San Francisco novelist named Tiffany Davis, for one.

"I was reading about it on ESPN.com," says Davis, a Nets fan and, like Mourning, a Georgetown graduate, "and I was like, Damn, he's fought so hard to keep playing, and now it's going down the drain. And I realized my blood type was O, too. So I was just moved to do it."

Davis dialed 1-800-633-6628, the Kidney & Urology Foundation of America, Inc., and heard about the 59,000 people waiting for a kidney, the 11 who die every day for want of one and the millions of Americans with kidney disease trying to stay off that dark list. Little crocodiles chewed at her insides.

"That's when I decided it doesn't have to be Alonzo who gets my kidney, it can be anybody," she says. "I mean, why not? I've got two. One is just hanging around." Now comes the hard part, she says, "telling my mom."

Prizefighter Jonathan Reid of Nashville is another one of those altruists. He was reading about Mourning in *USA Today* and decided it was time to "help a brother out."

"I just thought, man, this has got to be devastating to this guy," says the 31-year-old Reid, who is 33–1 as a middleweight. The more he found out, the more it pinched his conscience. And he came to a decision: "If it turns out Alonzo doesn't need my kidney," says Reid, a father of four, "I'd like to look into giving it to someone else. I mean, I'm healthy, right? I just can't tell my mom. She's a handwringer."

A boxer willing, for the sake of a perfect stranger, to fight with one kidney. What gets *into* people?

What would make Dr. Julian Lopez of Las Vegas call his dying buddy, Chicago White Sox owner Eddie Einhorn, out of nowhere last year and *insist* he take his kidney? "We're going to find out if chiles rellenos," the Albuquerque-born Lopez said, "go with bagels and lox."

They do. Today Einhorn, 67, feels 25 years younger. Come to think of it, so does Lopez. "I've learned a lot about what being a friend is," Lopez says. "It's more than just trading jokes and slamming cold ones. For me, Eddie was a golden opportunity to improve somebody else's life, and I just couldn't pass it up."

So what is Einhorn supposed to give as a thank you—Frank Thomas? "I got my friend back," says Lopez. "That's enough."

Something in all this bugs some people. David Garner's mother waited on the list 11 years before she got a kidney, then died when her body rejected it. "Where were all these people for my mom?" Garner says. "I don't care if you're a famous athlete or not, you should have to be on the waiting list just like everyone else. Is the life of an athlete worth more than the life of another person? I don't think it is."

Mourning will not affect the list, according to his nephrologist, Dr. Gerald Appel, because he'll almost certainly find a donor among his relatives and friends. "And then, I'm sure Alonzo will get up in front of the world," says Appel, "and say, 'Please, all of you who were willing to donate your kidney to me, donate it to someone else.'"

In truth, Mourning's fame won't just save *his* life, it'll save hundreds of lives.

My 25-year-old nephew, Reilly Capps, who writes for *The Washington Post*, wants to save one, too. He came home to Denver on Thanksgiving and announced he was going to donate his kidney to the next person on the list. And this time it wasn't just a mom wringing her hands—it was all of us.

But . . . but . . . but what about the way you ski? Going off cliffs and between trees? "I'll wear a kidney belt," he said with a shrug.

But . . . but . . . but what if your sister or brother needs your kidney later? "I'll hope somebody else will step up and help," he said, "just like I'm doing now."

But . . . but . . . but can't you wait until you've died? "Live transplants are way more successful than cadavers," he said.

But . . . but. . . . "Look," he said, "it doesn't hurt you. Life expectancy for kidney donors is the same as for those who don't donate. We don't need a second kidney. And I'm just not the kind of guy who can sit here and let people die."

And that's when I realized that, apparently, I'm the kind of guy who can. I mean, what kind of person would *do that*?

Postscript: At a book-signing in Phoenix in 2006, a man came up to me and said, "Can I show you something?" And he lifted up his shirt and showed me a scar on his back. "I donated my kidney because of you." He wouldn't even tell me his name. He said he just gave it to the general donor's bank and it went to somebody at the top of the list. Doesn't even know who got it. How cool is that? By the way, my nephew still hasn't donated his. And neither, I'm ashamed to admit, have I.

50

Crunch Time for Dad

JUNE 6, 2005

D AD? ¶ *YEAH, SON?* ¶WHAT'S THAT ON TV? ¶ OH, WELL, *pal, that's uh, that's the volume control. But we usually just use the remote.* ¶ No, Dad. The commercial. What's Viagrow? ¶ *Via-GRA. Well, that's, see, that's nothing you really need to know about until you're on, like, your third hip.*

Mom said I was supposed to ask you. Viagra, See Alice and Lavoris—she said to ask you about all of them.

Cialis and Levitra. She did?

Yeah.

Pal, have you ever really *looked at our ceiling down here? Because if you look at the ceiling tiles, you can make out animal shapes. Like, look right there, I see an elephant!*

What?

Hey, look, the game's back on! Let's just sit here and watch the game, want to?

(Pause.)

Hey! There it is again, behind home plate! It says Viagra.

Jeez, that's some amazing coincidence, huh?

What's it mean, on the Cialis ads, when they say you should call your doctor if you get a four-hour—

Hey! I just found a nickel in the couch! You want to look for more? You can keep anything you find!

Dad, does Levitra help you throw the football straighter? Because the guy in the commercial uses Levitra, and then he can throw spirals right through the swinging tire. Because that might help me make starting quarterback next year.

No, no, it's really not about football, buddy.

Well, how come Mike Dinka was always on TV talking about Levitra? He played football.

DIT-ka. I can't imagine how broke he had to be to do that ad, to be honest.

Doesn't Viagra help you hit home runs? Because the guy for the Orioles, Rafael Palmerror, he did ads for it. And he's got more than 500 homers!

Palmei-RO. Well, no, I don't think it helps you hit home runs. But you know what? I think SpongeBob SquarePants *might be coming on!*

Is it illegal or something? Is it like when Sammy Sosa corked his bat?

Is it like corking your bat? Well, kinda yes, but kinda no.

Did baseball players advertise Viagra when you were a kid, Dad?

No! I mean, I can't see Mickey Mantle doing a Viagra ad. "Hi, I'm Mickey Mantle! And whenever I have trouble becoming. . . . " Ah, never mind.

When we watch NASCAR, I see it on Mark Martin's car. VIAGRA. He got the pole position in the last race. Does Viagra help him get the pole position?

Psheesh! Really, son, don't worry about these ads for Viagra and all that, because a bill was just introduced in Congress to keep those commercials off our TV until after 10 p.m. So, you know, soon you probably won't be seeing them anymore.

Neither will you, Dad. You go to bed at 9:30.

Good point.

Justin says that somebody buys a Viagra nine times a second. Who's he talking about?

I don't know, but I'll bet he could really use a date.

What?

Nothing. Hey, I know, grab one of those copies of SPORTS ILLUSTRATED in that pile. You wanna go through it with me?

Sure! (Pause.) Dad, do all these girls in swimsuits play sports?
Well, some do. I—
How come this one's holding her swimsuit instead of wearing it? Does that make her swim faster?
O.K., forget that—
Wait! Here's an ad for Viagra, too!
Son, let's just drop this whole—
Might as well tell me, Dad. I can always go on the Internet.
(Sigh.) Well, uh, son, Viagra helps guys who—. See, Viagra is something that dads take when they're with moms and things aren't really happening—. See, uh, have I ever told you the story of Jack and the Magic Beans?
Where the magic beans make a huge beanstalk?
Yeah, it works kinda like that. Hey! It's time for SportsCenter! You wanna change the channel quick?
O.K.
Perfect! Let's just sit here quietly and check out what's going on in sports news.
(Pause.)
Dad, what's a Whizzinator?

Postscript: A congressman from Virginia wrote a bill to keep erectile dysfunction ads off TV sets until after 10 p.m., but support was soft and it couldn't push through.

51

Beyond the Pale

FEBRUARY 20, 2006

YOU'VE HEARD OF THE MOVIE *GLORY ROAD*, RIGHT? The inspirational story of the 1966 Texas Western basketball team that won the NCAA title with an unheard-of five black starters? ¶ Well, this is the flip side of that story. I was tipped off about it by *A Million Little Pieces* author James Frey. It's the Wyoming State University basketball team—the only NCAA Division I school in the country right now starting five white players.

"To be honest, it's been hell," says WSU's courageous black coach, Marlin Streeter, 43. "Some people just aren't ready to see five white guys out there. It triggers something deep inside them."

Wyoming State, located in Casper, is 17–5 overall yet has not cracked the Top 25. The Ghosts have been heckled, mocked and ridiculed everywhere they've played. They've heard, "Crackers!" and "Damn! Where's my sunglasses?" One sign read ALL WHITE? THAT AIN'T RIGHT!

"I was out there for the opening tip at Fresno State," says WSU's starting center Chip Lovington III, "and the ref goes, 'Son, five white guys isn't a basketball team, it's an insurance firm.' It gets old."

It's not like Streeter set out to thumb his nose at the you-need-blacks-to-win culture of college basketball. His team's makeup was born of desperation.

Because Wyoming State hasn't had a winning season in 14 years, and because Casper's black population can be counted on Bart Simpson's fingers, good black players weren't exactly wearing out Streeter's cell number. And then one day, while speaking at the Bemidji (Minn.) Elks Lodge, he looked out the window and noticed a 5' 9" white kid named Schuyler Olson making 20-footers like they were layups.

It took some sweet-talking to get him to come to Casper. Olson's father, Prescott, is the regional sales director for Wonder bread, and Schuyler had his future already mapped out. But when Streeter finally got him to sign with the Ghosts, the coach realized he might be on to something.

He started scouring the country for talented whites—at country clubs, squash courts and Volvo dealerships. He found power forward Chad Melman Jr. at his wife's book club. He persuaded point guard Cheddar Smithson to give up his beloved horseback riding and join the team. The white flight to Casper was on. And did it go over well with the team's previously all-black roster?

"Hell, no!" says backup forward Tayron Wilson. "We were like, 'You're bringing in all *white* guys? On *purpose*?' I kept looking for that *Punk'd* dude to show up!"

The interaction was rough at first. Streeter wanted the team to dress alike on road trips, but the black players refused to tie their sweaters around their necks. "And we told them they can stick their Docksiders!" says sixth man Antoine Davis. One night there were even fisticuffs over a John Tesh CD on the team boom box.

On the court it was worse. Streeter exhorted his starters to take the ball hard to the hoop and dunk it, but they'd insist on just laying it in. "It wasn't 'white men can't jump,'" says Wilson, "it was 'white men *won't* jump!'"

But when Wyoming State lost four of its first five games, a miffed Olson approached Streeter and said, "Coach, with all due respect to your expertise, and certainly with an understanding of your desires to grow this program, we feel we're not being allowed to play the style of game that will bring us success."

In other words, they wanted to make a minimum of 10 passes on each possession. Run backdoor plays. And wear very tight, high Larry Bird shorts.

And—*voilà!*—the changes worked!

The Ghosts reeled off 11 straight wins. Their games became the place to be for celebrities like Martha Stewart, Clay Aiken and Pat Boone. Then they got cocky, getting blown out at Air Force. "They were at the club all night," Streeter growls. "The Young Republicans club." After some serious stair-running as punishment, they've won five more since. Now they're white-hot. Ghosts cheerleaders even have a new chant:

Don't need no brothers
To stage a thrilla!
We rock your world with
Puuuuure vanilla!

All in all, it's been an amazing season in Casper. Streeter and his players have learned about prejudice, tolerance and, in the end, the common bond that makes them persevere: hoops.

And whether or not they win the NCAA title as Texas Western did, Streeter says he already feels like a winner. Why?

"I just sold the movie rights!" he says. The working title?

Glory Cul-de-sac.

Postscript: You wouldn't believe how many people thought this was real. So many people that the Casper Area Chamber of Commerce asked us to print a letter telling the people it was all fake. We did.

52

The Hero and the Unknown Soldier

MAY 3, 2004

ALL DAY, IN SAN JOSE, THE PARENTS OF LATE NFL star Pat Tillman were seeing their son get the kind of attention he would've hated: his face on CNN, teddy bear memorials, a tribute from the White House. ¶ *All day, in Bellaire, Ohio, the grandmother of former high school football star Todd Bates was living with a solitary ache she can barely describe: The boy she raised as her own came back from Iraq in a box, and nobody broke into a newscast to announce his death to a nation.*

Since 9/11, all Arizona Cardinals strong safety Pat Tillman wanted was to fight for his country. He took a potential $1,182,000 annual pay cut to jump from the NFL to the Army Rangers in 2002, and he refused all attempts to glorify his decision. He told friends that he wanted to be treated as no more special than the guy on the cot next to him. ("He viewed his decision as no more patriotic than that of less fortunate, less renowned countrymen," Arizona senator John McCain said.) Tillman even forbade his family and friends from talking to the press about him. News crews begged for photos, mere shots of him signing his induction papers or piling

172

out of a truck at Fort Benning, Ga., or getting his first haircut—anything. They got nothing.

Since he was a kid, all Bellaire High linebacker Todd Bates wanted was "to be somebody," his football team chaplain, Pastor Don Cordery, told the Associated Press. When you grow up poor and without your parents around, you get hungry to make your mark. He wasn't a good enough player to get a scholarship, yet he desperately wanted to go to college. So in 2002 he took the only road available to him—he left home and joined the Ohio Army National Guard. Nobody wanted to take a picture of him getting his haircut.

Tillman, 5' 11" and 200 pounds, joined the only team tougher than the NFL—the 75th Ranger Regiment. He served a tour of duty in Iraq, then went to Afghanistan. He was killed last Thursday in an ambush in the remote eastern Afghan province of Khost. His younger brother, also a Ranger, escorted his body home.

Bates, 6 feet and 250 pounds, walked eight miles a day with a 50-pound backpack to lose enough weight to join the Army, recalls his grandmother Shirley Bates, who raised him from a baby. He made it to Baghdad and was on a boat patrolling the Tigris River when his squad leader lost his balance and feel overboard. Without a life jacket Bates dived in to rescue him. Both men drowned. It took 13 days to find Bates's body, on Dec. 23, one month before his unit returned home.

Tillman's death shook the country like no other in this war. Makeshift memorials sprang up at his alma mater, Arizona State, and at the Cardinals' offices in Tempe. The club announced that the plaza around its new stadium will be named Pat Tillman Freedom Plaza. At the NFL draft in New York, commissioner Paul Tagliabue wore a black ribbon with Tillman's name on it. Some people talked about retiring his number, 40, league-wide.

Only friends and family grieved for Bates, but deeply. It so tormented Shirley's companion, 61-year-old Charles Jones—the man who helped her raise Todd—that he refused to go to the funeral. "If I don't go, then Toddie can't be dead," he kept saying. He refused to leave the house. He refused to talk much. He refused to eat. Four weeks later he dropped over dead without a word. "He died of a broken heart," says Shirley. She buried them in the cemetery up the hill from her home, side by side.

Tillman died a hero and a patriot. But his death is a wake-up call to the nation that every day—more than 500 times since President Bush declared

"Major combat operations in Iraq have ended," more than 800 times since the invasion of Afghanistan—a family must drive to the airport to greet their dead child. The only difference this time is that the whole country knew this child.

In the little house in Bellaire, any patriotism was swallowed up by sorrow. "There was no reason for my boy to die," says Shirley. "There is no reason for this war. There were no weapons found. All we have now is a Vietnam. My Toddie's life was wasted over there. All this war is a waste. Look at all these boys going home in coffins. What's the good in it?"

Athletes are soldiers and soldiers are athletes. Uniformed, fit and trained, they fight for one cause, one team. They take ground and they defend it. Both are carried off on their teammates' shoulders, athletes when they win and soldiers when they die.

Pat Tillman and Todd Bates were athletes and soldiers. Tillman wanted to be anonymous and became the face of this war. Bates wanted to be somebody and died faceless to most of the nation.

Both did their duty for their country, but I wonder if their country did its duty for them. Tillman died in Afghanistan, a war with no end in sight and not enough troops to finish the job. Bates died in Iraq, a war that began with no just cause and continues with no just reason.

Be proud that sports produce men like this.

But I, for one, am furious that these wars keep taking them.

Postscript: People either loved this column for its pathos or hated it for its politics. "Stick to sports!" they wrote. But I don't write about sports. I write about people who happen to be in sports. I write about human joy, sorrow, religion and politics as it weaves itself through sports. I couldn't have lived with myself if I'd written this without telling how I feel. I've been against the war from the moment it was planned. Hated the insanity of it, the injustice of it, the price of it. And when a war as wrong as this took a man as good as Tillman and many more like him each week, there's no way I was going to shut up. Of course, much later, we got to the sick punch line: Pat Tillman didn't die at the enemy's hands. He was killed by "friendly fire."

53

One Not-So-Shining Moment

AUGUST 23, 2004

W HY DO YOU ALWAYS HAVE TO BE SO NEGATIVE? Why not mention what I did right? ¶ For instance, I did not trip with the Olympic torch when I got my turn to carry it last Thursday outside Athens. ¶ Also, I did not burn down the Acropolis. And did I flunk a drug test afterward? No!

But you have to pick nits. You have to bring up the fact that after five continents, 27 countries, 78 days, 11,500 torchbearers and 50,613 miles, it was *me* who put out the flame.

That's true. But Olympic officials never should have let me near the thing! So whose fault is it?

The trouble started when so many corporations got scared about the possibility of terrorism in Athens. NBC, for instance, gave its Olympic advertisers the option of being entertained in bomb-free Bermuda during the Games, and about half of them took the network up on it.

That opened up torchbearer slots for people who had no business being around fire. Like me.

I immediately started working on Greek phrases I might need, such as *Eimai edo! Kato apo ta baza!* (I'm here! Under the rubble!)

The morning of the run, I got my instructions with about 50 other torch-bearers. "Do *not* hold the torch by the top—that part will be hot," the woman in charge actually said. "And do not go back the way the torch came. And if you want to buy your torch, it will be 360 Euros [$442], cash only."

O.K., so it's a sucker's game, but they got me. I now own an Olympic torch! I can't wait until I get it home. Imagine the possibilities. Donning the ol' uni and going backyard-to-backyard lighting neighbors' barbecues. Hanging around bars looking for people who have cigars to light. ("Oops! Sorry about your eyebrows, ma'am!")

And tell me it won't be handy if I have to lead a mob up to Dr. Frankenstein's house again.

Our group was taken by bus to the seaside suburb of Alimos. I watched as, one-by-one, the torchbearers were dropped off into throngs of happy Greeks, who rubbed the shoulders and soothed the nerves of each anxious runner for the 30 minutes until the torch came to their hero.

But when I was pushed out of the bus at my spot on the highway, there were no arms to fall into. In fact, nobody was there. Remember *North by Northwest,* when Cary Grant gets dropped off in the cornfield? This was lonelier than that.

I sat on the embankment and waited. Not exactly as glamorous a deal as I'd pictured. Eventually, a fat old woman with three teeth and wearing a bikini top came up and spat out what sounded like a question in Greek.

To which I replied, "No, the swimsuit issue is closed for next year, but thanks for asking."

Finally, with 10 minutes to go, citizens started coming around. Old men. Kids. A truck driver. They were mesmerized by my torch, even unlit. I let them hold it, run with it, play with it. These people are going to be about $10 billion in the hole after this little 17-day party. It's the least I could do.

Minutes later, after I lit my torch from the flame of Athens housewife Anastasia Gregoriadou, I felt suddenly swept up in everything the modern Olympics stand for—bribery, drugs and bizarre mascots.

Actually, I was proud to be a tiny part of an amazing human chain, even in the stupid Richard Simmons shorts and headband they gave me. Proud I was passing along the same flame carried—for the first time—in Africa and South America, carried by Tom Cruise and Billy Mills and Miss World 2002 before me, and by Nikos Kaklamanakis to the Olympic cauldron itself not 36 hours after me.

So what do you do when you're proud? You dance! You spin 360s! You run around trying to get cabbies to slow down long enough to show them the torch!

And what happens? All that flitting around puts the flame out!

Why? In Sydney a scuba diver carried the torch underwater. In Barcelona an archer shot it 35 yards. Yet my *little dance* put it out?

A very large Greek man came bounding out of a trailing van and grabbed me by the shoulders while a little guy with a Zippo relit my torch. "The torch serious!" the big man yelled into my forehead. "You not serious!"

Sorry, Avery Brundage.

I finished the rest of my 300-meter run more serious than Tom Ridge, handed off the flame to a Greek TV reporter and watched everybody peel away, leaving me alone again in a very stupid outfit.

Yes, I extinguished the Olympic flame. But I checked with IOC officials, and they said it does not necessarily mean the entire Games will have to be replayed.

Man, this thing's going to be *cool* at concerts.

Postscript: Man, having your own, real Olympic torch is more fun than monkeys on skis. You light that baby up, you are going to meet people. One night, in the main square in Athens, I must've taken 500 pictures with people holding it next to me. Some people were concerned. "You are lost? You should be in parade?"

Alas, it finally ran out of juice and now hangs on my office wall. Anybody know how to refill it?

54

Unsynchronized Swimming

OCTOBER 18, 2000

IN LANE 4, HEAT 10, QUALIFYING HEAT, WOMEN'S 50-METER freestyle, representing the Netherlands: Inge de Bruijn. ¶ In lane 3, heat 1, qualifying heat, women's 50-meter freestyle, representing Equatorial Guinea: Paula Barila Bolopa. ¶ De Bruijn, nearly six feet tall, has already won two gold medals and set two world records at these Olympics. Barila Bolopa, barely five feet, had never seen a 50-meter pool until this week.

De Bruijn, 27, trains in both Holland and Portland, Ore., with two world-class coaches, two masseuses, two physiologists, a nutritionist, a sports psychologist, an agent and a personal trainer. Barila Bolopa, 18, trains in the 20-meter pool of the three-story Hotel Hureca in Malabo, her home in Western Africa. That is, until the hotel guests want to use the pool. Then she swims in the ocean and her coach keeps an eye out for sharks.

De Bruijn loves the Olympic pool. "It's fast," she says. Barila Bolopa loves the Olympic pool. "It's easier to swim without always having to turn so often," she says.

De Bruijn is equipped with the best equipment science has developed:

$250 Speedo FastSkin suit, proven to take as much as half a second off a 100-meter time; expensive goggles; lycrex hat; practice drag suit; and rubberized water-pumping cool-down suit. Barila Bolopa is equipped with almost nothing. She came to Sydney without a swimsuit. A week before the Games a volunteer drove her and her teammate, Eric Moussambani, to the Adidas outlet store in Sydney and bought them swimsuits, swim caps, warm-ups, flip-flops and towels.

De Bruijn's dive off the starting block, analyzed and improved by physicists, is an explosion of twitch and nerve. She is in the air .41 seconds after the gun fires, an almost clairvoyant head start. Barila Bolopa has never stood on a starting block. She fairly belly flops off it, then surfaces almost perpendicular to the water. If the depth of the pool weren't two meters, she might've touched the bottom with her feet. The other swimmers in her heat are already two lengths ahead.

De Bruijn's power makes you check for mermaid fins. She nearly hydroplanes across the water, seeming more to skim across it than through it. Her stroke and kick feed her down her lane so fast it looks as if she's being pulled by a high-speed winch. Perhaps it's some elaborate David Copperfield trick.

Barila Bolopa barely gets her head wet. She swims with her face fully out of the water the whole way, turning this way and that as her arms flail, her feet a good three feet beneath the surface and dropping.

De Bruijn finishes with a fury. When she hits the wall, she spins to see her time: 24.13, a mark that not only breaks her own world record by almost one-fourth of a second but also brings her to within 2½ seconds of the men's world mark, unthinkable a few months ago.

Barila Bolopa isn't even halfway across the pool at 24.13 seconds, and the huge crowd at sold-out Sydney Aquatic Centre begins to clap, yell and cheer for her to finish. Unlike her Equatorial Guinea teammate, Eric the Eel, as he became known, she doesn't look as if she'll drown, but the poolside volunteers edge a little closer just the same. Finally, she touches the wall to a thunderous ovation: 1 minute and 3.97 seconds, making Barila Bolopa the slowest swimmer of these Olympics.

De Bruijn is thrilled with her race: "I saw my time, and I said, 'Holy smokes.' It's ridiculous. It's crazy. Someone asked me what my limits are, and I don't know."

Barila Bolopa is thrilled with her race: "I got very tired at the end, but the crowd urged me on. They are very serious about swimming here. I wish we had something like this in my country."

De Bruijn says, "It feels like a dream to me." Barila Bolopa says, "I had no idea it would all be so big."

De Bruijn packs up her swim bag, emblazoned with the name of the company that pays her big guilders to carry it, and prepares to return to the Olympic Village, where she will eat meals that have been studied to within a calorie of their lives, then answer fan mail. "This is definitely my year," she says.

Barila Bolopa packs up her school backpack and prepares to return to the Olympic Village, where she wonders how much is left of the $220 that the entire six-person Equatorial Guinea delegation has for the Games. "What can I say?" she says. "Some have and some do not have."

De Bruijn says she has never heard of Paula Barila Bolopa.

Barila Bolopa says she has never heard of Inge de Bruijn.

Postscript: The one they called "Paula the Crawla" was in the Olympics only through an organized effort to build programs in third-world countries. Her teammate was more famous—Eric (the Eel) Moussambani, who was so bad people crowded around TV sets all over the world just to see if he'd drown. Bolopa wasn't exactly Esther Williams. She swam like a four-year-old in a Minnows class. She finished in last place in that heat by almost 50 seconds. De Bruijn went on to win the gold in Sydney and then again four years later in Athens. Bolopa hasn't been heard from since.

55

Bred and Buttered

MAY 10, 2004

I'VE SEEN PAMPERED, SPOILED AND CODDLED ATHLETES BEFORE, but the ones I got stuck covering last week make me sicker than the third floor of hospitals. ¶ Nobody ever tells them no. They get more strokes than an ICU. Everything has to be perfect or they go triple Liza. ¶ No, not the Lakers. Not the Yankees. Not even the Williams sisters.

A group of athletes much worse. Thoroughbred racehorses.

At last Saturday's Kentucky Derby a horse named Smarty Jones made $5.9 million for 124 seconds of work. Then he went back to his Churchill Downs stall and got more hands laid on him than a $10 stripper: a warm soap-and-water sponge bath, a massage and a nice helping of hot mash, all of it from grooms who generally live in backstretch hovels with hot-and-cold-running cockroaches.

Across the way, in Barn 17, the colt Tapit had spent Derby week eating organic carrots, breathing purified air and munching sod trucked in from his home farm in Maryland. He slurped Guinness beer and farm-fresh raw eggs. (Good grass and beer, followed by eggs? Sounds like breakfast at Hunter S. Thompson's house.) He finished ninth.

181

How's this for a sweet gig? Six, seven naps a day. Winters off. Seven or eight races a year. No wonder the jockeys wanted to strike this Derby. Compared to the horses, they're Malaysian shoe stitchers.

Put it this way: How would you like to retire at four (about 24 in people years) to a life of having sex with the most fit females in the country, three times a day? From February to June, that's all you'd do. Then you'd take July off (phew!), and if you're good, maybe fly to Australia and start again with the sheilas down there until Christmas. Nobody this side of Wilt turns that down.

And you don't even have to mess around with foreplay! A teasing stallion takes care of that. He gets things heated up, as it were, and when the mood is right, you waltz in like Elvis and bada-bing! Nice work if you can get it.

One time the late *Dayton Daily News* columnist Si Burick was watching Secretariat pull away to another easy win. "Jeez, I hate Secretariat," he grumbled. "He's good-looking, still has all his hair, and his whole sex life is in front of him."

With all that, you'd think the beasts would be happier than Ted Kennedy trapped in the Sara Lee factory, right? Wrong.

"Be 15 minutes late with their meal, and by God, they let you know," says Roland Nixon, who heads up the crew that works on Derby entrant Friends Lake (finished 15th). "They'll kick the walls, whinny, scratch the ground. Or if they smell the littlest thing wrong in their feed, they'll cause a ruckus. Oh, yeah, they're spoiled."

The track has a lipreader, Barb Borden, whose job is to read the I.D. number tattooed inside the upper lip of each thoroughbred before every race. The way they stomp and jump when she comes near them, you'd think Borden was trying to drag them to the glue factory. "I get bit at least once a week," she says.

And you thought Neon Deion was vain? Even the rear ends on these beasts get the Hollywood treatment. Some get their butts combed in lovely designs. Others get their manes elaborately braided. Their inner thighs are coated in cream to keep them from chafing. You think anybody ever did that for John Kruk?

They have the best in critter comforts. They get acupuncture treatments and chiropractic work, and sleep with magnetized blankets. They fly in roomy, specially designed stalls in customized 727s. Remember how much room you had on *your* last flight, stuck between two BEFORE Subway sandwich models?

Some get their favorite bottled water flown in. Others have music in their stalls. (Friends Lake prefers the Beach Boys.) Plus, unlike many Americans, they get to choose whom they sleep with, even if it's a dog or a goat or a Shetland pony. Imperialism (third in the Derby) is so spoiled that his 21-year-old trainer, Kristin Mulhall, sleeps in the stall with him. Now, I ask you, what chance does her boyfriend have?

With everybody treating these horses like the King of Siam, you figure they'll run through a wall for their trainer, right? Please.

Last Friday supertrainer Bob Baffert discovered a tiny bump, smaller than a dime, on the leg of his Derby entrant, Wimbledon. The vets said it was a knot on the tendon, so Baffert pulled the horse from the Derby and will rest him for the next—get this—90 *days*. Biggest race in the world, and a bump scratches him. Los Angeles Rams defensive end Jack Youngblood played in a Super Bowl with a broken leg!

And even when you get them to the starting gate, nothing says they'll go in. "They all think they're the biggest horse in the race," says Churchill Downs official starter Roger Nagle. "Hell, it's no wonder. These trainers never make 'em do anything they don't want to do. You pull on Smarty Jones and he just backs up!"

Of course, once he was in the gate last Saturday, Smarty Jones didn't back up. He ran his perfect record to seven for seven. In fact, he'll probably go on to win the Triple Crown, make more money than ExxonMobil, retire immediately and wait for the preheated babes to start showing up.

Jeez, I hate Smarty Jones.

Postscript: Smarty Jones retired in August of 2004 and is now a stud at Three Chimneys Farm in Midway, Ky. He's in the same stall where Seattle Slew was pimped out for years. Smarty's first foals were born in 2006 and will start racing in 2008. Lucky bastards.

56

Half the Size, Twice the Man

OCTOBER 3, 2005

YOU THINK YOU'VE SEEN REFS AS BLIND AS NEWBORN moles? You think you've seen officials make bizarre calls? You've seen zebras who are as boneheaded as a box of hammers? ¶ Well, you ain't seen blind, bizarre and boneheaded until you've seen this.

It's halftime of a game in Dayton on Sept. 16—Colonel White High against Mount Healthy. After Colonel White leaves the locker room, the refs approach the coaches on the sideline. Crew chief Dennis Daly announces, "Number 99 cannot play in this game anymore. He's not wearing shoes, knee pads or thigh pads."

Head coach Earl White just stares at him.

"But he doesn't have any legs!" White says.

"Sorry," Daly says. "It's the rule."

Number 99 is senior Bobby Martin, backup noseguard, a starter on punt coverage and a kid, yes, born without legs.

Doesn't slow him down much. He runs on his hands about as quickly as his teammates do on their feet. Strong as a John Deere in the chest and arms, he benches 215 and will wrestle for the varsity this winter. Wants to go out for track in the spring in the shot put. And now they were telling him he couldn't play without shoes?

"I didn't get it," says Bobby, 17. "The ref could look at me and see I don't have feet or knees. How can I wear shoes if I don't have feet?"

"A rule is a rule," Daly said. Bobby was disconsolate as he sat on the sidelines and Colonel White lost 41–12.

How can you throw a legless kid out of a game for not wearing shoes? Can you throw an armless kid out for not wearing wristbands? And even if he were suddenly to produce shoes and knee and thigh pads, where was Bobby supposed to wear them? From his ears?

In fact, Bobby did borrow a pair of cleats and came out during the third quarter with them tied to his belt. *You want me to wear shoes, I'm wearing shoes.* But the school's athletic director, Carolyn Woodley, took them off, telling him that it was "undignified." Though, by the refs' own black-and-white logic, it should've worked. Where is it written that the shoes have to be worn on the feet?

Is there anything worse than a whistle-worshiping, self-important stiff who can't see past his precious rule book to the situation that stands in front of him? Even if that "situation" is a kid who stands about three feet tall and weighs 112 pounds, 101 of it heart?

Wait. I take that back. The only thing worse is talk-radio goofs like Cincinnati's Andy Furman, who told his listeners the whole thing was "a charade and a freak show."

"The rule says you have to wear shoes and pads, period," Furman told me. "He can't play. He's handicapped. There's certain things handicapped people can't and shouldn't do, and one of them is play football. Would you put Stevie Wonder behind the wheel of a car? No! Who in their right mind would put this kid out there?"

Hey, Andy, you've *got* to cut back on the glue sniffing.

It'd be nice if any of these people actually took five minutes to get to know Bobby Martin before deciding what he can and can't do with his life.

He bowls, dances and does flips and cartwheels. He flies off staircases on his custom-made skateboard. He weaves down the hall between classes on it doing one-handed handstands. He built his own computer, ground up. He's the guy you go to when your car stereo won't work. Your car, too, for that matter.

Whatever he lacks in height, he makes up for in humor. The other day, one of the coaches, who happens to be missing a front tooth, told the players, "O.K., everybody take a knee. Even you, Bobby."

To which Bobby cracked back, "Sure, coach. Right after you go and visit an orthodontist."

But along come knee-jerk Barney Fifes like Furman and Daly (who didn't respond to my interview request) who decide it's their place to put a leash on the kid.

"The ref said they were doing it for his safety," Coach White says. White tried to explain that Bobby had passed his physical and already had clearance to play from his doctors. But the referees kept saying, "We can show you the rule." White took his broken-up player aside and said, "Don't worry about this. You'll be back playing next week."

He was right. On Sept. 19 the Ohio High School Athletic Association said the officials were wrong and sent White a letter, which he'll keep in his back pocket, just in case. Furman should get a copy, too, for his cave.

Everything was back to normal last weekend. Bobby Martin was happy again, back playing without shoes. And official Dennis Daly and his crew were back reffing, without brains.

Postscript: The tip on this one came from one of SI's photographers in Ohio. He was shooting a high school football game and e-mailed that he couldn't believe what he saw. Like Jake Porter, Bobby wound up with an ESPY and an Arete courage award. I know it's hard to believe, but the kid really can play. He finished his senior season with 41 assisted tackles, seven solos, three sacks, six hurries and a fumble recovery. And he was named homecoming king. Who'd have thought it? The kid with no legs stands taller than everybody else in school.

57

In Lehman's Terms

SEPTEMBER 3, 2001

WHY IS IT THE WORST THINGS HAPPEN TO THE best people? ¶ Tom Lehman, who is 3–0 in Ryder Cup singles matches and has never even made a *bogey* in a singles match, wasn't chosen to play in this year's Ryder Cup. And that wasn't within a par-5 of the worst thing that happened to him this summer.

On July 23 Tom drove his five-months pregnant wife, Melissa, to the hospital. Twenty-five hours later Samuel Edward Lehman was delivered stillborn. Tom sat in a rocking chair and held Samuel as though he were alive. He held the 10-inch-long baby in his big hands for two hours, rocking and touching and weeping worse than any infant in that maternity wing.

That day also happened to be the sixth birthday of the Lehmans' son, Thomas, and that's what made it hurt even more. Lying there in his dad's arms, Samuel looked identical to his big brother.

Tom had the funeral, had two weeks of crying, and then had to go on. He put his golf clubs on his sagging shoulder and headed out the door. With two tournaments to go, he had to protect his place in the top 10 of the Ryder Cup point standings. *Had to.* Nobody wanted to play this Ryder Cup, in Sutton Coldfield, England, worse than Lehman did.

See, to Europeans, Lehman had become the symbol of rude American behavior. They had singled him out as the head hooligan in the celebration on the 17th green at the 1999 Ryder Cup, after Justin Leonard holed his 45-foot putt to seal the U.S. win. The Europeans howled that José María Olazábal could have canned his 20-footer to tie but had no chance amid the hug riot. "And Tom Lehman calls himself a man of God," chided Sam Torrance of Scotland, who happens to be the Euro captain this time around.

That ate at Lehman. Even Olazábal admitted later that the ruckus didn't affect his putt. And what did Lehman's religion have to do with anything? "That *really* was uncalled for," Lehman says. "I was like, You guys can take that and stick it where the sun don't shine. I'm telling you, I couldn't think of anything sweeter than to go over there, let my clubs do my talking, put the *hammer* on somebody, win the thing and celebrate on the 18th green, right in front of their fans."

But as he set out to keep his spot on the team, he had Samuel and Melissa on his mind and a big hole where his fire was supposed to be. He missed both cuts, including the final one at the PGA Championship, which dropped him from 10th to 11th and out of the automatic spots. "I was emotionally spent," Lehman says. "I was running completely on empty. I'm not going to apologize for playing poorly. I couldn't dig down. I had nothing in me."

Then came U.S. captain Curtis Strange's phone call on Aug. 19, just 45 minutes after the PGA had ended. Strange had two wild-card selections to make. "Seems like you've been struggling," Lehman says Strange told him. "I'm not picking you."

At first Lehman thought Strange was joking. Next he was shocked, and then crushed. Still, Lehman didn't make a peep. "I'm pulling for you guys," he told Strange, "and I'll be watching." Lehman hung up and nearly threw the phone through the window.

"If he's going to judge me on my play over the last few weeks, that's a little shortsighted," Lehman said two days later. "I know I've been down, but by the time of the matches nobody was going to have more incentive than me."

So to recap, Lehman won't be playing at The Belfry on Sept. 28–30, despite having more Ryder Cup points than Strange picks Scott Verplank (who ranked 14th) and Paul Azinger (22nd). He won't join a U.S. team whose members, without Lehman's 5-3-2 record, have a losing cumulative Cup mark of 36-38-15. He's not going even though he played in the last three Ryder Cups, while Azinger hasn't played in one in eight years or won a singles match in 10, and Verplank has never been in a Ryder Cup. "Scott's inclusion has surprised me," Torrance said. "It's an intimidating atmosphere, and he'll find it an . . . experience."

At the 1995 Ryder Cup, Curtis Strange made three bogeys on the last three holes when a par on any one of them would have kept the Cup in the U.S. It was the worst brain-lock of his career.

Until now.

Postscript: Been doing this for almost 30 years and I've never come across a kinder, more decent man than Tom Lehman. I caddied for him for my book Who's Your Caddy? and he would sneak breakfast out from the player's locker room for me every morning. When he borrows your locker for a tournament, he leaves you four shirts, four dozen balls and four gloves. He still plays great golf, so great he probably should've abandoned the 2006 Ryder Cup captaincy and played on the team himself. Instead, despite all his preparations, the Europeans crushed his American team. I texted him: "Remember, 1.5 billion Chinese don't care."

58

Nothing but Nets

MAY 1, 2006

I'VE NEVER ASKED FOR ANYTHING BEFORE, RIGHT? WELL, SORRY, I'm asking now. ¶ We need nets. ¶ Not hoop nets, soccer nets or lacrosse nets. Not New Jersey Nets or dot-nets or clarinets. *Mosquito* nets. ¶ See, nearly 3,000 kids die every day in Africa from malaria. And according to the World Health Organization, transmission of the disease would be reduced by 60% with the use of mosquito nets and prompt treatment for the infected.

Three thousand kids! That's a 9/11 every day!

Put it this way: Let's say your little Justin's Kickin' Kangaroos have a big youth soccer tournament on Saturday. There are 15 kids on the team, 10 teams in the tourney. And there are 20 of these tournaments going on all over town. Suddenly, every one of these kids gets chills and fever, then starts throwing up and then gets short of breath. And in seven to 10 days, they're all dead of malaria.

We *gotta* get these nets. They're coated with an insecticide and cost between $4 and $6. You need about $10, all told, to get them shipped and installed. Some nets can cover a family of four. And they last four years. If

190

we can cut the spread of disease, 10 bucks means a kid might get to live. Make it $20 and more kids are saved.

So, here's the ask: If you have ever gotten a thrill by throwing, kicking, knocking, dunking, slamming, putting up, cutting down or jumping over a net, please go to a special site we've set up through the United Nations. The address is: UNFoundation.org/malaria. Then just look for the big *SI's Nothing But Net* logo (or call 202-887-9040) and donate $20. *Bang.* You might have just saved a kid's life.

Or would you rather have the new Beastie Boys CD?

You're a coach, parent, player, gym teacher or even just a fan who likes watching balls fly into nets, send $20. You saved a life. Take the rest of the day off.

You have *ever* had a net in the driveway, front lawn or on your head at McDonald's, send $20. You ever imagined Angelina Jolie in fishnets, $20. So you stay home and eat on the dinette. You'll live.

Hey, Dick's Sporting Goods. You have 255 stores. How about you kick in a dime every time you sell a net? Hey, NBA players, hockey stars and tennis pros, how about you donate $20 every time one of your shots hits the net? Maria Sharapova, you don't think this applies to you just because you're Russian? Nyet!

I tried to think how many times I have said or written the word "net" in 28 years of sports writing, and I came up with, conservatively, 20,000. So I've already started us off with a $20,000 donation. That's a whole lot of lives. Together, we could come up with $1 million, net. How many lives would that save? More than 50 times the population of Nett Lake, Minn.

I know what you're thinking: *Yeah, but bottom line, how much of our $1 million goes to nets?* All of it. Thanks to Ted Turner, who donated $1 billion to create the U.N. Foundation, which covers all the overhead, "every cent will go to nets," says Andrea Gay, the U.N. Foundation's Director of Children's Health.

Nets work! Bill and Melinda Gates have just about finished single-handedly covering every bed in Zambia. Maybe we can't cover an entire Zambia, but I bet we could put a serious dent in Malawi.

It's not like we're betting on some scientist somewhere coming up with a cure. And it's not like warlords are going to hijack a truckload of nets. "Theoretically, if every person in Africa slept at night under a net," says

Gay, "nobody need ever die of malaria again." You talk about a net profit.

My God, think of all the nets that are taken for granted in sports! Ping-Pong nets. Batting cage nets. Terrell Owens's bassinet. If you sit behind the plate at a baseball game, you watch the action *through* a net. You download the highlights on Netscape and forward it on the net to your friend Ben-net while eating Raisinets. Sports is nothing *but* net. So next time you think of a net, go to that website and click yourself happy. Way more fun than your fantasy bowling league, dude.

One last vignette: A few years back, we took the family to Tanzania, which is ravaged by malaria now. We visited a school and played soccer with the kids. Must've been 50 on each team, running and laughing. A taped-up wad of newspapers was the ball and two rocks were the goal. Most fun I ever had getting whupped. When we got home, we sent some balls and nets.

I kick myself now for that. How many of those kids are dead because we sent the wrong nets?

Postscript: The response to this has given me goose bumps—almost 17,000 people contributed nearly $2 million dollars, enough for 150,000 nets. Most were hung in Nigeria, one of the poorest and most disease-riddled countries in the world. So I went there too, to make sure the net results were what we'd all hoped for. The people were deliriously grateful. They fell on their knees and kissed our hands. They threw us festivals and soccer matches and dances. One prefecture king said, "Thank you for dee nets. All my wives use dem!" Turns out he had four wives, and 23 kids. The one thing we heard the most was, "We need more!" So the giving continues. The NBA signed on, as well as the United Methodist Church. Then Bill and Melinda Gates kicked in $3 million, so we're over $5 million. Still, to cover the entire continent would take 300 million nets. Hey, why dream small? Go to NothingButNets.net, send $20. Beats losing it to your bookie, right?

59

Fair Game

DECEMBER 23, 2002

I LOVE HUNTING. MAN VERSUS NATURE. MY CUNNING AGAINST the animal's. That's why I take only the most basic gear, because I believe in the hunter's code of "fair chase." ¶ For instance, some hunters who track coyotes use semiautomatic rifles that fire 30 to 40 shots in about 10 seconds. That's not hunting. The magazine on my Browning semiautomatic ($690) limits me to only five shots every two seconds. And don't forget: It takes at least another 10 seconds to reload.

I believe in the burden of the hunt before the glory of the kill. That's why I won't use camouflaged remote digital movie cameras when deer hunting. How hard is it to sit in the cabin and watch on a monitor until the deer show up? I use only my motion-activated Buckshot 35 Infrared Scouting still camera ($380) with date and time stamping.

Of course, in the interest of maintaining a fair and equitable hunt, I do allow myself some of the same advantages as the game. For example, deer can maneuver their ears to pinpoint sound. To make up for that, I allow myself to use the Game Finder Mega Ears Hearing Muff ($160), which allows me to hear a bug's arthritic knees creak.

And because deer can see better than us in low light—their eyes can gather 10 times as much light as humans'—it's only fair that I use the U.S. Night Vision 441 riflescope ($2,570) with infrared light source. With one of those puppies I could see to the back of a Tora Bora cave. In daylight I'll switch to my Bushnell Mini HOLOsight ($250) scope, which projects a red laser dot on the hide of the target. Hey, if a deer could use one on me, you don't think the sonuvagun would?

Deer are a worthy adversary because of their keen sense of smell. That's why I feel forced to put every stitch of my ultrawarm hunting clothing through the charcoal-filtration system of my portable Scent Master ($160) to remove all human odors.

I'll also wear my Primetime Scent Wafers ($9)—now in cow elk urine! I'll use my Scent Machine ($50) to release a precisely measured aerosol spray of scent every 3.5 minutes as I walk. And when my Wildlife Research Ultimate Scrape Dripper ($20) drips doe urine scent, it convinces bucks that there's a doe around, not me. You ought to see the bucks' faces when their date with a hottie becomes a date with hot lead! Doh!

O.K., I admit I allow myself a few creature comforts. For instance, I'll hunt from my heated camouflaged tree stand ($240) with cushioned back, armrests, lumbar support, umbrella and footrest, but at least I didn't do what some guys do and add a DVD player. Like I say, I'm a purist.

And true, I'll pack my handheld Global Positioning System device ($350) with electronic compass, barometer and database; my radio-controlled, 400,000-candlepower spotlight ($216); my hands-free, voice-activated, two-way radio ($130); my Carry-Lite Deer Decoy ($140); my Rattlin' Antlers ($23); my Cough Silencer ($20); and my Grunt-Snort-Wheeze Deer Call ($15). But what are you going to do, put the genie back in the bottle?

It's a battle of wits, I tell you. Sure, some of my hunting buddies laugh at my full-length Shaggie camouflage coat and hood ($150)—the one that makes me look like Cousin Itt from *The Addams Family*—but think about the risks I take wearing it! Some tanked-up yokel sees what looks like a giant pile of leaves clomping through the forest, you don't think he'll fire on me like I'm in a carnival shooting gallery? And remember, Bobby Knight could be out there!

It's the same with duck hunting. Those ducks are smart! I don't think there's anything wrong with leveling the playing pond a little with my remote-control Mallard Machine ($190) that I can make swim, bob, shake, thrash and dive, with the touch of a button, from my duck blind. I mean, everybody has his tricks. Charles Schwab planted hundreds of acres of rice on his property just to lure ducks he could shoot—and he got a federal subsidy for planting the rice!

Besides, think of this: I *could* use an amphibious, eight-wheel rover ATV ($7,000 to $12,000), complete with gun rests for firing on the run, but I don't. I take a six-wheeler.

Because for me, hunting is not about ease, comfort or tilting the scales to satisfy a hunter's thirst for a trophy. That's why I won't go to one of those awful 100-acre, fenced-in "canned hunting" ranches that are springing up around the country. These privately owned clubs simply truck the game in, and the members hunt until they bag something. It's like hunting at the Milwaukee County Zoo. Even Shaq, among many thousands of Americans, has done it.

No, I refuse to go to that kind of place. The land I hunt is far more fair and honorable. It's 500 fenced-in acres. I could be out there for more than an hour before I bag my kill. Do you know what that does to my bunions?

But, hey, that's the price you pay when you choose to respect the honor, dignity and honest competition of true hunting.

God, I love this sport.

Postscript: Every time I make fun of hunters or the NRA I get a few idle death threats. They usually come into the writers' secretary in SI's New York office, who relays them to me by phone. One year, we had a secretary with a wind tunnel for a brain. She'd take these threats but not realize what they were. "Uh, Rick, a very nice man called from Alabama and he wanted to make sure to tell you never to walk alone," she'd proclaim. Oh, well, thanks. "Yeah, and then a really sweet man who's in prison left you a voicemail and said you should be really careful opening your mail. Isn't that nice?"

60

Boy Meets Girls

FEBRUARY 2001

TRAILING IN ALL THE FATHER OF THE YEAR POLLS, I decided to take my 14-year-old son, Kellen, to a swimsuit photo shoot. Fourteen is about when you start realizing that the annual swimsuit issue is not just something that gets in the way of your NHL coverage. Fourteen is about when you realize that the NHL coverage is getting in the way of your swimsuit issues.

Kellen is like a lot of teenage boys—a terrific kid, but inexplicable by science. How is it possible that sagging jeans four sizes too big somehow stay up on what are only rumors of hip bones? How does a person sleep only slightly longer than a drugged mastodon? How can a kid navigate a snowboard at 50 mph and then trip on a tiny crack in the kitchen tile?

So, Kellen and I found ourselves on a plane bound for Hawaii's North Shore, his young id unable to imagine the glories that lay ahead. He had finally stopped telling his buddies he was going. None of them believed him. His mom wasn't too sure about the trip, either, but we said we were doing it so we could both learn to surf.

"Yeah," said Kel. "Surf."

She didn't buy it for a second.

We landed at about 3 p.m. and got to the hotel about 4:30. "Kel," I said, "if you want, we can try to make the sunset shoot."

"Sure," he said, shrugging. "What else do we have to do?"

We walked about a mile along a deserted beach until we came to a craggy point. We climbed that and, beneath us, discovered thong paradise. There, on an impossibly beautiful beach, were impossibly gorgeous models, either 1) posing with nearly nothing on, 2) getting ready to pose with nearly nothing on or 3) changing nearly nothing swimsuits behind nearly nothing towels held by, sometimes, one another.

I looked at Kel. His eyes widened to the size of saucers. He tried to stay cool. We strolled down to the shoot, pretending that the all-you-can-see feast spread before us was nothing new. This was my fourth shoot, so I was a little used to it. But for a 14-year-old, six-foot, 150-pound man-child perched sweetly on the windowsill between Legos and *Legs*, it was knee-buckling, life-altering, vertebrae-snapping heaven. It got worse. The models started coming over to him. Turns out they thought he was kind of shy and cute. Pretty soon, women hot enough to ignite concrete were shaking Kel's hand with their right hands while trying to cover up their nude top halves with their lefts—and these were not the kind of halves easily covered up with one left hand.

Kel seemed to have ceased breathing. It got worse. One model was changing out of her suit behind a towel. When she kicked off her bikini bottom, it went flying in the air, did a 2½ gainer and landed on Kel's shoulder. He grinned. She grinned. In many states she could do three to five for that. I was thinking that if she did it to me, I would gladly do the time.

It got worse. Photographer Walter Iooss needed Kel to come stand next to him and hold a sun reflector. So, now, what you had was a purple Hawaiian sunset, a deserted beach, a too-fabulous-to-dream-about model in nothing but a thong and a black top hat, me stuck behind the *Entertainment Tonight* crew, unable to see a damn thing because of some damn sun reflector, and Kel, a ninth-grader who'd never even been to a prom, making swimsuit calendars. It was possibly the greatest Take Your Children to Work Day in the history of American commerce.

During a quick break, as the makeup man moved in to spray more "sweat" on the model's derriere, Kel's eyes caught mine. I would say they were now the size of 1952 Nash Rambler hubcaps.

That night, back in the room, I was beat. Kel, however, seemed energized. "So," I said with half a wink, "you want to do the sunset shoot again tomorrow night?"

He stopped cold. "Dad," he said, firmly, "we've *gotta* be at the sun*rise* shoot."

"What?!" I protested. "That's a 4:30 wake-up call! You haven't been up before noon since you were six years old!"

"Dad," he said, firmly and responsibly, "they *need* us."

We finally did learn to surf—on the beach where they filmed *Baywatch Hawaii*, as bra-busting actresses and models practiced jogging, tanning and heart-stopping on the beach in front of us. God, this kid owes me.

On the flight home I wondered if I'd ruined him for life. After all, what was he going to say to the freshman girls back at his high school? "Hi, Amber. Hey, how come you're not backlit?"

Postscript: To this day, I get offers from 53-year-old orthopedic surgeons and 44-year-old accountants, asking me to adopt them. "I'll clean my room every day, make my bed and pay your mortgage," one begged. "All I ask is that I get to go next year."

61

No Doubt About It

I BELIEVE BARRY BONDS. ¶ I BELIEVE BONDS NEVER *KNOWINGLY* took steroids. ¶ I believe Bonds—a man who won't eat buttered popcorn unless he knows its saturated fat content—would put any old thing into his body that his trainer, Greg Anderson, told him to. "I never asked Greg" what the products contained, Bonds told the grand jury for the BALCO steroids case, according to the *San Francisco Chronicle*. "I just said, 'Whatever.' " Sounds like the carefree, trusting, tune-whistler we all know and love.

I believe Bonds—a man who has his own nutritionist and won't eat from the postgame spread, a man who studies his body the way a rabbi studies the Talmud—really thought he *was* using "a rubbing balm for arthritis," as he told the grand jury, not a steroid. That's why it surprises him that the elderly can't bench-press their Oldsmobiles.

I believe it was just a crazy coincidence that Bonds went from never hitting more than 49 homers in a season to belting 73 about the same time he befriended BALCO weasel Victor Conte Jr., extolled him in a muscle maga-zine article, gained 35 pounds and went from Ben Hogan to Hulk Hogan.

I believe Bonds didn't recognize documents, in Anderson's handwriting, detailing his alleged performance-drug use. "I have never seen anything written by Greg Anderson on a piece of paper," he told the grand jury. Hey, Bonds has only known Anderson since they were kids. How many chances do you get to see a friend's handwriting?

I believe Bonds paid Anderson $15,000 in cash for "weight-lifting services." And you're just a cynic if you think he might have paid cash for steroids because he didn't want to leave a paper trail.

I believe Bonds had *no* idea there were BALCO documents that allegedly detail his use of human growth hormone, testosterone and Clomid, a drug for female infertility. And so what if there were? Maybe he's trying to start another family—in a Pyrex beaker.

I believe New York Yankees star Gary Sheffield lied when he told the feds that Bonds hooked him up with the designer steroids ("the cream" and "the clear") and with "red beans," identified by prosecutors as Mexican steroid pills. Besides, *cream, clear and red beans* could be special meal number 5 at El Torito, right?

I believe that even though Yankees star Jason Giambi admitted to the grand jury that he took steroids given to him by Bonds's trainer, and that Sheffield admitted that he used the steroid cream given to him by Bonds himself, Bonds was utterly innocent, like the schlub who explains to the cops he was only holding the bag of Rolexes until the thief came back.

I believe baseball commissioner Bud Selig really *is* going to get something done about steroids this time, and not just because six MVP seasons since 1996 now look more suspicious than carnival-stand diamonds.

I believe the players' union bosses when they say they really are concerned about the health of the players, not just the health of their portfolios, even though they block effective steroid testing at nearly every turn. In fact, if players start dying, I'm sure they'll start a flower fund.

I believe ESPN baseball analyst Tim Kurkjian is right for saying Bonds would *still* be voted into the Hall of Fame on the first ballot, while adding, "but that's not to condone anything." I also believe in rehabbing peeping toms by locking them up in Carmen Electra's house, but that's not to condone anything.

I believe Bonds should go straight to the Hall of Fame, too, even though I know that he's a cheater and that the second half of his career was as phony as Cheez Whiz. Hey, at least he didn't cheat like Pete Rose by betting on his team several times to win. Now *that* will kill a sport.

And I believe track star Marion Jones when she insists she never took a steroid, even though Conte has said that he hooked her up with everything but liquid Drano and saw her inject human growth hormones into her quad. Hey, Conte's old and wears glasses. Maybe it was some other statuesque three-time Olympic gold medalist.

And I believe Jones should be able to keep all her medals and Bonds all his MVP awards because it will give them something to hang on their cell walls if they perjured themselves in front of a grand jury.

And I believe Sammy Sosa would've gotten tested for steroids that day, in July 2002, I invited him to go to a private lab. He freaked out only because he thought I wanted to check his bats, too.

And I believe Ron Artest never meant to hurt anybody, Notre Dame didn't really want Urban Meyer, and that wasn't Carmelo Anthony's weed in his backpack.

And I believe reindeer fly, President Clinton did not have sexual relations with that woman, and Rogaine really *can* regrow your hair.

Now, if you'll kindly move out of the way, I believe I'm about to get sick.

Postscript: Having said all that, I still believe Bonds's records should stay in the books. With a little syringe next to every one.

62

Extremely Big Red

OCTOBER 11, 2004

Y OU GO TO A COLLEGE FOOTBALL GAME. YOU FIND YOUR seat. You stand and cheer. No big deal. ¶ But when you are Patrick Deuel and three months ago you weighed 1,072 pounds, going to a college football game is not just a very big deal. It's what you live for.

Deuel's goal is to be able to attend the very first Nebraska football game of his life, inhale the fresh air and "become part of that sea of red," he says.

That's a lot of red. This is a man who weighed 90 pounds in kindergarten, whose arms weigh 120 pounds apiece and who can't wait to fit back into his XXXXXXXXXXL Huskers T-shirt. And you thought you were Nebraska's biggest fan.

It's not going to be easy. Until June, the 42-year-old former pancake house manager hadn't been out of his bed in at least seven months. Hadn't been out of his house in Valentine, Neb., in seven years. (The doors weren't big enough.) Couldn't lie on his back to sleep because there was so much fat on his chest that his lungs couldn't expand. Couldn't roll over without the help of two or three people.

"He was terminal," says his doctor, Frederick Harris. "He was going to die."

For 14 years, Patrick and his wife, Edith, had been begging for help. Insurance companies he approached kept saying that treatment for his morbid obesity—partly the fault of his genes—was "cosmetic" and refused to help.

No hospital within 400 miles of Valentine was willing to take a man who weighed almost as much as the entire Nebraska defensive line. The Deuels were trapped. Meanwhile, adults and high school kids drove by the house shouting obscenities at Patrick.

Enter Dr. Harris, who refused to let Deuel die. Harris pleaded with Avera McKennan Hospital in Sioux Falls, S.Dak., to take Deuel, even though the facility wouldn't be able to collect the hundreds of thousands of dollars his care would cost. When the hospital said yes, the problems really began.

It took a specially equipped ambulance—one of only six in the country—to transport the half-ton man. When the vehicle got to Deuel's house, a local rescue team had already cut down the wall between the garage and his bedroom with a saw.

"Patrick was facing a wall not a foot and a half from his face," says Dan Gray, the man in charge of the move for American Medical Response. "That's what he'd been staring at for months."

"I was sure I was going to die in the ambulance that day," says Deuel. His skin was stretched so thin, a cut or a hernia could kill him. Lying in the wrong position could kill him. Edith was scared, too, but she couldn't be there with him because she had to work.

"They'd said their last goodbyes the night before," Gray said. "They thought this was the end."

Six strong men pulled Deuel onto a Hovermat—a mattress that floats inches above the ground on a cushion of compressed air. The mattress was lowered onto a stretcher that was pulled into the ambulance by a winch.

Then they drove four hours to Sioux Falls—"We couldn't give him food," says Gray, "but he never stopped smiling"—where the hospital had already widened the door to his room and laid a king-sized mattress across two reinforced beds clamped together.

Placed on a strict 1,200-calories-a-day diet, Deuel began losing a toddler a day: as much as 20 pounds. Tell Jared from Subway *that*. Deuel just keeps getting thinner. "He really wants to go to that Nebraska game," says Harris.

Last week he was down to 684 pounds, which meant he had lost 388 pounds, which meant he could finally ride in a reinforced wheelchair (weight limit: 700 pounds), which meant he could actually be wheeled *outside* now. It was the first time he'd regularly felt sunshine on his face since 1997.

If he can lose another 334 pounds, he'll be at 350, which he hopes will allow him to walk proudly, on his own, into Memorial Stadium.

Nebraska had better hold a bunch of seats. Deuel and his sunny face have made so many friends, everybody wants to be there for his moment. Nurses, doctors, hospital janitors.

"My crew and I are coming," says Gray. "We love Patrick. He's a very smart, eloquent man. He's the favorite call we've ever made."

He's still a mile from pulling it off. "He's just getting to the hard part," says Tina Ames, a hospital spokesman. To help him live a normal life, Harris plans to perform risky gastric bypass surgery (stomach stapling) on him soon.

We college football fans whoop for and worship the athletes on the field. But just this once, could we stand and cheer for a fan?

After all, wouldn't it be great to go to a game where the goosebumps comeback victory happens *before* kickoff?

Postscript: Deuel is thriving now. He's lost the equivalent of a third-grade class. He's down to around 400 pounds, thanks to all the pounds he lost through his emergency crash diet, his gastric bypass, regular walking and now, believe it or not, biking. At one point he lost 81 pounds just from doctors surgically removing a mass of fat and loose skin. O.K., maybe that was more than you wanted to know. But the great news is, he finally did attend a game: Nebraska's 34–20 homecoming win over Missouri on Nov. 4, 2006.

63

Fear Factor

JANUARY 31, 2005

I N GOLF, BOGEYS HURT. BUT BOGEYS NEVER HURT ANYBODY the way they hurt Sean O'Hair. ⁊ For him, a bogey might mean a backhand to the face, a bloody nose, another mile to run, another silent 500-mile car ride. Because Sean O'Hair had the world's toughest coach to answer to when he made a bogey—his dad, Marc. "No kid should ever have to go through what I went through," says O'Hair, 22, a rookie on the PGA Tour. "I can't tell you how many times I wanted to quit. But what was I going to do? I read about women who stay [with husbands or boyfriends] even though they're getting beat up all the time. I think that was me. I was always afraid of my father. He's 6' 3", 230. He's a big guy."

At 16 Sean was the nation's second-ranked junior amateur. At 17, prodded by his father, he pulled out of his Bradenton, Fla., high school, turned pro and set about trying to qualify for events in golf's bush leagues. Grinding 90,000 miles a year in his Ford sedan, Sean's father was his coach, trainer, cook, high school teacher and full-time tormentor.

Though he was never in the service, Marc treated his son as if he were in the army. Reveille for Sean was at 5 a.m., followed by exercise, then a strict practice regimen before playing a course, with Marc caddying. For every shot he finished over par, Sean would have to run a mile after the round. (One time Sean played in New Orleans when it was 93°, shot 80 and had to run eight miles. Playing the next day, he could hardly walk.) After the punishment run, there was weightlifting and then supper, which was chosen and cooked by Marc on a portable stove in their hotel room, followed by homework and bed.

"I had no friends," Sean remembers. "I had no driver's license. I had nothing. My life was golf, golf, golf. It was just so tense. How are you supposed to play good in all that?" He usually didn't, and often there was a price to pay on the way to the next Red Roof Inn. "Anytime I disagreed with my dad, he considered it back talk," says Sean, "and he slapped me around."

Though he refused comment when I contacted him, Marc admitted to *The Orlando Sentinel* that he had hit his son. Sean told me his dad's smacks gave him a bloody nose "20 times—at least." And that was just the physical pain. "It's weird, but when I got hit, I thought I was the problem," Sean says. "I thought he hit me because I was bad."

He felt trapped. When Sean was 17, his father made him sign a contract giving him 10% of Sean's earnings "for life." Sean also signed an agreement to pay his dad back "about $100,000" to cover various expenses. "I felt like I had to sign. What else was I going to do? I was 17."

Then in 2001 Sean met Jackie Lucas, a Florida Atlantic University golfer, on a course in Coral Springs. For two weeks he couldn't bring himself to ask her out. After all, at 19 he'd never been on a date. It took him three months to kiss her.

She couldn't believe Sean's life. "It was boot camp," says Jackie, 23. "There wasn't a single decision he could make for himself."

"She opened my eyes," Sean says. "She made me understand that I didn't deserve this, that I had a right to be happy."

Finally, on the road one night in 2002, Marc said something ugly about Jackie. For the first time Sean got in his dad's grill. "I was scared," he says, "but I didn't back down." Sean told Marc to shove it. Their relationship was done. Sean went out and bought his first pair of jeans. Six months later he and Jackie married.

You'd be amazed how freely you swing when 230 pounds comes off your back. Sean and Jackie took all their wedding-gift money and tried a mini-tour in New England. Golf became what he did, not who he was, and he started to love the game again. At the second stage of Q school last fall, he birdied the last three holes to make it to the final round, then finished an astonishing fourth to earn his PGA Tour card. He's played two tournaments, including the Buick Invitational last week, and made one cut. Pressure? The Tour is tiddlywinks compared to the pressure he has known.

Sean hasn't spoken to his dad in two years, and Marc told the *Sentinel* he may send copies of the contract with his son to major media outlets. "I intend to crucify him in the media," says Marc, 52, "because what he did to me is not right."

And guess what? Sean doesn't care, "as long as he stays out of my life." See, Sean's too busy being happy. He and Jackie just bought a house in Boothwyn, Pa. His new caddie—Jackie's dad, Steve—only kids him about bogeys, then takes him out to dinner. Even better: Jackie is due on Feb. 17. "I know one thing," Sean says. "If I ever give my kids money, I'll never expect anything back."

He misses his mom, Brenda, and sister, K.D., who live with Marc in Lakeland, Fla. Word is, 16-year-old K.D. has a killer voice. She sang the anthem at an Orlando Magic game. "We think she has a chance to be something special," Marc told *Golf World* last week.

God help her.

Postscript: Happily married, his father out of his life and his father-in-law carrying his bag, O'Hair became the PGA Tour Rookie of the Year in 2005.

64

Dribblephilia

NOVEMBER 25, 2002

HE'S RANKED NO. 1 NATIONALLY IN HIS CLASS. Basketball coaches ask about him constantly. He'll play more than 80 games this year around the nation. ¶ And he's 11 years old. ¶ His name is Kendall Marshall. He's 5' 1", weighs 90 pounds and is known as Butter for the way he spreads the ball around. He likes macaroni and cheese but not girls. In June, Hoop-ScoopOnline.com, one of the best-known websites covering blue-chip recruits, ranked him the No. 1 fifth-grade player in America for last season.

You didn't know fifth-graders were ranked? Where you been? Tora Bora?

"Some kids in the neighborhood told me about it," says Kendall, now a sixth-grader who will be the first. . . uh. . . man off the bench for the Evangel Christian High *varsity* this winter in Woodbridge, Va., despite being six years younger than many of his teammates. "I didn't know what to think. I guess it's cool."

The very fact that someone ranks fifth-graders tells you how nutso all of us have become about sports.

"Who does this benefit?" says Will Robinson, the coach at nearby Woodbridge High. "If the kid pans out, is that a feather in somebody's cap? And who does it hurt? It hurts the kid. He's got these expectations the rest of his life."

Kendall says, "Sometimes kids come up to me and go, 'Hey, you're not all that.' One kid tried to get me mad so I'd fight him, but I didn't." Can't you see the poor kid if he doesn't lead every list from now until college?

Fan No. 1: That kid Marshall. So much potential, but what a bust.

Fan No. 2: I know. He didn't even make Playboy's *Sixth-Grade All-America team this year.*

"To rank a kid that young," says Kendall's dad, Dennis, a computer network administrator, "who would do that?"

Clark Francis, that's who. He runs HoopScoopOnline.com, a service that 150 coaches pay to read.

"Of course I haven't seen every fifth-grader," Francis says. "But the best ones go to the big camps and the AAU nationals. You see them. You hear things."

Francis says he doesn't really want to rank fifth-graders, but "the college coaches who pay my bills want to know. So you put kids' names out there, and if they turn out good, then you were the first to write about them. It helps."

But why, for the love of God, do coaches want to know about kids still in SpongeBob Squarepants pajamas?

"Let's say you're a college coach," says Francis. "You know that you have to beat Kentucky, Duke or North Carolina. To do that, you have to get the star players onto your campus when they're in junior high."

Can't you see it?

Kendall, welcome to Trey State. Check it out! Bunk beds! All the Lucky Charms you can eat! And I know a guy who can get you the key to the Slurpee machine at night!

And it's not just college coaches who want them tagged and identified. High school coaches want to know so they can recruit (often illegally). AAU coaches want to know so they can win national titles, like the 11-and-under championship that Kendall led his team to this year. Shoe companies want to know so they can get a leg up on the race for soles. Even sleazy street agents want to know so they can start turning heads.

Look, kid. You could use a nice new Schwinn, am I right?

It might be funny, if it didn't make you want stick forks in your brain. Back when the fifth-grade list came out, Kendall was a 4' 9" point guard. It's trouble when the list is taller than you are.

And you just know, somewhere, somebody's got a scouting report on the kid: *Great spot-up J, quick hands, cries when he skins his knee.*

What will they rank next? Tall couples who have really good genes!

It's this kind of hype that tricked Leon Smith and Korleone Young—both of whom were ranked No. 1 in their class as middle-school players—to go pro out of high school. Now both are out of the NBA and wondering where their futures went.

"The problem is these kids start to believe their press clippings," says Francis. "Then they stop working on their game. They're like, 'I'm 6' 10", I can shoot, pass and dunk. And I'm in eighth grade. I've made it.' "

If you think the hype can't get to a kid's melon, you haven't heard of the legendary O.J. Mayo, from Huntington, W.Va., who tops most eighth-grade lists, signs autographs daily, has his own website (and a moustache) and plays at a Christian school that isn't even in his state—along with five other out-of-state teammates.

Uh, Sister Magdalene? Can I be excused from math today? I gotta do MTV's Cribs.

Hopefully, it won't happen with Kendall.

"No, sir, I haven't gotten too excited about the whole thing," he says, " 'cause I know I got my whole life ahead of me."

That figures, huh? The one person in all of this who is not acting like a sixth-grader is the sixth-grader.

Postscript: The kid isn't 5' 1" anymore and he probably doesn't wear pajamas either. Last I checked he's 6' 1" already. He's lived up to all that hype and then some. Hoopscooponline.com rates him as a Top 10 recruit in the class of 2010. The kid's 15 and he's been famous for four years. At 15 my greatest accomplishment was burping the alphabet.

65

Canada's Goose
Is Cooked

APRIL 30, 2001

W HOA, CANADA! ¶ YOU WENT TOO DAMN FAR this time. First you tried to pawn off that bad ham as bacon. Then you stuck us with Celine Dion and no instructions on how to turn her off. But when you started booin' our national anthem, Bubba, you peed on the wrong leg.

It happened five times last week. Vancouver Canucks fans roundly booed *The Star-Spangled Banner* before two home playoff games against the Colorado Avalanche, and Edmonton Oilers fans booed it before three home games against the Dallas Stars.

Hey, Roseanne wasn't even singin' it!

I know it's not easy playin' Paul Shaffer to our David Letterman, but we don't deserve this. Don't we keep our border open to you people? Put up with that gross Tom Green and his televised testicles? Let you park your Zambonis anyplace you want?

O.K., our anthem isn't the catchiest tune, but it's *ours*. We don't like Muslim point guards sittin' down while it's played, and we don't like Canadians like Robert Goulet forgettin' the words to it, and we sure as *hell* don't like a bunch of plaid-wearin', moose-speakin' McKenzie brothers booin' it. Don't forget, we've got a Texan on the button now.

Nobody's quite sure why you're booin'. Maybe you think if you disrespect somebody else's country, it makes you more patriotic. Maybe Vancouver is hacked off about losing its NBA Grizzlies to a U.S. city. Maybe Edmonton fans have had it up to their earflaps with gettin' punked by the Stars in the playoffs four straight seasons. Or maybe fans hear the rumors that the Oilers are the next Canadian hockey team that's going to pack up and move across the border. Or maybe you drink about three dozen too many Labatts before the games. But you buncha lumberjacks just crossed a 3,987-mile line.

Well, I know what it is. You're sore at how we're whippin' you at your game. A Canadian team hasn't won the Stanley Cup since 1993. You've only got six teams left out of the 30 in the league, and those six are lookin' paler than a Saskatoon stripper. None of 'em have a snowball's chance this year, and most are broker than Braniff. Meanwhile, there are teams in such hockey hotbeds as Dallas, Miami, Phoenix (you remember that team, right? Used to be in Winnipeg), San Jose and Tampa.

Your dollar is worth, what, 65 cents now? How many pesos is that? And now a Coloradan, George Gillet Jr., is trying to buy your crown jewel, the Montreal Canadiens. Is that beautiful? Hope he starts serving tacos and Bud and slappin' all those snooty French Canadians on the back with, "How's it hangin', Hoss?"

You had to be pretty desperate to boo ol' Frank Key's jingle. The Avalanche (you remember that team, right? Used to be in Quebec) was on its way to sweepin' out the Canucks four-zip, and most of the Colorado players are Canadians anyhow. You even pissed off Avalanche captain Joe Sakic, and he's from suburban Vancouver! You're booin' your next-igloo neighbor. Plus, you've been runnin' those Molson beer "I Am Canadian" ads up there the last three years, takin' shots at us, callin' Canada "the best part of North America." One ad mocked us for our basic friendliness, like when you tell us you're from Canada, and we say, "Hey, do you know Suzy? *She's* from Canada!"

O.K., we do know one guy you might know—Wayne Gretzky. Owns a piece of the Phoenix club. You thought he'd come back after he'd seen Hollywood, the beach and Janet Jones naked? Yeah, right. He figured out early on that he was stayin', especially after his Canadian buddies came to his house in L.A., saw the long, steep driveway and moaned, "Wayner, you'll never get up this in the winter."

I notice Larry Walker hasn't moved back, either. Or Michael J. Fox. Or Jim Carrey. Gee, can't imagine why. Other than fat taxes, tiny temperatures and the fact that a big Saturday night is sittin' next to a hole in the ice waitin' for a lunk to come along while keepin' your bait warm in your mouth.

You know what a Canadian guy asks before he agrees to a blind date? "Does she have her own jumper cables?" You know how to spell Canada? C, *eh*? N, *eh*? D, *eh*?

So that's it. Burn the Peace Bridge. This is war. Your only job was to stay quiet up there, send us the occasional smoked salmon and protect us from invasion by Greenland. But you went and ruined it. You think we can't take all them sissy Mounties? We can whip them with Rulon Gardner alone.

Tell you what. We either get an apology by the morning, or you hosers can forget about becoming our 51st state.

Postscript: Boy, Canadians sure are touchy. They didn't seem to get into the spirit of this one at all. So to make amends, I will point out that when Justin Morneau of the Minnesota Twins was voted MVP of the American League for 2006, it meant that three of the four MVPs in the big four pro sports were Canucks—Morneau, the Phoenix Suns' Steve Nash, and the San Jose Sharks' Joe Thornton. Free bacon for everybody!

66

Van Earl Wrong

MARCH 1, 2004

AS A KID I NEVER WANTED TO BE JOE NAMATH OR Jerry West or even Jim Murray. All I wanted to be was Curt Gowdy, sports announcer and god. ¶ Sadly, upon puberty's pummeling, I abandoned the dream. Sportscasters were dashing baritones. None had a tin voice whining through a can-opener nose under a forehead tall enough to fit a 72-point MAN WALKS ON MOON!

But then ESPN gave us *Dream Job*—its reality show that had 10,000 amateurs vying for one spot at the *SportsCenter* desk. It's down to 11 this week, and a few of the finalists look like mooks you'd use to fill a police lineup, Brillo-haired and neckless.

My hopes rose. I begged ESPN for a tryout, just to see what the *Dream Job* guys were up against. "Sure," said ESPN senior vice president and executive editor John Walsh. "We put ugly people on TV all the time!"

Uh, swell!

He gave me a shot last Friday night, in the much-desired midnight-to-12:30 a.m. slot on ESPNEWS. Perfect. So few people would be watching, it might as well be E-SPAN. Yet it would be live. The ESPN guys suggested that I come to network headquarters in Bristol, Conn., and train for two weeks. I suggested two days. I mean, how hard could it be?

The first guy I talked to when I got there on Wednesday was Chris Berman. "You're going to make a million mistakes," he said. "Just remember: They're off to Pluto. Let 'em go and move on."

Then I met the anchor who would be my partner for the half hour, Stan Verrett, who said our audience would be about 500,000 (gulp). On Thursday he let me sit just off-camera during one of his telecasts. Somehow, while directors yelled into his earphone, Verrett seamlessly called highlights he hadn't seen before, involving hockey players whose names looked like a spilled Scrabble box.

When I tried just a seven-minute rehearsal—with nobody in my ear—I fell behind twice, used the same stupid "Take that, Lex Luthor!" on all eight dunks I called, and covered the desk in spittle.

I sincerely missed my DELETE key.

"Don't worry about it," said *SportsCenter* anchor Scott Van Pelt. "A lot of the people watching you will be in bars, drunk, with no sound. They'll think you're great!"

I rehearsed again on Friday and was worse. I kept saying, "Now watch this!" as if people were suddenly going to start staring at the hat rack instead of the TV. I yelped a dunk line—"Somebody get us a new peach basket!"—when we were already into the Detroit Red Wings highlights. I gave three scores, two of them wrong. "Where'd you go to school again?" asked my senior coordinating producer, Barry Sacks.

I had nightmares about sitting at the desk, pantsless, as someone was saying in my ear, "O.K., the Serbian all-star hockey game. In 3, 2, 1. . . . "

Still, it was cool to be living inside a SportsCenter ad. George Karl was shoehorned into a tiny cubicle. Digger Phelps fumbled for change ahead of me in the cafeteria line. Stuart Scott was changing in the men's room. "Just don't be one of those guys with 25 ways to say *dunk*," said Scott.

"No way!" I said, hiding my list of 25 ways to say *dunk*.

But when midnight struck, something serendipitous happened. Maybe the last of my ephedra kicked in. For no good reason, everything went right!

On a splendid floater by Carmelo Anthony: "You had me at Mel-lo." On a long trey by Tracy McGrady (singing): "We're goin' to Sizzler!" On the five goals that beat St. Louis Blues goalie Reinhard Divis: "Hey, Reinhard, we'll keep the light on for you!"

Verrett was laughing, so I kept firing. One shooter was "hotter than a $3 pistol!" A hole in one was "allergic to daylight!" And John Daly just set a record—"the 117th straight day he didn't marry anybody!"

O.K., so I still got behind on some highlights. And, true, I said a hockey game was in the "first half," and then, instead of letting it go to Pluto, recoiled at the horror of my gaff and blurted, "second *quarter*—I mean, second *period*."

And, yes, perhaps it was wrong, when asked on-air by Verrett if I was nervous, to say, "You know, I had a fifth of Scotch right before the show, so I feel pretty good."

But, still, I was thinking Curt Gowdy would've been proud—until I came out of the studio and saw Sacks looking like he'd just swallowed a moth. "Uh, I'm not sure you can say somebody beat a goalie 'like Liza's ex,' " he said.

Oops.

"And even though it was about his assists, you can't call Greg Ostertag 'your neighborhood dealer,' " he said. "And I'm not sure I'd let you call BALCO ' 'Roids R Us' again."

If it had been a different reality show, he would have added, "You're fired!"

I was watching myself in the newsroom and saw, for the first time, just how vast my forehead appeared on camera. "My God, that looks like Half Dome," I moaned.

SportsCenter anchor Linda Cohn happened to be standing there. "Yeah," she said, sympathetically, "imagine what it'll look like in high definition."

Postscript: Maybe I wasn't that bad. ESPN actually offered me an on-air job afterward. There are weeks, when it's Deadline Friday and I still don't have a good idea and I've started and abandoned four different columns, and Bobby Knight hasn't slapped anybody, that I wished I'd taken it.

67

Fan Power

THERE'S A BILL OF RIGHTS FOR U.S. CITIZENS, CHILDREN, taxpayers, consumers, home owners, travelers, mental patients and animals. Which leaves only one important group without one: sports fans. ¶ Until now.

AMENDMENT I: Owners shall make no seat in a stadium narrower than John Madden's butt; nor name said stadium after some soulless brokerage house; nor install trough-style urinals in said stadium without little shelves to set cold beers upon.

AMENDMENT II: A good seat being necessary to the pursuit of happiness, any fan may move down to a better one after halftime, including courtside, and not get the hook from a 17-year-old, $5.15-an-hour-making, Clearasil-jonesing usher who thinks a spiffy jacket suddenly makes him a member of the Marines Security Guard.

AMENDMENT III: No fan shall suffer strikes, lockouts, seat licensing fees, male cheerleaders, ticket-price hikes after losing seasons, drastic last-minute changes in starting times to accommodate ESPN3, team-logo changes within one year after said fan has plunked down $75 for a jersey with the *old* logo, mascot arrests, vendors handing over lukewarm beers with thumbs in them, 6' 10" yokels wearing novelty cowboy hats in the seat in front of said fan, drunk carnies constantly screaming "Run the flea-flicker!" in said fan's ear, or ejection from the arena or stadium by a security guard because of said fan's T-shirt, even if it says POHLAD DATES FARM ANIMALS.

AMENDMENT IV: The right of the fan to a short national anthem shall not be violated; nor shall the anthem be "personalized" to hell and back; nor shall said singer be the owner's niece; nor shall the guy in the music booth continue to play *Na Na Hey Hey Kiss Him Goodbye* or *We Will Rock You* year after year after year.

AMENDMENT V: No fan shall be required to answer questions from spouses, such as why the garbage disposal is still stopped up, during crucial situations, such as the second half; nor shall said spouse interrupt at such times to get a pickle jar opened or to "mention" a "little, teeny-weeny nothing accident" with the new Mustang knowing full well that said fan is only pretending to listen in such crucial situations, such as *SportsCenter*.

AMENDMENT VI: The fan shall be afforded a fair and speedy baseball game and not suffer through human glaciers like Nomar Garciaparra stepping out of the batter's box to readjust his hat, sleeves, gloves, groin and stirrups after every pitch; nor shall the fan suffer TV camera closeups so tight that said fan can see the piece of spinach on a pitcher's tooth, all the while leaving said fan no idea that the infield has shifted and the first base coach is on fire.

AMENDMENT VII: In lawsuits it shall be judged that any ball, bat or muffler that ends up in the seats shall be permanently the property of the fan who first comes into possession of it, not the meathead who wrestles it away. In case of said wrestling away, said meathead will be subdued, stripped, wrapped in the Iraqi flag and dropped off at the nearest Harley bar.

AMENDMENT VIII: There shall be no such thing as a traffic lane between the TV and the fan watching the game. Use the off-ramp behind the sofa. In addition chips, wings and cold beer shall be readily available to said fan, though rising to get said items shall not constitute an offer by said fan to get same for lard-ass brothers-in-law in close proximity.

AMENDMENT IX: No fan shall be made to feel like a jerk just for wanting to shake the hand of an athlete said fan has spent all his time and money idolizing, just because said athlete happens to be 7' 1" and 325 pounds with footwork Baryshnikov would've guzzled turpentine for.

AMENDMENT X: The fan shall not suffer parking places that are $4 cab rides to the arena door; nor shall the cost of four tickets, four hot dogs, four sodas, four programs and four souvenir hats to any game exceed that of a 2003 Ford Focus; nor shall old phone books, sliced diagonally, slathered in picante sauce and topped with green goo, be sold as a $9.95 Fiesta Mexicana; nor shall the beer be anything but very, very cold.

It would also be nice if somebody explained the Davis Cup to the fan, preferably Anna Kournikova.

These powers delegated to the fan shall not be construed to mean that said fan can streak, holler "You da Man!," participate in Father-Son Night pummelings, ask for autographs if over the age of 12, or wear those hideous striped Zubaz pants.

Ever.

68

The Comeback of All Combacks

APRIL 3, 2006

THE POINT GUARD NEARLY DROWNED IN HIS OWN HOUSE. ¶ The coach lost his home. ¶ The shooting guard spent five weeks in a cramped hotel room with no power or water. ¶ Their leaky gym had no heat. ¶ And they almost killed each other. ¶ So you tell me: How in the *world* did Ehret High win the Louisiana state basketball championship?

"When you think about where we started," says Ehret's coach, Allen Collins, "it's nothing short of incredible."

Where they started was in Marrero, La., 10 minutes from New Orleans, on Aug. 28, 2005, the day Hurricane Katrina turned the whole area into a watery hell. "I was afraid for my life," says Ehret guard Gary Davis, who was trapped for days on the second floor of his house in New Orleans. "Choppers saw us and kept going past. I just kept thinking about hoops. It was the only thing that made me happy."

Hoops? The gym at Ehret High was a wreck. There would be no time for conditioning or weightlifting. But Collins wanted to try to play anyway. "I made a commitment to coach 'em, and I was gonna coach 'em," he says.

Problem was, only four of 'em were left. The rest of his team was scattered as far away as Atlanta.

He found a couple of transfers and got the roster to six, but nearly every game was on the road. The team didn't have a single home game until January. And since there was no money in Ehret's budget for athletics, Collins couldn't even buy his kids postgame pizza. They made do with Salvation Army meals and cold MREs donated by military personnel stationed at the school. "It's not like I could take 'em to McDonald's. All the McDonald's were closed," he says. Ehret even had to withdraw from a Thanksgiving tournament. Couldn't afford a bus driver.

Remarkably, things got worse. Most players had no transportation. For a while, only senior guard Randy Verdin had a reliable car, and if he couldn't round everybody up, there'd be no practice. Players were living from one friend's couch to another. Transfers came in but would have to leave again with their unsettled families.

Hundreds of phone calls later, Collins finally quilted together a patch-work team—10 kids from five schools, including a cocky inner-city transfer named Brian Randolph whom nobody on the team liked. The feeling was mutual.

"He just had an attitude all the time," says Ehret's star forward, Christian Wall, who still lives in a trailer on his front lawn. The Ehret kids bickered almost daily with Randolph and the non-Ehret kids. It was like *West Side Story* in Reeboks.

They lost early and they lost often, then started 1–2 in the district. "We were at a point of no return," Collins said. So before a must-win game, he threw them all into a room and told them, Work it out, or the season is lost.

And lo and behold, they did. Almost to a man, the players say it hit them, in that room, that they could lose clothes and homes and trophies to Katrina, but they just couldn't bear losing hoops.

Randolph backed down and became a passer and a screener and a re-bounder. Transfer Nicholas Washington, who'd been a star at Cohen High, swallowed hard and let Wall become the go-to guy. Everyone else chipped in as best he could. And they won 10 of their next 11.

"Other coaches would ask me, 'How are you doing this?'" Collins recalled. "I'd say, 'It's not me, it's them.' All I did was try not to let them get too low. No yelling. They've had enough negative stuff."

Next thing you know, Ehret was in the state 5A championship game, playing Woodlawn of Baton Rouge, a school whose biggest distraction all year was cheerleader practice. And while Woodlawn and the other semifinalists were happily snuggled in their hotel rooms near the Cajundome in Lafayette, Ehret commuted 2½ hours each way back to their couches. They couldn't afford rooms.

Yet somehow, against all logic, Ehret beat Woodlawn, the most powerful team in the state—with the clinching dunk coming from none other than Brian Randolph. It was hard to decide who was crying harder, the players or their emotionally spent parents. "A mismatched bunch of riffraff won it all," Collins beams. "It's like *Hoosiers*!"

Actually, it's bigger than that. Ehret's Katrina Comeback has been a little patch of blue sky for a ravaged city, a symbol of how things can be rebuilt when you don't care who gets the credit.

"We showed New Orleans that different parts of the city can come together and do something great," Randolph says. "I mean, I know Katrina might be horrible for some people, but it was a blessing for us."

Postscript: After this column hit, I was inundated with calls from movie types who wanted to do a film about the team. I sent all of them on to coach Collins. At press time, there was still no definite deal. But ESPN invited the entire team to Hollywood, where they received an award presented by Matthew McConaughey and got to hang out with him at the ESPYs and meet Reggie Bush, LeBron James and Shaun Alexander.

69

Attention, Please!

APRIL 4, 2005

O K., EXPERIMENT TIME. WHAT ARE THE ODDS THAT I can spend an entire morning with the most dominant athlete in the country—in public, no disguises—without that athlete being hailed, photographed or bugged for a single signed napkin?

The athlete? Annika Sorenstam, of course, who is doing to women's golf what the boll weevil did to the South. She just tied Nancy Lopez's record of five straight LPGA wins with her *eight*-shot victory in the Nabisco Championship on Sunday. She just won her fifth major out of the last eight. She's won 36 times since the 2001 season began. Nobody's won that much since Mickey Wright and Kathy Whitworth beat fields full of P.E. instructors in the 1960s.

9:05 a.m. I greet Sorenstam in the coffee shop at the JW Marriott in Denver. Already done with her 1,000 crunches for the day, she's wearing her logo-laden golf hat and sweater. Yet the waiter doesn't even blink twice. In the lobby we meet one of her managers, David Livingston. People are everywhere, yet they walk by her as if she's Ms. Nadine Nobody.

9:32 a.m. We go to the headquarters of a huge grocery-store chain, where she'll do a meet-and-greet with company honchos. She is stopped on her way into the offices. "Ma'am," says the security guard, "do you have a visitor's badge?"

Sorenstam actually prefers her Annika-nymity. When she was a kid, she'd purposely finish second in tournaments to avoid having to make a speech. This winter, at her home in Lake Tahoe, a burly guy knocked at the door and Sorenstam answered.

"Oh, uh, hi," he said, startled. "Hey, does anyone ever tell you that you look a lot like Annika Sorenstam?"

"Who?" said Annika Sorenstam.

"It's a golfer who supposedly lives around here."

"Oh."

"Can I blow your roof?"

10:08 a.m. At a studio to record a radio ad, the engineer says over the intercom, "O.K., let's get Anna on the mike so I can get some levels. Anna? Anna?"

Anna? This woman has won 59 times on the LPGA tour and once shot a 59. Pal, you're an idiot anna moron.

"That's nothing," the Swedish-born Sorenstam says. "I was in Milwaukee the other day, and I was 'Anee.' I've also been Anita, A-nee-ka [it's pronounced AH-nih-kuh]. Sometimes I'm Monica. I'm also Soren-son a lot. I've been Soren-strum. One time I got, 'So, A-nee-ka, how do you pronounce your last name?'"

This is a golfer who has won 15 more times than Tiger Woods since the beginning of 2002. Can you imagine someone saying, "So, Teeger, how do you pronounce your last name?"

10:43 a.m. Starbucks is packed. If it were Phil Mickelson, people would be begging to lick the bottom of his peppermint mocha. But does Sorenstam get even a half shot of love? Nope.

Love is hard to come by lately. She just filed for divorce from her husband (and former caddie), David Esch. She won't talk about it, but she will talk about what's next.

"I can't see myself playing past 50," she says, keeping an eye on Livingston. She waits until he's distracted, then whispers to me, "Actually, 40."

Then she wants kids. "I don't know how many," says Sorenstam, who is

34. "But I can see myself going to a Little League game and screaming until my husband has to put a sock in my mouth."

How the hell Sorenstam will retire is a mystery, because she has the same disease Michael Jordan had—an addiction to winning. Golf, Ping-Pong, cards in a hat, doesn't matter. She is to a "friendly game" what a Doberman is to a bowl of sirloin. When she hits a tennis ball into the net, she looks as if she wants to break the racket. When she loses at chess, she sweeps the pieces off in a rage. "That's going to be my problem when I quit golf," she admits. "I get to the tee to play a relaxing game, and this little demon is inside my head screaming, 'You gotta win!' "

Of course, if Sorenstam really does want to retire at 40, she's going to have a hard time breaking the sexiest record in women's golf: Whitworth's alltime record for LPGA wins, 88. Then again, if she keeps averaging eight wins a year (her average the last four years), she'll reach 88 by the time she's 38. Then she could marry and get pregnant in the off-season, go win one more and be 10 centimeters dilated by 40.

Not to be pushy or anything.

12:30 p.m. Last event before lunch: a press conference at Cherry Hills, site of this year's U.S. Women's Open in June. Colorado governor Bill Owens's wife, Frances, reads a proclamation that ends grandly with, "Therefore, this day is hereby declared Annika Sorem-stum Day!"

Somebody needs to find this Sorem-stum lady. She's going to be *thrilled*.

Postscript: Anna ... Aneeka ... whatever. She continued to blow away the record book in women's golf. At press time, she had 69 career wins, only 19 short of Whitworth's 88. But as she hinted that day, she's starting to focus on more than the center of the fairway. After divorcing her former caddy, David Esch, she began dating agent Mike McGee, the son of ex-PGA player Jerry McGee. And for the first time in years, she did not win the LPGA Player of the Year, Lorena Ochoa did. That's O.K. One less speech to make.

70

The Weak Shall Inherit the Gym

MAY 14, 2001

N OT TO ALARM YOU, BUT AMERICA IS GOING SOFTER than left-out butter. Exhibit 9,137: Schools have started banning dodgeball. ¶ I kid you not. Dodgeball has been outlawed by some school districts in New York, Texas, Utah and Virginia. Many more are thinking about it, like Cecil County, Md., where the school board wants to ban any game with "human targets." Personally, I wish all these people would go suck their Birkenstocks.

Human targets? What's tag? What's a snowball fight? What's a close play at second? Neil Williams, a physical education professor at Eastern Connecticut State, says dodgeball has to go because it "encourages the best to pick on the weak." Noooo! You mean there's weak in the world? There's strong? Of course there is, and dodgeball is one of the first opportunities in life to figure out which one you are and how you're going to deal with it.

We had a bully, Big Joe, in our seventh grade. Must have weighed 225 pounds, used to take your underwear while you were in the shower and parade around the locker room twirling it on his finger. We also had a kid named Melvin, who was so thin we could've faxed him from class to class.

I'll never forget the dodgeball game in which Big Joe had a ball in each hand and one sandwiched between his knees, firing at our side like a human tennis-ball machine, when, all of a sudden, he got plunked right in his 7-Eleven-sized butt. Joe whirled around to see who'd done it and saw that it was none other than Melvin, all 83 pounds of him, most of it smile.

Some of these New Age whiners say dodgeball is inappropriate in these times of horrifying school shootings. Are you kidding? Dodgeball is one of the few times in life when you get to let out your aggressions, no questions asked. We don't need less dodgeball in schools, we need more!

I know what all these NPR-listening, Starbucks-guzzling parents want. They want their Ambers and their Alexanders to grow up in a cozy womb of noncompetition, where everybody shares tofu and Little Red Riding Hood and the big, bad wolf set up a commune. Then their kids will stumble out into the bright light of the real world and find out that, yes, there's weak and there's strong and teams and sides and winning and losing. You'll recognize those kids. They'll be the ones filling up chalupas. Very noncompetitive.

But Williams and his fellow wusses aren't stopping at dodgeball. In their Physical Education Hall of Shame they've also included duck-duck-goose and musical chairs. Seriously. So, if we give them dodgeball, you can look for these games to be banned next:

•*Tag.* Referring to any child as *it* is demeaning and hurtful. Instead of the child hollering, "You're it!" we recommend, "You're special!"
•*Red Rover.* Inappropriate labeling of children as animals. Also, the use of the word *red* evokes Communist undertones.
•*Sardines.* Unfairly leaves one child alone at the end as the *loser*—a term psychologists have deemed unacceptable.
•*Hide-and-seek.* No child need hide or be sought. The modern child runs free in search of himself.
•*Baseball.* Involves wrong-headed notions of *stealing, errors* and gruesome *hit-and-run.* Players should always be safe, never out.
•*Hopscotch.* Sounds vaguely alcoholic, not to mention demeaning to our friends of Scottish ancestry.
•*Marbles.* Winning others' marbles is overly capitalistic.
•*Marco Polo.* Mocks the blind.

•*Capture the flag.* Mimics war.
•*Kick the can.* Unfair to the can.

IF WE let these PC twinkies have their way, we'll be left with:
•*Duck-duck-duck.* Teacher spends the entire hour patting each child softly on the head.
•*Upsy down.* The entire class takes turns fluffing the gym teacher's pillow before her nap.
•*Swedish baseball.* Players are allowed free passage to first, second or third, where they receive a relaxing two-minute massage from opposing players.
•*Smear the mirror.* Students take turns using whipped cream to smear parts of their reflection they don't like, e.g., the fat they have accrued from never doing a damn thing in gym class.

Postscript: Dodgeball fell back into favor not long afterwards. Ben Stiller made a very funny movie about it and there was a move afoot to start a professional dodgeball league. My highlight memory of the whole thing was going on the Today show by satellite with an actual red rubber dodgeball hidden under my chair. When the precious professor made some ridiculously wimpy point, I pulled it out and whipped it at the camera. I'm fully expecting a civil suit.

71

Illegal Use of Hands

SEPTEMBER 10, 2001

WITH LITTLE OR NO NFL EXPERIENCE AND FEW days to prepare, the league's replacement officials may not be ready for prime time, but as of Monday it looked as if they'd be around for a while. That's why the commissioner's office issued these replacement-referee hand signals you'll need to know.

No coin flip. Used silver dollar for bus fare.

Starving. Send down two free hot dogs.

ILLUSTRATIONS BY JEFF WONG

229

Just got Melissa
Stark's home
number.

Can you believe the
NFL is stupid enough
to pay us for this?

Timeout to look up
obscure Dennis
Miller reference.

Change channel.
Sex and the City
is over.

Had no idea there would
be this many big, mean
guys. Want to go home.

Call 9-1-1.
Pacemaker on fritz.

NFL's check cleared.
Can finally pay off
'77 Gremlin.

Not sure if it was a
fumble. Rock-paper-
scissors will decide.

Calling bookie to change bet on this game.

Timeout to look through peephole at Eagles cheerleaders.

Ran off with Eagles cheerleader.

Loss of lunch. Had no idea I'd be running this much.

Blew call. Cost Bucs game. Warren Sapp wants to kill me!

Game over. Have to get these clothes back to Foot Locker.

72

You Make the Call

THIS ACTUALLY HAPPENED. YOUR JOB IS TO DECIDE whether it should have. ¶ In a nine- and 10-year-old PONY league championship game in Bountiful, Utah, the Yankees lead the Red Sox by one run. The Sox are up in the bottom of the last inning, two outs, a runner on third. At the plate is the Sox' best hitter, a kid named Jordan. On deck is the Sox' worst hitter, a kid named Romney. He's a scrawny cancer survivor who has to take human growth hormone and has a shunt in his brain.

So, you're the coach: Do you intentionally walk the star hitter so you can face the kid who can barely swing?

Wait! Before you answer. . . . This is a league where everybody gets to bat, there's a four-runs-per-inning max, and no stealing until the ball crosses the plate. On the other hand, the stands are packed and it is the title game.

So . . . do you pitch to the star or do you lay it all on the kid who's been through hell already?

Yanks coach Bob Farley decided to walk the star.

Parents booed. The umpire, Mike Wright, thought to himself, Low-ball move. In the stands, Romney's eight-year-old sister cried. "They're picking on Romney!" she said. Romney struck out. The Yanks celebrated. The Sox moaned. The two coaching staffs nearly brawled.

And Romney? He sobbed himself to sleep that night.

"It made me sick," says Romney's dad, Marlo Oaks. "It's going after the weakest chick in the flock."

Farley and his assistant coach, Shaun Farr, who recommended the walk, say they didn't know Romney was a cancer survivor. "And even if I *had*," insists Farr, "I'd have done the same thing. It's just good baseball strategy."

Romney's mom, Elaine, thinks Farr knew. "Romney's cancer was in the paper when he met with President Bush," she says. That was thanks to the Make-A-Wish people. "And [Farr] coached Romney in basketball. I tell all his coaches about his condition."

She has to. Because of his radiation treatments, Romney's body may not produce enough of a stress-responding hormone if he is seriously injured, so he has to quickly get a cortisone shot or it could be life-threatening. That's why he wears a helmet even in centerfield. Farr didn't notice?

The sports editor for the local *Davis Clipper*, Ben De Voe, ripped the Yankees' decision. "Hopefully these coaches enjoy the trophy on their mantel," De Voe wrote, "right next to their dunce caps."

Well, that turned Bountiful into Rancorful. The town was split—with some people calling for De Voe's firing and describing Farr and Farley as "great men," while others called the coaches "pathetic human beings." They "should be tarred and feathered," one man wrote to De Voe. Blogs and letters pages howled. A state house candidate called it "shameful."

What the Yankees' coaches did was within the rules. But is it right to put winning over compassion? For that matter, does a kid who yearns to be treated like everybody else *want* compassion?

"What about the boy who is dyslexic—should he get special treatment?" Blaine and Kris Smith wrote to the *Clipper*. "The boy who wears glasses— should he never be struck out? . . . NO! They should all play by the rules of the game."

The Yankees' coaches insisted that the Sox coach would've done the same thing. "Not only wouldn't I have," says Sox coach Keith Gulbransen, "I didn't. When their best hitter came up, I pitched to him. I *especially* wouldn't have done it to Romney."

Farr thinks the Sox coach is a hypocrite. He points out that all coaches put their worst fielder in rightfield and try to steal on the weakest catchers. "Isn't that strategy?" he asks. "Isn't that trying to win? Do we let the kid feel like he's a winner by having the whole league play easy on him? This isn't the Special Olympics. He's not retarded."

Me? I think what the Yanks did stinks. Strategy is fine against major leaguers, but not against a little kid with a tube in his head—whether you know he had cancer or not. *Just good baseball strategy?* This isn't the pros. This is: Everybody bats, one-hour games. That means it's about fun. Period.

What the Yankees' coaches did was make it about them, not the kids. It became *their* medal to pin on *their* pecs and show off at *their* barbecues. And if a fragile kid got stomped on the way, well, that's baseball. We see it all over the country—the overcaffeinated coach who watches too much *SportsCenter* and needs to win far more than the kids, who will forget about it two Dove bars later.

By the way, the next morning, Romney woke up and decided to do something about what happened to him.

"I'm going to work on my batting," he told his dad. "Then maybe someday *I'll* be the one they walk."

Postscript: This column got a huge response at SI—*more than 1,200 letters in the first month. The week it was published, the story played all over the country—on CNN, MSNBC, CBS, etc.—and the family, the coaches and I were swamped with calls about it. SI.com even ran an unscientific poll that drew more than 27,000 voters. Sixty-one percent voted,"Pitch to the slugger," and 39% said, "Walk the slugger."*

What's funny is that it proved to be one of the best things to ever happen to Romney. The L.A. Lakers called, offering to host him at a game, where Kobe Bryant signed a jersey for him. The Miami Heat sent him a ball autographed by the NBA championship team. And the Boston Red Sox asked him to be part of a ceremony in which Johnny Pesky threw out the first pitch and Romney delivered the game ball to the mound.

73

Corpo-Name Disease: Stop the Plague!

JANUARY 15, 2001

W ANT TO GET IN ON A HEX? THIS ONE'S A KILLER. It's ruined more companies than blonde receptionists and three-Stoli lunches combined. ¶ All you have to do is repeat after me: "I, [your name], do hereby invoke the Oprah of all curses on all companies that for greedy profit slap their monikers on stadiums that used to be named for our heroes, our history and our cities. May they all go down the drain faster than New Coke."

I invoked the hex the day I heard that Oakland Coliseum had been changed to Network Associates Coliseum. Yes, the spleen-ripping, child-eating Raiders now play out of Network Associates. Al Davis: *"Just associate, baby."*

That, plus the awful truth that 1) the Baltimore Ravens play at a stadium called PSINet, which, I believe, is an extra-hold hair spray; 2) the Seattle Mariners play at Safeco Field, which is one in a chain of Mister Rogers-approved kids' playgrounds; 3) there are arenas or stadiums in this country named PNC, PGE, P&C, MCI, RCA and HSBC; 4) Louisville plays football at—I swear this is true—Papa John's Cardinal Stadium; and 5) three venues are named for Alltel and three for Pepsi.

I had no choice. I hexed the bejesus out of those companies. Using two strands of Marge Schott's chest hair, a gallon of French's mustard and an old Brian Bosworth quote read backward, I hexed their top brass and their bottom lines. I prayed they'd crash and burn faster than the McRib sandwich.

The results were hexcellent! Twenty-three of the 51 companies that ponied up huge bucks to put their names on pro stadiums and arenas have lost at least one quarter of their stock price over the past year! PSINet has dropped 98%! The stock options for Qualcomm (the stadium in San Diego) and Conseco (Indianapolis) are so far underwater, they're growing gills! Savvis (St. Louis) is down 93%! CMGI (New England Patriots) has fallen 97%, and the stadium hasn't even been built!

And it's not just me. People across the U.S. are rising up against corpo-name disease. In Denver a skinny restaurateur named John Hickenlooper heard that the new publically funded Mile High Stadium was going to become Invesco Field or some such cheesiness and thought, Hey, wait a minute! How much is the name Mile High Stadium worth to this city? How many people hear Al Michaels go, "Live, from Mile High Stadium . . . " and think, I'm going to live there, or I'm going to visit there? He commissioned a poll, which showed that most Denverites agreed with him. Then the mayor agreed. Then Hickenlooper helped pay for 50,000 signs, handed out at a Broncos game, that read MILE HIGH STADIUM: BEST NAME BY A MILE. Now, no corporation with half a focus group will touch it, lest it risk the Oprah of all boycotts.

So rise up, Chicago! The Bears want to hyphenate the newly renovated Soldier Field. Don't let them! Put it this way: Would you take your World War I veteran great-grandfather to Samsung-Soldier Field?

Rise up, Boston! Not only are the Red Sox going to abandon the greatest ballpark of all, Fenway, but they're talking about naming the new stadium Polaroid Park! Sounds like an amusement park for flashers!

Rise up, citizens of Canada and the U.S.! After all, do you really need nine North American sports venues named after airlines? Do you really want vapid, soul-sucking names that will change more often than a Madonna hairstyle? (The Philadelphia 76ers and Flyers played in the Spectrum, CoreStates Center and First Union Center in four years.) Don't your heroes

(Joe Louis, RFK, Connie Mack) and your favorite places (The Stick, Three Rivers, Market Square) mean more to you than a fourth vacation home for one more cigar-snipping marketing director?

So find the Hickenlooper inside you! Hex from the bottom of your hexer the community-crumbling megacompanies that try to steal your sense of who you are and where you are! Vow never to let a single corpo-name poison your lips!

Because if you don't stop them now, I guarantee the corporate fat cats will rename everything. You'll visit the Statue of Liberty Mutual. Kids will go to school at P.S. Century 21. And you'll find yourself saying, "O.K., you take a left at Our Lady of Midol and a right onto Frito Lane, and we're the house shaped like Colonel Sanders."

Postscript: The hex lives. How'd Enron do once it paid to become the home of the Houston Astros? The Miami Dolphins' home became Pro Player Stadium and then Pro Player went out of business. And so the Dolphins played for six years under a brand that didn't exist! In fact, since 2001, 45 stadiums and arenas in the big four pro sports have changed their names, many because the name sponsor either went belly-up or was bought out. Which has left us with a sports landscape where the name of a stadium means absolutely nothing. There's no there there. When you tell your buddies, "I took the kids to see Quicken Loans Arena [home of the Cleveland Cavs], for the first time," do you have any idea where the hell he's talking about? By the way, Mile High Stadium did become Invesco Field at Mile High. Of course, now Invesco is defunct. But Hickenlooper's not. On the strength of his efforts to save Mile High, he ran for Denver mayor and won in a rout.

74

Seventh-Inning Stress

SEPTEMBER 8, 2003

MIKE DITKA MANGLED IT. BEA ARTHUR SMOKED IT. Mel Gibson risked his life trying to do it. *NSync asked to do it. Oprah refuses to do it. On a 90° day Joe Frazier *froze* in the middle of it. ¶ What is *it*? ¶ It's Singin' the Stretch at Wrigley Field—standing in the broadcast booth after the top of the seventh inning and leading more than 35,000 people in *Take Me Out to the Ball Game.*

Astronauts to Little League champs have done it, Miss America to George Will, Bozo to Barney and back again. Jeannie (Barbara Eden), Mary Ann (Dawn Wells) and the Beaver (Jerry Mathers) have all taken a whack at it. So did Muhammad Ali and George Foreman, whose ham-fisted rendition was introduced by Michael Buffer. *Let's get rrrrrready to mumble*!!!

Nearly all of them have one thing in common: They butchered the song.

One hockey coach (the Cubs can't remember which one) began this way: "Bring me out to the ball game." Ditka yelled the whole thing in 15 seconds, turning the lyrics into a kind of overcaffeinated halftime screech. He was so bad that when former Bears linebacker Dick Butkus tried it, he started by saying, "Well, I can't be worse than Ditka." And, then, sadly, he started singing. Blackhawks star Denis Savard got so flustered he resorted to French.

But they're all off the hook now, thanks to Ozzy Osbourne.

He tried Singin' the Stretch recently and sounded like a surgical patient in the last moments before the anesthesia takes hold. He was not just awful. He was 42 exits past awful. He had the words right in front of him, but, well. . . . "Mr. Osbourne has obviously lived a very full life," explains Joe Rios, the Cubs' marketing assistant who handles the celebs, "and the moment kind of consumed him."

According to the *Chicago Tribune*, here is exactly what Mr. Osbourne, er, emitted:

One. Two. Three.
Let's go out to the ball game. Let's go out to the bluhhhhhn.
Take me a ee-yan eeya [humming] the field.
I don't care if I ahh-uhn ack.
Da da da da duh da da da eam. Duh ee, da da da da dahhh.
For a fee, two, three strikes you're out at the old ball game!

Somewhere, Harry Caray was weeping.

The original idea came up five years ago as a way to honor Caray, the late Cubs announcer who had made the seventh-inning sing-along at Wrigley famous. The team decided to play a tape of Caray singing the song, but the crowd just couldn't get into it. So Cubs marketing director John McDonough hit on this idea: Each game invite a different celebrity to come watch the Cubs and sing. For one day the celeb could eat, drink and be Harry.

The idea was a smash hit. If Wrigley is baseball's time capsule, Singin' the Stretch is its warbling soundtrack. Thus, Dick Clark has done it, as have KC and the Sunshine Band, and Eddie Vedder. Not to mention Vanna White and Cyndi Lauper, Chuck Berry and Kenny Rogers, Roger Ebert and Macho Man Randy Savage.

And not one of them was paid a dime or expenses to do it. Most of the time their performances were worth every penny. "Right now," says McDonough, "we're at *abysmal*. We're trying to move up to *bad*."

It's just that as the seventh inning approaches, the gravity of the situation starts hitting the poor celeb. "With two outs in the top of the seventh inning, some of the greatest athletes of our time turn white sitting next to me," McDonough says. They're handed the mike, the countdown begins, and suddenly 35,000 people are turning, as McDonough says, "to watch you do something you can't do."

Frazier froze so badly his security guard had to take over. KC gagged. "My heart was beating so fast," he admitted. *NYPD Blue* tough guy Dennis Franz melted into a puddle. "The moral of the story," says McDonough, "is that Harry wasn't as bad as we thought."

Some, though, chew up the ivy. Gibson got so into it, he was hanging out of the booth with only his legs braced against the windowsill to keep him from falling. ESPN's Chris Berman sang, "I don't care if I never go back-back-back!" Former Bears defensive tackle Steve McMichael used the forum to berate the home plate ump for a controversial call the inning before. The umps wanted him ejected. My God, where were they halfway through Ozzy?

The Ozzy thing has some people's boxers in a bunch. The *Tribune* called for an end to the use of celebrities, basically saying it was embarrassingly painful. Uh, hello? We're talking about Cubs fans here! Highest pain threshold in the majors, 95 years in a row!

Anyway, next time you're in Chicago, take the day off and go watch the carnage at Wrigley. You won't care if you ever ahh-uhn ack.

Postscript: The Cubs actually asked me to sing it once. They issued the invitation two days before the will-you-take-a-steroid-test-Sammy-Sosa? column hit newsstands. I decided against it, since a man leaning out of a box at a baseball game is a very easy target for snipers.

75

The Guns of Augusta

DECEMBER 2, 2002

N OW THAT THE FIRE IS OUT, THE RIOT HAS BEEN quelled, the paramedics are gone, the jails are locked down and the National Guard is in control, I have to say that the 2003 Masters was an absolute Hootie. Wouldn't you? ¶ And it all started so innocently. ¶ Martha Burk wrote a little letter asking Augusta National to get a female member. Club president Hootie Johnson answered by saying, basically, "When Hell gets a bobsled team." Feminist groups promised to picket the Masters. *The New York Times* demanded that Tiger Woods boycott the event. And Jesse Jackson said he'd be there for the women.

For their *cause*, I mean.

So the tournament started, and for the first time in history, there were throngs of protesters outside the gates of storied Magnolia Lane. There were two main groups: Martha's Mothers, who carried signs saying things like WELCOME TO THE MS.STERS, and Hotties for Hootie, who were led by Anna Nicole Smith because, as one said, "she's so great with the octogenarians."

Then Ben Wright showed up and said that women couldn't fit into the members' green jackets because "their boobs get in the way." Gloria Steinem hit him over the head with a Big Bertha, and you had yourself a good old-fashioned throwdown.

That convinced CNN to set up a makeshift studio at the new Piggly Wiggly across the street, with Wolf Blitzer at the desk. They called the show *Insane at the Lane* and started broadcasting nonstop. Next thing you knew, everybody who had a bone to pick with Augusta showed up at the gates.

There were picket signs saying that Augusta was unfair to Asians, Native Americans, Eskimos, North Dakotans, South Dakotans, New Mexicans, Mexicans, gays, poor people and Donald Trump (none of whom are members). Banned CBS analyst Gary McCord was there holding an AUGUSTA UNFAIR TO ME sign.

Jesse Jackson was there, chanting, "We don't want surplus cheese! We just want women's tees!" And Newt Gingrich was walking around handing out NEWT'S FOR THE COOTS! bumper stickers. All the billionaire CEOs who are members of the club had to sneak past the press by pretending they were pimento-cheese-sandwich deliverymen.

Then Phil Mickelson had a plane fly overhead pulling a sign that read, TIGER OUT OF AUGUSTA NOW! And NOW was there with T-shirts that read, A WOMAN'S PLACE IS AT THE (PRACTICE) RANGE. Then Kenny G showed up, but the fur people mistook his hair for a coonskin cap and hurled a bucket of blood at him. Some of the blood got in the eyes of the old Pinkerton guard manning the gate, and while he was temporarily blinded, Winona Ryder lifted the old guy's keys and let everybody in.

That's when it started getting nuts.

Burk and her adjutants occupied Ike's Cabin—which the other side sarcastically renamed Dyke's Cabin—and Hootie and the members holed up in the men's grill, firing black-eyed peas at anybody who wasn't wearing one of their T-shirts that said THE ONLY IRON A WOMAN SHOULD HOLD IS A STEAM IRON!

In the middle of all this, the players were trying to win the tournament, which wasn't easy with Johnnie Cochran running all over the place yelling, "How come the balls are white? Where are the balls of color?" and Pat Buchanan holding a prayer vigil at Amen Corner, and PETA down at Rae's Creek trying to save the fish swimming in the green-dyed ponds.

I *still* can't figure out why Hans Blix and his U.N. inspectors were there.

People kept having to explain to Jimmy Carter that there *were* no hostages to free. They finally had to get an ambulance for CBS anchor Jim Nantz. Hootie had decided to televise this Masters without any ads, to take the heat off his sponsors; the E.R. guy said no TV announcer could handle the stress of going that long without re-moussing.

But the most frustrated person at Augusta was Tiger Woods, who was trying to become the first man in history to win three straight Masters. He led by 35 shots at one point, despite having to constantly step over and around Dusty Baker's kid, who kept running along the fairways trying to pick up Tiger's ball and bring it back to him.

Hootie finally canceled the whole damn tournament Sunday afternoon, mostly on account of Richard Gere's Tibetan monks meditating in the bunkers, the pile of burning bras on the 18th green (which somebody tried to put out with Andy Rooney) and the desecration of the membership log by Burk, who wrote herself and 50 of her friends in as members.

Tiger had only a four-footer left on 18 when Hootie shut it down. Tiger didn't take the news well. It was the first time anyone had seen a guy come for the green jacket and get taken away in a straitjacket instead.

Still, I think Hillary will make a terrific membership chairwoman, don't you?

Postscript: The reality of the 2003 Masters was possibly more ridiculous than this fiction. It had to be the oddest year in the tournament's history. I'll never forget the pathetic sight of Burk showing up at the muddy protest field she'd been stuck with. She arrived with a bus carrying maybe 25 protesters—total—and began pleading her case to 75 reporters, 100 cops and even a guy from the KKK. And right in the middle of it, as the poor thing is fumbling along, some guy stands right in front of her with a huge sign that reads FIX MY DINNER.

76

No Man's Land

SEPTEMBER 16, 2002

IT'S OUT-AND-OUT DISCRIMINATION! TO BE BARRED FROM A golf club based on your genitals is an outrage! And for 78 years now! ¶ Augusta National? Nah. The Ladies' Golf Club of Toronto. Since it opened in 1924, the Ladies' Golf Club has *never* had a male member. Thousands of men have wanted to join. Are you kidding? You'd give your left Titleist to be a member. The course is gorgeous! Located on the outskirts of Toronto, it's lined with huge trees and has steep elevations.

But unless you have ovaries, don't even apply.

I know. I tried. The waiting list is one year—unless you're a man, in which case the waiting list is forever and a year.

"We do not accept men," the receptionist said when I called. "However, if you know a member, she can sponsor you to become a guest-card holder. If you're approved, you can play before 8:30 a.m. and after noon, except on weekends, when you can play after 3. And you pay full greens fees as well."

Wait a second. Restricted tee times? Extra fees? What am I, some kind of second-class citizen?

Still, I badly wanted to play the course. I did know, barely, one member, Sandy Guluk. Like most women, Sandy has only one thing on her mind—golf. She plays five days a week, 36 holes if she can, unless she can play 61, which she did once. She said I could join her for one (1) round last week.

Driving up to the course, it hits you that the Ladies' Golf Club has the most beautiful entrance north of Magnolia Lane. The driveway weaves under the huge trees and up a hill to a graceful, white-and-green, 82-year-old clubhouse. Seems oddly familiar, doesn't it?

But if you happen to be a man, don't try to park in the main lots. Those are female-only lots. Not members only, *female only*. A $9 hooker asking directions can park right up front, but I had to drive another 200 yards around back and park on gravel.

And that was just the start of the humiliation. The women's locker room takes up almost the entire top floor of the clubhouse and has a beautiful veranda overlooking the 18th green. The men's locker room is way in the back, behind the pro shop. It's the size of Gandhi's closet—one lousy urinal, no TV, no radio, one crummy golf painting on the wall, no shoeshine guy and no attendant.

"We're lucky we have *this*," said guest-card holder Bruce North. "Until three years ago all we had was an old shack. There weren't any showers or lockers. You just hung your clothes on a hook. We used to have to sneak beer in and keep it on ice."

Men aren't allowed on the driving range. Or at the member-guest events. Husbands and boyfriends are not allowed on the grounds without a member. And you can just *guess* how many times men ask to play through.

"They better not," said one of the club's 650 members. "Or they get the boot!"

Women are pigs.

Sandy was polite, but there was tension from the start. Our group included a seventysomething woman, and Sandy had to ask, in a whisper, if she'd mind playing with a you-know-what.

"A what?" the old lady yelled.

Sandy whispered louder.

"A *man*?" the old lady creaked. Then she peeked around Sandy's elbow, glared at me, crinkled her nose and said, "I guess."

This joint makes Augusta seem like the ACLU.

Twice Sandy found my ball 50 yards behind where I was looking. "Typical male," she muttered. And she didn't seem to appreciate the little chipping tip I gave her. "Just like my husband," I think she grumbled.

Still, it was such a good course. Why should some old-girls' network keep men out? True, it's believed to be the only ladies-only private golf club in North America, but, hell, 78 years from now there could be another!

Men, let the girlcott begin. Until this is resolved, withhold sex. When your wife brings you your home-cooked dinner, refuse thirds. Upon settling into your Barcalounger, snap it back brusquely.

Look, any Neanderthal knows it's wrong to keep women out of Augusta National. As soon as Martha Burk can find a woman willing to eat peach cobbler with a lot of dandruffs wearing flammable green coats, I say let her in.

As soon as they let one of us into theirs.

I loved the role-reversal of this place so much I decided to set parts of my third novel, Shanks for Nothing, at it. Poor Lenny (Two Down) Petrovitz is stuck serving drinks in the women's grill, getting his butt pinched and parking a quarter of a mile away in the gravel lot. Serves him right.

77

It's Not Easy Being Santa

DECEMBER 27, 2004 / JANUARY 3, 2005

I T'S THAT TIME OF YEAR AGAIN, WHEN OUR THOUGHTS TURN to that lovable plus-sized elf with the ruddy red cheeks, the white hair and the belly of jelly, the one who never needs an airplane. ¶ John Madden. ¶ No, actually, Santa Claus. ¶ This holiday season the morals of a lot of athletes are lower than flounder droppings. The other day I heard a worried announcer say, "What must kids think of the way we adults are behaving?" But you really can't ask kids because when a kid is asked a question by an adult, the only thing the kid thinks is, How *huge* are this man's nostrils?

Kids trust Santa, though. They'll tell Santa anything. So I set out to conduct the Santa Sports Survey. Disguised as Saint Nick, I would spend 90 minutes at each of three Boys & Girls Clubs in metro Denver. I loaded the trunk with toys and trinkets, borrowed a Santa suit from the Cherry Creek Mall and called Susen Mesco of Amerevents.com, which runs one of the best Santa Schools in the country.

"Don't *play* Santa," she advised. "*Be* Santa."

She also said something odd. "Never ask what the children want for

247

Christmas." Huh? "Ask, *What would you like to tell Santa?* Because a lot of times, what they want has nothing to do with toys. For instance, what will you do if a child says, 'Santa, I want you to bring my mommy back to life'?"

(Silence)

"You say, 'Sorry, Santa can't do that. But you know what? Sometimes our sleigh flies so high, we pass right by heaven. What do you want to tell your mom, and I'll give her a message.' "

I wasn't sure I was ready for this.

The clubs were all in poor sections of the city. At each club I was given a room and about 70 squirmy kids, ages six to 10. And right away I learned something—I make a lousy Santa.

"Who are you?" one girl asked.

"Since when does Santa drive a sedan?" a boy said, suspiciously.

"Uh, that hurts," another girl said as I tried to tickle her.

One kid wanted to know how old I was. "Just turned 1,310," I said. His mouth flopped open like a drawbridge. I said, "I know, I don't look that old."

"No, you *do*," he said.

One little girl wanted to know where Rudolph was. "Rudolph pulled a hammy," I said. "This year the sleigh is going to be guided by Sylvester, from the temp agency."

(Blank stare)

I kept trying to ask my state-of-sports questions, but I might as well have been asking about pork-belly futures. Not one of them knew about Barry Bonds's BALCO connection. In fact, if I were running baseball, I'd be worried. Not one kid had a favorite ballplayer. Not one of them wanted a bat or glove. Few of them even had favorite pros in any sport: Local hero Carmelo Anthony of the Nuggets was mentioned the most, followed by two Philadelphia stars, Terrell Owens of the Eagles and Allen·Iverson of the Sixers. The athletes the kids most wanted to spend time with were their dads.

"Could you bring me a fishing pole so my daddy will take me fishing with him?" one little girl asked. Another wanted a soccer ball, " 'cause I think my dad would play soccer with me then."

I kept trying to hit them with survey questions like, "Do you view athletes as role models in this age of . . . ," and they kept hitting me with real life.

"Santa, for Christmas could you make the bill collectors stop coming?" one boy said. "It makes my mom cry."

A little girl said, "Santa, could you bring us a new house? The one we have now leaks all the time."

Lots of kids wanted hats and shoes and coats. "I want clothes," said one boy. *What* kind? "The warm kind," he said.

Another kid wanted to be an NBA star and make "a million dollars."

"What would you spend it on?" I asked.

"Doctors," she said, "for my cousin. She's four. She has cancer."

I told one seven-year-old boy, "Last year I came by and you were still awake, so I had to go do Dallas first until you fell asleep. So this year I want you to go right to sleep."

And he said, "That's not true, Santa. Last year you forgot my house."

I learned nothing new about sports, but plenty about how spoiled my life was, how Scroogish my spirit, how narrow my vision.

One somber eight-year-old girl was making her first visit to the club. She'd been sent from another state to live with her uncles because there were "issues" at home. She looked as if somebody had just sat on her birthday cake.

"What can Santa make you this Christmas?" I asked her.

She turned and looked at me with huge, hopeful eyes.

"Happy?" she asked.

Be Santa.

78

Mountain Lion

JULY 30, 2001

W HEN YOU ARE LANCE ARMSTRONG AND you've survived 12 tumors on your lungs, two on your brain and a cancer-ravaged testicle the size of a lemon, the French Alps start to look like speed bumps. When you are Lance Armstrong and you keep an expired driver's license in your wallet because it shows you in Death's lobby, your face paler than 1% milk, your eyebrows and eyelashes and hair missing, and your eyes as two yellow moons, a six-hour ride up and down murderous mountains sounds like a Tupperware party.

So no wonder Armstrong delivered two of the most remarkable days in Tour de France history last week, tearing through the French Alps as if he were double-parked somewhere, dancing on his pedals, nobody coming within a yodel of him. No wonder he took both classic mountain stages, l'Alpe d'Huez and Chamrousse, and crumpled them in his riding gloves, making up 22 minutes on the leader in two days. No wonder he breezed through the next three stages, in the Pyrenees, taking possession of the leader's yellow jersey last Saturday and opening up a five-minute, five-second lead on Sunday. Unless the Eiffel Tower falls on him, Armstrong will become the fifth man to win the Tour de France three years in a row. "It's just so much fun," he said.

Unless you're trying to catch him. "We keep waiting for this man to have a bad day," said the director of rival Team Telekom, Rudy Pevenage, "but the only bad day he has is the day after celebrating in Paris."

Did you expect any less? Could the Alps do anything to Armstrong that cancer didn't? Could they give him more stitches, sweats, shivers? Could they be more cruel? Could they leave him more swollen, aching, broken? Don't the mountains and the disease both call for heart monitors and doctors at the ready and unending attention to red-blood-cell counts? Don't you need an unbending will, a strength deep inside to get you through both?

No, the Alps separate men like Armstrong from the rest, and he knew it and he waited for them, waited through nine stages of meadows and flowers, waited in 24th and then 23rd place, waited to get to the point in the Tour de France when hearts are truly measured. He waited until the sixth hour of stage 10 on July 17, waited until he got to the base of the unforgettable 12-mile, straight-up, 21-switchback Alpe d'Huez, waited in the back of the peloton and bluffed, pretended to be winded, grimaced every time a Telekom rider drifted by to spy on him, kept pretending to suck air for the cameras on the motorbikes, kept conserving his energy in a game of two-wheeled Texas hold 'em.

Then he turned and eyeballed his greatest rival, Germany's Jan Ullrich of Telekom, eyeballed him cold, as if to say, *Let's cut to the chase*, and took off up the mountain as if he had just knocked over a 7-Eleven. Within minutes he reeled in the leader, France's Laurent Roux, who was six minutes ahead of Armstrong when the attack began. "I had the feeling I was being passed by a motorcycle," said Roux. Armstrong won the stage by two full minutes—think Dallas 52, Buffalo 17—beat one rider by 42 minutes (seven others never finished) and worried that he had spent too much. "I may pay for this," he said.

However, the very next day after his Huez-cide ride, he whipped the time-trial field in "The Ride of Truth" to the top of Chamrousse, the ski resort where Jean-Claude Killy won three gold medals in the 1968 Olympics, as though he'd spent the last 24 hours lying by the pool. "America doesn't understand," said Armstrong's U.S. Postal Service teammate, Tyler Hamilton. "What he did here these last two days was like John Elway winning those two Super Bowls."

They understand in the chemo rooms. "I know they're out there," Armstrong said. "Sitting there with those damn drip poles, lying in those La-Z-Boys thinking, *This guy had the same exact thing I do. If he can do it, I can do it.* I think of them all the time. I want to motivate them. They motivate me."

Not that he needs it. That night, after melting the Alps, he had to do something hard. He and his wife, Kik, nervously opened an envelope from her obstetrician. The cancer treatment had left Armstrong sterile, but inside was news that the in vitro had worked again, that she was carrying *twin girls*.

That's the thing about being Lance Armstrong—once left for dead and now more alive than any other man in sports, once broken and now more than whole—every day is an envelope you can't wait to tear open.

Postscript: My five most important athletes in American history are Babe Ruth, Babe Didrickson, Muhammad Ali, Tiger Woods and Lance Armstrong. All of them were bigger than sports, more important than the games. Of the five, Armstrong's story may mean the most. He is a hope machine for cancer victims all over the world. You're with him and people just try to touch him, hoping some shred of his unkillable will might rub off. But once you know him and can get past him as a god, you realize he is just an overcaffeinated maniac who can't sit still. He drives 100 miles per hour, wants to beat you at everything and never relaxes. When he's not training or parenting his three kids, he has his hands in everything. He's always online, which makes it easy to torture him whenever you want. Two weeks after his record seventh straight Tour de France win, I e-mailed him the following urgent message: Me: Bad news. Paris authorities say they've discovered something in your hotel room that's banned in France! Him: That's bull! What? What'd they find? Me: Soap.

79

In Like Flynn

FEBRUARY 11, 2002

COMING TO THE BIG EASY, 72-YEAR-OLD DION RICH had sneaked, weaseled, conned, bluffed, tricked and bamboozled his way into 32 straight Super Bowls, the record for a man refusing to touch his wallet. ¶ Wait. Not just into the games, but often onto the fields and into the locker rooms. That's Rich on the winner's podium with Vince Lombardi and Pete Rozelle after the first Super Bowl. That's him helping to carry Cowboys coach Tom Landry off the field after XII. That's him whispering sweet nothings into coach Joe Gibbs's ear as the Redskins run off after winning XVII.

Wait, wait. It's not only Super Bowls. Rich has gone ticketless into World Series games, title fights, America's Cup races, Kentucky Derbies and 14 Olympics. Basically, he's Red Smith without the deadlines. He's also crashed eight Academy Awards, as proved by pictures like the one of him with his arm around Gwyneth Paltrow after she won her Oscar. He even has a snap of himself at the Playboy Mansion, in Hugh Hefner's bathrobe.

It's not that Rich is poor. He's made boatloads in real estate and other things. "But why pay when you don't have to?" he asks.

Then came Super Bowl XXXVI, hard on the heels of 9/11. The NFL spent $7 million on a mammoth security effort manned by the Secret Service, the FBI, FEMA, the National Guard, U.S. Marshals and dozens of state and local law-enforcement agencies. The week looked bleak for the Sneak Streak.

It got worse. Everywhere Rich looked, there were Jeeps, Humvees and even tanks. There were more wands around than at a fairy godmother convention. Security was *triple* anything he had seen before. A 10-foot-high chain-link-and-barbed-wire fence was put up around the perimeter of the Louisiana Superdome.

Welcome to the Big Hard.

Dion cased the Superdome and declared it tighter than Joan Rivers's eyelids. How could any of his tricks work? The wheelchair? Claiming to be a ref? Pretending to be with the team, the band, the stadium crew? The Coke-bottle bifocals? The bag of press credentials? "If every Super Bowl were like this," he sighed in a media center he wasn't supposed to be in last Thursday, "I'd retire."

Not only that, but he was sure he was being followed. The NFL admits it has tailed him. "Oh, yeah, I've heard of him," Milt Ahlerich, the league's vice president of security, grumbled. The NFL once told Rich if it ever caught him on the field again, he'd be finding out if he could sneak out of jail. He agreed to stay off the fields—but he never said anything about stadiums.

A streak is a streak, wartime or peace, and the Gate Crasher knew what lay before him: He must descend into hell and pull the devil's teeth. It was Clyde Barrow versus Fort Knox. Roseanne versus the Waldorf Sunday brunch. Wearing a blue blazer and a tie, Albert Einstein's haircut and glasses on the end of his pointy nose, Rich set off to penetrate the most impenetrable fortress in U.S. history.

The fortress lost. Rich was inside in six minutes. I followed him the whole way. It was pure art.

He doddered, darted, acted addled and hurried, slunk through tiny spaces and sped through unguarded ones. He was Frogger Senior. He never stopped walking and never started hearing. He nudged his way through the masses at the first security checkpoint and ticket check, waited until a young guard (he always looks for the youngest) had her head buried in a bag, sidestepped past her and through the one-foot gap between the metal detector and a fence. Then he buttonhooked a distracted wand man, did a pirouette around a bored National Guardsman that would've made Fred Astaire weep and then beat it up a ramp. He was never security-screened. Thank God he's on our side.

Now he had to get by the ticket rippers. He found a bank of unmanned doors locked from the inside, waited until a supervisor came barreling out of one, lithely slid his loafer into the gap before it closed and stepped through it as casually as if he were entering his own kitchen. "When am I going to learn never to bet against myself?" he said, grinning.

Make it 33.

Memo to NFL commissioner Paul Tagliabue: $7 million wasn't enough. Memo to Salt Lake Olympic Committee: He'll be there this week.

I didn't hear from Dion again until midnight. He called from inside the Rams' postgame party, gobbling free gumbo and sipping gratis merlot. Hey, at least they had one winner in there.

Postscript: The 2002 Salt Lake City Olympics followed on the heels of this Super Bowl, and Dion Rich was Public Enemy No. 1 there. Security even posted two-inch photos of him on the metal detectors at all the venues. "The jig is up," he moaned on the phone. "Every security guy here is looking for me. I'll never get in." But he did. Olympic security had him rounded up and brought into the ceremonies, as a guest. They didn't want any sneaking-in stories on their watch. Poor, poor Dion. He had no choice but to watch the Olympics without paying.

80

Color Scheme

AUGUST 12, 2002

I F YOU'RE A BLACK PRO ATHLETE WHO OWNS A SWEET RIDE AND lives in a ritzy neighborhood in this country, chances are good you've been busted for DWB. ❡ Driving While Black. ❡ "It happens to me all the time, especially in Tampa," says outfielder Gary Sheffield, who grew up in Tampa. "I go home to see old friends, and I get stopped. Or if I'm driving slow, looking at my old neighborhood, I get stopped. It never happens in my truck, just in my nice cars."

Defensive tackle Trevor Pryce says an officer followed him home once, pulled him over and said, "I don't think this is your car." And Pryce replied, "Why, because I'm black and driving a Corvette?" Pryce has been pulled over for DWB so many times he has a new strategy. "I pull up right next to cops," he says, "roll down my windows and play my music as loud as I can. Nobody would do that driving a stolen car, right?"

"It's happened to me eight or nine times," says NBA guard Jim Jackson. "I asked one cop in Dallas why he pulled me over, and he goes, 'Oh, we're just doing random checks.' Right. Random checks of black men in nice cars."

When comedian Chris Rock was pulled over on a DWB, he jokes, "It scared me so bad, I thought I *had* stolen my car!"

Three times this summer, Miami Dolphins running back Ricky Williams says, Fort Lauderdale police have stopped or hassled him for nothing more than the color of his skin.

"One cop pulled me over for no other reason than I was a black man driving an expensive car [a Hummer]," says Williams, the former Heisman Trophy winner who moved to south Florida after being traded to the Dolphins in March. "They said later it was because my tags were expired. But it was a handwritten temporary license they couldn't *possibly* have been able to see. For that they call the drug dogs and I get handcuffed?" The stop and search lasted an hour and a half, Williams says, and then he was ticketed for expired tags and for not having his driver's license and proof of insurance in his possession.

Twice cops have knocked on his front door to tell him his garage was open, Williams says, and then asked him for proof that he owned his cars. They questioned him about what he did for a living and how much he paid for the cars. It's the kind of frustration that white athletes never have to deal with.

Williams has started taking the long way to work so he doesn't have to drive past a police station. Other guys just give up and drive crappy cars. Sometimes these guys don't even have to be in a car.

"You go into a Tiffany's in the mall," says Jackson, "and right away you notice the lights [brighten]. Then the clerk follows you around, pretending she's just cleaning up. I came out of a restaurant once and the valet goes, 'Man, what did you do to get a car like this?' I was like, 'I got a job, that's what I did!' "

The dreadlocked Williams says that when he flies first class, more times than not attendants ask to see his ticket, assuming he's in the wrong seat. NBA forward Glen Rice wasn't allowed to check into a five-star hotel by a woman behind the desk who insisted, "I know what you're about."

"What am I about?" asked Rice, who refused to leave until he was given a room. The desk clerk called police, who recognized Rice and advised the woman to give him a room. That's when Rice said no thanks and walked out.

Says Jackson, "I don't think most of white America understands how it feels. You work hard to be successful, to get some nice things, and people treat you like you stole them."

"I guess cops think we're drug dealers," says Latrell Sprewell, the New York Knicks guard. "It pisses you off, but what pisses you off more is that when they see who you are, they suddenly change it to, 'Uh, I pulled you over to, uh, can I have your autograph?' "

When you mix cops with young men who feel persecuted, things can get volatile. "I feel myself boiling over," says Jackson. "But if I started yelling at the cops, next thing you know, I'd be in jail." Or worse. Remember the four young unarmed black men on their way to a basketball tryout who were profiled by troopers and stopped on the New Jersey Turnpike, then had 11 shots fired into their van, wounding three of them?

Williams was so frustrated by his treatment after one DWB stop that he started to walk home in protest, got a block and a half, then sat down on a curb and cried. "It hurts your feelings," he says. "Nobody likes to be treated like a criminal."

And we wonder why so many black athletes are angry.

Postscript: Not to beat a dead horse, but this will give you an idea of what Barry Bonds is like: I asked dozens of athletes the same question—"Have you ever been arrested for DWB?" But when I asked Bonds, he wheeled on me and snapped, "Get the f--- out of my face! What kind of motherf------ question is that?" I tried to explain what it was, but he wouldn't let me speak. Finally, teammate Ellis Burks stepped in and said, "Damn, Barry, relax! It means 'Driving While Black.' Racial profiling?" Bonds never looked up at either of us.

81

Regretlessly Yours

MAY 8, 2006

S TAR ATHLETES TEND TO GET THEMSELVES IN MORE HOT
water than Top Ramen. Last week alone Keith Hernandez,
Kenyon Martin and Delmon Young all had to do major dam-
age control for bad behavior.

But now, thanks to the discount law firm of Wheezle, Wangle and Dodge,
stars can save boatloads of p.r. and legal fees with the first-ever Do It Yourself Athletic Apology—the No-pology™.

It's the best way to say "I'm sorry" without really meaning it. Try it next time
you're busted!

(Clear throat and read sincerely.)

THE NO-FAULT APOLOGY

Ladies and gentlemen, let me begin by saying I'm acutely aware of the accusations that I (pick from Menu A) . Let me state categorically and on the record that (one from Menu B) . What everybody involved needs to clearly understand is that (Menu C) . And I refuse to let the (Menu D) win. Still, if (Menu E) , then I would definitely like to take this opportunity to (Menu F) . But I'll tell you one thing, I (Menu G) . Peace. Out.

Menu A OFFENSES
• tested positive for every chemical on the element chart
• insulted an entire (race/gender/religion)
• beat the bejesus out of that meter maid
• groped most of the Rockettes
• threatened to kneecap my coach
• kneecapped my coach

Menu B EXCUSES
• I have no recollection of doing any of that
• it is what it is
• my meds were way off
• that's just (my name) being (my name)
• it was the arthritic rub
• I had to do something; they dissed my peeps

Menu C RATIONALIZATIONS
• people just build you up to knock you down
• things got blown way out of proportion
• I didn't know that the damn thing was loaded
• people should be curing cancer, not hassling me
• nobody would've said a word if I were (name different race)
• nobody told me cops can dress like hookers

Menu D SCAPEGOATS
- media
- haters
- liberals
- terrorists
- Girl Scouts
- voices in my head

Menu E DISTANCING PHRASE
- my actions were somehow misinterpreted
- my T-shirt was taken out of context
- people are that PC
- one little flag-burning offended the mouth-breathers
- my Rosie O'Donnell impression bothered anybody
- the wildfires have become a distraction

Menu F NO-POLOGY™
- turn the page and move forward
- in a way, apologize, up to a point-ish
- express regret that it even happened
- feel bad for these morons
- ask you what you want me to say
- leave it in (Jesus/Allah/Vishnu)'s hands

Menu G THE LAST WORD
- sure as hell ain't apologizing to that nun
- will pick a batboy next time who can take a punch
- didn't even know those people were considered a minority
- won't ever ride my Harley in Nordstrom again
- will not torpedo any more Smirnoff/Zoloft shooters ever again
- had my fingers crossed

82

Trade You Eight Reillys For a Vick

AUGUST 22, 2005

ARE YOU AN AVID COLLECTOR OF SPORTS MEMORABILIA? If so, what you're going to hear next is going to make you take up a new hobby, perhaps sword swallowing. I now have my own football trading card. ¶ Sadly, this is true. Donruss has a series of cards called Fans of the Game, and this year they asked me if I'd like to be on one. They said my picture and my alltime favorite team (the extinct Los Angeles Rams) would be on it. This is a sickening trend in trading cards: putting nonathletes on them and causing 10-year-old boys everywhere to take up needlepoint.

Last year, for instance, Topps put out a series of World Treasures that included Pope John Paul II, Nelson Mandela and Princess Diana. The only card signed by the Pope went for $10,400 on eBay last weekend.

I broke the news about my card to my 16-year-old daughter while trailing five feet behind her at the mall. "Rae, your dad is going to have his own football card!" I yelled up.

And she whispered back to me, "Dad, you promised to keep a gap between us at the mall! In case my friends see me!"

262

"There is a gap between us!"

"No! A Gap *store.*"

O.K., the kids weren't impressed. But when I was a boy, my baseball and football cards were my life. I'd put them in three shoe boxes according to worth—KEEP, FLIP and KNIFE.

Keeps were any Ram or totally cool player, like Joe Namath (who wound up being both). Flips were ammunition for lunchtime games of Match It, which you could play as long as the nuns didn't catch you and match you with the school paddle. And the Knife cards were doomed to be thumb-tacked to the door of the room my brother, John, and I shared. He could stand 10 feet away and flip his pocketknife so that it stuck in the door. I can remember his sticking the Baltimore Colts' John Mackey in the right eye, a feat so amazing that Mackey remained pegged to the door for near-ly a month, a hapless one-eyed Jack.

And then, 37 years later, my brother is waking me out of my daydream with a phone call.

"Guess what I just bought on eBay!" he says. "Your football card!"

"Oh, crap," I moan.

"Guess how much I paid?"

"Please don't tell me."

"One cent!"

"One cent? Who sells anything for one cent?"

"Well, he got me for $3 shipping."

So between my brother and my kids, a good bit of the glory was gone by the time a box of 750 cards came. Secretly, it was a minithrill, except there were no stats or cartoon on the back of my card. You know? Like, on the old cards, they'd have Jim Taylor's yards per carry, plus a funny drawing of him getting pulled through the water by a fish with the caption, *Jim once caught an 800-pound marlin!*

Of course, what were they going to put on mine? My adjectives per para-graph? And maybe a drawing of me, sitting stubble-faced at a laptop, with a bottle of Dewar's and a blank balloon over my head? *Rick's drinking tends to worsen with writer's block!*

I autographed 250 cards and sent them back, and Donruss sprinkled them among the other 1,000 they printed and put in packs of NFL cards. Can't you see some kid paying $2.99, hoping for Michael Vick (worth as much as $1,600 signed) and getting me instead? No wonder there's so much youth violence today.

A few weeks later I got an e-mail from Tracy Hackler of Beckett's collectibles magazines. He said they had priced my autographed card at $50, ahead of those of other Fans of the Game like Erik Estrada of *ChiPs* ($30) but "slightly behind" Tony Danza's ($250). Ouch.

He said my unsigned card, at $2.50, compared favorably with those of such current NFL stars as Ryan Moats, Brock Berlin and Chris Rix. And I had two thoughts about that:

1) Take that, Ryan Moats!

2) Who the hell is Ryan Moats?

With 500 cards to get rid of, I went to Denver's hot new watering hole, Elway's, and started handing them out to perfect strangers. "Hang on to that," I told them. "That could be worth seven or eight cents someday."

And every person looked at me and said the same thing: "Will John Elway be here tonight?"

So far, I've gotten one (1) card in the mail to sign. From Jeff Majeski of Fairmont, Minn. I called him up. He said he has some great signed cards, including a Joe Montana, which he keeps in a safe. Others he puts under the glass on top of his desk. "You're in my bottom drawer," he said, sheepishly.

Hey, beats the Knife box.

Postscript: I'm down to my last 617 of these, if anybody's interested.

83

The Devil Went Down
To Pittsburgh

NOVEMBER 6, 2006

P
LEASE ALLOW ME TO INTRODUCE MYSELF. ¶ I AM LOU Siffer, agent for a Mr. Roethlisberger, Pittsburgh Steelers quarterback. And I'm coming to you, the fans, for help. Mr. Roethlisberger is in breach of our contract, even though I've held up my end of our bargain.

He stomped into my office two years ago, after he had dropped to the 11th pick in the draft, behind two other quarterbacks—Mr. Manning (the first pick) and Mr. Rivers (the fourth). "I know I'm better than those guys!" he yelled. "And Pittsburgh? The Steelers are pure hell for quarterbacks! They *run* the ball, dammit!"

My eyebrows arched.

"This is *not* how my career was supposed to happen!" he moaned. "I mean, I'd give *anything* to change this!"

"Anything?" I asked.

He spun and looked me right in the eye, slapped his palms on my solid-bone desk and barked, "Anything!"

I punched the intercom. "Miss Jones? Will you kindly bring in the

265

standard contract for me to see? It's just like the one in Mr. Tyson's file."

Immediately, the world was his own personal Eden. His coach, Mr. Cowher, started him in just his third game, even though he'd normally rather start a Mafia target's car than a rookie quarterback. In fact, Mr. Roethlisberger went 13–0 in his first year, unheard of in the NFL.

He became the toast of Pittsburgh. More than that, he was the lunch—somebody invented a Roethlis Burger, and the whole city gobbled it up. He began dating a gorgeous pro golfer, Ms. Gulbis. I'd made him a star.

He came to see me again. "This is good," he said, with a demonic gleam in his eye, "but I want it *all*."

So, in 2005, I gave it *all* to him. And as he was being carried off the field—the youngest quarterback ever to win the Super Bowl—I yelled up to him, "Happy?"

"Yeah, dude! Thanks for everything!"

"You still have the devil to pay," I mentioned.

And this is when he started to get weaselly.

"You know, Mr. Siffer, I checked with the players' association, and they said that a contract like that isn't legal."

And he disappeared, leaving me very unsatisfied.

Of course, right then and there, I could've sent him swimming for eternity in a river of boiling blood, or had crows gnaw on his head forever, but I didn't. Call me a softy. Besides, I wanted him on my team for a few years, sewing discontent, selfishness and greed. (We're very happy with Mr. Owens on that score.)

So I started with some subtle stuff. You know, gave his cell number to Larry King, put Ben-Gay in his jock, threw a new red shirt in with his whites, things like that.

Still, Mr. Roethlisberger wouldn't come around. So I took it up another notch and had his girl break up with him. And I made sure two of his best teammates—Mr. Bettis and Mr. Randle El—left the team.

Nothing.

Then I lost my temper and tried to kill him. Four months after that Super Bowl, I smashed him and his motorcycle into a Chrysler New Yorker at 40 mph.

But the damned kid lived. And as he lay in critical condition at the hospital, an even worse thing happened: You fans started praying for his soul. I just can't tell you how much that complicates things.

I complained to God while we were playing racquetball one day. Even showed him my signed contract. But He just shrugged and said, "What can I do? People like the guy!"

But Ol' Beelze doesn't quit easy, Bub. Three months later I put a pox on Mr. Roethlisberger's appendix. It nearly burst, but he survived. I had his backup, Mr. Batch, make like Joe Namath, just to spite him. But two weeks later, Mr. Roethlisberger was right back in there. So, I made him start throwing like Marie Antoinette. At one point his passer rating was 34.3. My pet serpent could do a 34.3. The Steelers' record fell to 1–3, but you just kept right on loving him.

Two weeks ago I sent three Falcons to knock him loopier than King George. Mr. Roethlisberger had to be taken off in a cart. Last week I even had him lose to the Raiders. (Al Davis is a friend.)

But he still wouldn't budge.

I'm stuck. I humbly ask for your help. I know it's not easy to have sympathy for the agent, but Mr. Roethlisberger and I had an agreement. Stop bailing him out with your infernal prayers and hope and faith in him. Please?

Or how about a compromise? I won't lodge him forever in a minotaur's colon, but can I at least trade him to Buffalo?

Postscript: It only got worse. A couple of weeks after I wrote this, he was sacked nine times–nine!– by the Baltimore Ravens in a 27–0 shutout. People were actually bellowing for Charlie Batch to start ahead of him. That's like screaming for Tito Jackson to take over for Michael. I say give the guy a break. Yeah, he sold his soul to the devil, but at least he didn't sign with Drew Rosenhaus.

84

It's Men Just Being Men

NOVEMBER 7, 2005

WENT ON *OPRAH* THE OTHER DAY. IT'S TRUE. ALL I can figure is she thought I was *Pat* Riley. Like I'm going to set her straight? ¶ The show was called *Why Do Men Go to Strip Clubs? And Other Burning Questions.* Jay Leno, singer Brian McKnight and I were dragged onto her stage in front of hundreds of seething women and made to answer for our gender.

You remember the scene from Hitchcock's *The Birds*? When the guy tiptoes through thousands of birds who are ready to tear out his pancreas at the slightest misstep? That's what the *Oprah* set was like.

Why do men go to strip shows so much? a woman would bark. (My answer: "I only go once a year, to look at the new fall line of shoes.") Or *Why don't men cuddle after sex?* ("*Much* too hot.") And *What do men think about after sex?* ("Is Subway open this late?") Suffice it to say, my pancreas was living on borrowed time.

The problem was, we never got to the show that Oprah *should* have done: *Why Do Men Obsess So Damn Much about Sports That Women Want to Clamp Their Noses in Curling Irons?* I'll open it up for questions now.

Q: Why can my husband discuss the Vikings for two hours but us for only two minutes?

A: Men like things simple. Black/white. Win/lose. But relationships are gray/slippery. Not once has a ref brought the two coaches together and said, "While it's true you won 49–0, I felt the way you treated him in the third quarter was a projection of your own insecurities, so, actually, you lose and he wins. Shower up."

Q: Why do baseball players touch their groins with the same frequency as Michael Jackson?

A: When Randy Johnson's 97-mph fastball is about to be hurled at you, you tend to check and secure your valuables.

Q: Why did my husband cry when the Red Sox won the Series but not at our wedding?

A: If you had turned him down for 86 years, he might have.

Q: Do men consider belching a sport?

A: Yes.

Q: What's the deal with men and the remote?

A: See, when we were boys, we had popguns, dart guns, BB guns. Now most of us only have the remote. It feels good in our hands. We're not switching channels to see what else is on, we're shooting the thing that is on. *Bang. You're dead. Next victim.*

Q: Why do men wear jerseys to the game? Do these nimrods think the coach will suddenly put 135-pound accountants in?

A: For the same reason women wear tennis outfits to the U.S. Open. What, you think Martina is suddenly going to say, "Hey, you, in the $500 Neiman Marcus tennis dress and $5,000 tennis bracelet, I need a doubles partner"?

Q: My boyfriend is constantly saying, "Hold on, Honey, only a minute left in the game." Twenty minutes later it's still on. How fricking long is a sports minute?

A: An NFL minute is 17.3 minutes in real time. An NBA minute is 43.8. Neither of these, though, is as long as the "I-only-need-a-minute-to-fix-my-hair" minute. When men hear that, we take our coats off and finish doing the taxes.

Q: Why must our infant son wear eye black during Eagles games?

A: Most men don't fight wars anymore. But there's something embedded deep within our cerebral cortex that still drives us to storm castles, wear ridiculous paint and chant lustily. O.K., so now it's White Castles and eye black and J-E-T-S! But you get the idea.

Q: What is my husband thinking when he takes his sand wedge to bed with us?

A: He's thinking, What if there's a fire in the garage?

Q: Why does my husband always insist that I touch the calcium deposit on his clavicle?

A: I'm not sure you're grasping the historic significance of that calcium deposit. It's from the Slippery Rock B Division Intramural Flag Football Championships. It was his diving catch that forced the overtime that allowed Phi Psi Delta to go on and defeat Six Guys Your Girlfriend Wants. He broke his collarbone on that play. That's his Purple Heart. Indulge him.

Q: When is my husband's high-school linebacker teammate, Hurl, ever going to get off our couch? It's been two months!

A: You don't understand. They're Walla Walla High Fighting Panthers. They vowed to *never, ever* give up on each other. And aren't you glad he's big on vows?

Q: Will the trash take itself out?

A: Babe, there's only a minute left in the game.

Postscript: The reach and power of Oprah's show is astonishing. More than a year later, I was still getting waitresses tossing my plate down and going, "You're the guy who says it's O.K. for husbands to play golf on Christmas Day. Jerk!" (It was a joke!)

85

Bored of the Rings

MARCH 14, 2005

T HEY MEAN MORE THAN ANYTHING ELSE IN SPORTS. "I'M all about the ring," athletes say. *Sure, Dan Marino set hundreds of records*, fans gripe, *but he never got a ring*. After 18 years Karl Malone left a team and a city that he loved to try to get a ring. ¶ Well, you know what? I've got three championship rings, and they suck!

First, they're so big it's like attaching a steam iron to your finger. You can't eat, write or play clavichord with them on. Second, they hurt to wear. Your knuckles start to look like a Benihana trainee's. Third, they're so gaudy, pimps look at you and go, "Bro . . . tacky."

How did *I* get them? From Jostens, one of the leading makers of title rings for pro and college sports. They were gullible enough to let me borrow three for 14 days to see what's so damn wonderful about them that an athlete will sell his liver to get one.

Jostens makes samples of every championship ring they produce and uses those to trigger more sales. I was sent duplicates of Michael Jordan's 1993 and 1998 NBA championship rings plus last year's Patriots Super Bowl ring.

The first Jordan ring is half pretty, but too big—with a jumbo garnet Bulls logo set against 50 diamonds (in the samples they're replaced by cubic zirconia) on the top and Jordan's name on one side. The '98 Jordan is even huger, and so blingy you can't read your watch for the glare.

But the Patriots' is the Ring That Taste Forgot. It's the approximate size of a Subaru Forester. It might look good around Hulk Hogan's calf, but that's about it. Cast in 14-carat white gold with diamonds crammed *under* other diamonds (104 in all), it's worth $20,600. They should pay you that to wear it.

Before this, it shocked me when players sold their rings. Steelers running back Rocky Bleier, for instance, unloaded all four of his Super Bowl rings while in the midst of divorce and bankruptcy proceedings. Lester Hayes sold his Raiders Super Bowl XVIII ring for $2,000 because he had a toothache he wanted fixed. Giants receiver Bobby Johnson pawned his Super Bowl XXI ring for $500.

But after two weeks of living with these Mr. T starter kits, worrying about some thug relieving you of your fancy fingers with chain cutters, I can almost see why players sell them.

"Plus, they hurt when you shake hands," says John Elway, who has worn his two Broncos Super Bowl rings for a total of three days. "And you can't get your hands into your pockets. And they're so gaudy it feels like you're wearing a trophy on your hand." There is one small advantage, though. "My kids liked taking them to show-and-tell."

Besides, what fun are they when nobody believes they're real?

"Yeah, right," a pawnbroker told me. "I'll give you $150 for the big one."

"Yeah, right," one homeless-looking guy outside a pharmacy said, "and I got one of Mike's rings in my pocket."

The Jordan rings fascinated people. One sportswriter put on the '98 and declared, "I have this sudden urge to gamble." One girl my son knows put it on and said, "Does this mean I can dunk?" I ran into an ESPN anchor I know. "Dude, if you can't get sex wearing that," he whispered, "give it up."

I kept hoping to run into Jordan himself, just so I could say, "Hey, man, did you drop this?"

The same way hockey players won't touch the Stanley Cup until they've won it, ballers want zero to do with somebody else's ring. "You're just teasin' me," said the Denver Nuggets' Earl Boykins, who refused to touch it.

The Phoenix Suns' Shawn Marion pulled back from the ring like it was kryptonite, saying, "You're all bling-bling in my face with that, huh?"

I asked Shaq how much he'd give me for the Pats ring. "Nothin'," he grumbled, " 'cause I didn't *earn* it."

Worse, one day I was going through arena security and flipped the Jordan '98 into a basket—and the zirconia-glutted faceplate came off. What, a $12,000 ring gets $1.98 Elmer's glue? Cost me $4 to, uh, fix it. Made me wonder why I went to all the trouble of winning the title in the first place.

But there was one fun thing about showing them around: kids. I blew away one boy sitting by himself at a bus stop when I let him put one on his finger. For him, it was the opposite of Bilbo Baggins—this ring made him *visible*. He lit up like a neon sign when he put it on. *How's it feel?* "Powerful!" he yelled.

One girl from an inner-city school made a fist with the Pats ring on and said, "I'd like to see somebody fight me now!"

My buddy brought over his two sports-freak boys, eight and 10, just to see the rings. Boggle-brained, they held them for a minute, then put them down, sprinted to my Pop-A-Shot and started firing up jumpers.

Hey, you've got to *earn* it.

Postscript: The poor guy who sent me the rings got in all kinds of trouble for it. And it didn't help that I lost one of them for three weeks. Finally found it in the bottom of my backpack. Wonder if that ever happens to Jordan?

86

The Parent Trap

JULY 31, 2006

I WENT OUT TO GET MY PAPER THIS MORNING AND FOUND my neighbor Dalton instead. ¶ He was slumped on my stoop, looking as though he'd slept under a marching band. His eyes sported five-pound bags, his right hand was bandaged and bloody, and his face was sunk like a bad soufflé.

"My God!" I said. "What happened to you? You look like a 20-car funeral!"

"Youth lacrosse happened to me," he grumbled. "The Competitive Elite Lacrosse League. My little Ashley made one of those 'travel teams.' Pray it never happens to you, dude."

He explained. "See, I really never thought Ashley was all that hot at lacrosse, and she's only 14. But when she made this competitive team, all the parents said it was a big honor. They said it's the only way to make your high school varsity, and it's the road to a scholarship, and it looks great on your résumé.

"I'm not even sure Ashley wanted to do it. But all of her friends made it, so she just *had* to do it. What was I gonna do? Tell my little girl no?

"Next thing you know, I'm writing a check for $1,500. Then it turns out, they practice or play seven days a week on these things. And it's clear across town, so pretty soon I'm standing on the sidelines every day of the week.

"My wife can't do it 'cause she has to take Justin to hockey every day. Why an eight-year-old nearsighted kid needs a 42-game schedule is beyond me. What is he, Wayne Gretzky? Plus there's pylon camp and forecheck camp and backward-skating lessons with his personal coach, Hans.

"So pretty soon I got no life. Family dinners? Forget it. Every meal is in the car—righthanded Taco Bell. I almost *never* see my wife awake. When I do, I have to ask for I.D.

"Then this lunatic lacrosse coach schedules an extra 6 a.m. practice every day. It's like the old bottle-feeding days. I'd be like, 'I got her last time. You get her.' And Denise would moan, 'I had to stay up for Midnight Madness last night. Your turn.' Then, at night Ashley is so tired, we end up doing her dang homework! And we're gettin' C's!

"Anyway, Ashley and I started flying to all these stupid tournaments— Dallas and Baltimore and, my God, Ottawa!—and every one is billed as 'the recruiting event of the year!' And do you know who we see at these tournaments? The same damn girls we used to play in our *neighborhood* league! Essentially, we're flying across the country to get our ass kicked by the same exact people!

"So I start talking to these girls' parents, and it turns out they don't really want to be there either, but *their* kids were saying we were going to do it, so *they* had to!

"But then my wife gets to talking to some other moms at Justin's slap shot workshop, and they say we're crazy if we don't have a 'performance-enhancement specialist' for our kids. So she signs them both up with one. Then she finds out most of these girls have 'recruiting consultants' who make highlight reels of kids and send them to college coaches. I'm like, 'She's 14!' And my wife is like, 'You're gonna tell our little girl no?' Then we add a rating-service guy and a sports psychologist and a webmaster.

"Well, what with me working half time and all this crap I'm paying for and all these trips, I had to take out a second mortgage. Denise can't work because she's spending every waking moment in a freezing ice rink, which makes her joints stiffen up. Luckily, Hans knows some New Age massage technique that makes her feel better.

"So now I'm getting no sleep, turning my stomach into a Dumpster and having less sex than a dead monk. But before I can put my foot down, my boss does. He fires me! And as he's firing me, he adds, 'By the way, the average lacrosse scholarship is $1,000, you putz!' So I punch him, and now I think my hand might be broken.

"I stomp out and go find Ashley to say, 'It's over.' And she goes, 'Whatever. I quit today anyway. My sports psychologist says you guys push me too hard.'

"Nice. So I go home to tell Denise, but she's not there. Three days go by. I figure she's at the Elite Competitive Hockeypalooza in Cheyenne. Turns out she moved in with Hans. Says she wants to be with someone who 'knows' her. Oh, and she *really* likes massages.

"So now I get home and somebody changed the locks! Probably the mortgage company, since I'm *way* behind.

"And do you know what I learned from all this, man? I learned that the most viciously competitive sport in the world is parenting.

"Anyway, what I wanted to ask you is—you wanna buy some lacrosse sticks?"

Postscript: My buddy in Denver gave me this idea when he called me from Philadelphia with the following voice mail: "Can you explain to me why I had to fly my whole family to Philadelphia to watch my daughter get beat by a team from Denver?

Hey, it takes a village to write a column.

87

Fear Strikes Out Again

SEPTEMBER 9, 2002

A SAILOR MUST NAVIGATE THE BERMUDA TRIANGLE. A climber must scale Half Dome. A drunk must conquer Oktoberfest. ¶ And if you think of yourself as a hitter, you must face Nolan Ryan. ¶ The other day, having kielbasa for brains, I did. ¶ It seemed like such a good idea at the time. Ten lucky Baby Ruth customers won an all-medical-expenses-paid trip to face Nolan Ryan, the greatest strikeout pitcher in history. A p.r. guy wanted to know if I'd be the 11th.

I thought, *Well, what could be more fun than facing the greatest fastball pitcher of all time wearing a pathetic plastic Baby Ruth helmet?*

To prepare, I took hitting lessons from a former New York Yankees farm-hand named Bill Stearns, who kept saying, "You're gonna do great! Just keep your head in there!" Uh, Bill? You heard this is Nolan Ryan, right? Once threw a pitch clocked at 100.9 mph? Tossed a record seven no-hitters? You keep *your* head in there. I'll be bailing like a *Titanic* crewman.

So there we were at The Dell Diamond in Round Rock, Texas, home of the minor league Express, which Ryan owns a piece of. We started off hitting in the cage against Nolan's son Reid. And I was just flat *raking* it. Thank you, Bill Stearns. Line drives. Opposite field ropes. Two bombs, the last of which I stood and admired. After all, how often do you see a ball fly almost all the way to the warning track?

That's when I heard this voice from behind: "You admire one like that against me and I'll give ya an earful."

It was Nolan Ryan himself.

Would anybody have a Tums?

O.K., so he's 55 now. And he had double bypass surgery 2½ years ago. And he hasn't pitched in the big leagues since 1993. But his arm still has 90 mph in it. "It's just the rest of me that fails," he said. I made the mistake of asking him if he'd ever hurt anybody badly.

"Yeah, one time a guy squared around to bunt, and I hit him right in the head. He was out eight weeks. I mean, I know I'm capable of killin' somebody."

O.K., kids! Who's ready to step in?

The 10 winners tried their luck. They hit only one pitch past the infield, an anemic bloop Willard Scott could've run down. Suddenly, sickeningly, it was my turn.

At first, it seems kind of cool. He peers in at you, menacingly. *Wow! I've seen him do that 1,000 times!* you think. Then he starts that familiar leg kick. *It's like I'm inside SportsCenter!* But when you see that right hand rear back behind his hip, you realize, *Jesus, Mary and Joseph! He's throwing it toward me!*

I crushed his first pitch, a fastball, off the knuckles. My hands felt as if they'd been run over by the Ohio State marching band. The ball went approximately 15 feet, hit right of the chalk and spun nearly back to my feet.

I've got to get on a better steroid program.

Then I took a called fastball on the outside corner. I never saw that pitch. To me, it's still only a rumor. I looked at the catcher. "Gas," he said, grinning. The third pitch was going right for my head when it suddenly broke off the countertop and just missed on the inside corner. Sitting on my butt, I looked at the catcher again. "Nasty hammer," he said, laughing.

On the next pitch, parts of my body were in mutiny.

Feet: *Screw this. We're out of here.*

Me: *Please stay. At least until he starts his windup?*

Colon: *Uh, we may have a problem.*

I whiffed on a curve only a chiropractor could love. Strike three. The next time up he fanned me on four pitches, including two curves and a sick circle change. The third time up, on an 0–2 count, I squared to bunt when I suddenly remembered what happens to people who bunt on Nolan Ryan. Somehow, I bailed out and bunted at the same time, fouling it off, strike three.

So. . . three ABs, three K's, 11 pitches.

Hey, thanks for stopping by the booth!

Afterward Ryan sat down next to me on the bench, sweat-soaked. "Whoo-ee," he laughed. "I threw some good pitches to you!"

O.K., so I was humiliated. But I'm *still* going to tell people I took Ryan to the warning track, twice.

Who says I have to mention *which* Ryan?

Postscript: Just because it hurt so much, I left the comedian Tom Arnold, then the star of FOX's Best Damn Sports Show, *completely out of this one. Arnold was also there and he swung like a man swinging a Buick fender. But, somehow, some way, despite missing nearly all of his batting practice pitches, he actually hit a dribbler to second base when it counted. Of the 10 of us, he was the only one who actually hit a ball into play. There, I said it. Now I must go weep.*

88

Listen Up, Grads

MAY 17, 2004

DEAR 2004 GRADUATING CLASS OF SPORTS FANS, jocks, wannabes, willbes, players, playaz and everybody in between: Thank you for allowing me to deliver your commencement address. ¶ Someone once said, "Free advice is worth every penny." So as you embark on a great new adventure, follow closely these little instructions I'm about to give you, and your life will be more screwed up than that of any member of the Jackson 5.

GIVE DON KING power of attorney.

When interviewing for a job in the sports industry, always arrive wearing your favorite throwback jersey. Also, grab your crotch a lot and say, "Word, bossman!" It lends authenticity.

And always begin those interviews with the question, "You don't have any kind of screwy *drug* policy here, do you?"

Always be an hour late for everything. It adds mystery.

Bet big on the Chargers.

And remember, if your kitty gets low, you can always make it back with a big move on the Monday night game.

Keep up with the Joneses. In fact, make it your sole goal in life to kick the Joneses' ass.

Never *ever* take crap from Mike Tyson.

Do what Michael Jordan and Tiger Woods do: Never take a stand on anything, because you might make somebody angry and screw up your endorsement possibilities.

Buy all your Rolexes from out-of-breath vendors near Shea Stadium.

Never miss a single game of your beloved Boston Red Sox, even if it means staring at the Internet radio feed on your computer for four hours. Tucking in your three-year-old can wait. You've got to keep your score book up to date.

Try to please everybody.

Move to N.Y. or L.A. right away. That's where all the important people are.

Don't play basketball. Play *EA Sports NBA Live 2004* basketball. Don't join a football team. Get in a fantasy football league. Don't shovel the walk. Drive 20 minutes to the athletic club, and get on the sim-snow-shoveler 2000.

Find a cigarette brand, and stick to it, dammit.

Men, when you get your first apartment, nail your baseball cap collection up on the wall. Chicks dig it.

Supersize everything.

Get more tattoos than Allen Iverson. They age you gracefully.

And wear enough jewelry to set off the airport metal detector from the Hertz lot.

Once you're married, never go to bed mad. It's important that you settle, once and for all, who forgot to tape the Cavaliers' game.

Get deeply involved in world championship wrestling.

Let Bob Knight be your moral compass.

Buy a great big house on a great big wide street with a three-car garage. Then anchor yourself in a La-Z-Boy, and vow to never miss a *SportsCenter* or meet the neighbors.

Remember, charities only want your check, not your time.

And never do community service without being sentenced first.

Get involved with the Big Brother program. They'll take you to the ball game and buy you ice cream cones.

Secretly tape all your conversations with your agent and hitmen. And keep the tapes where prosecutors can easily find them once the trial starts.

Always get one for the road.

If you get pulled over by a cop, be sure to say, "You're not gonna check in the trunk, right?"

Keep your grudges handy.

Buy the biggest freakin' SUV you can find. If your kids want to talk to you from the backseat, they can use their cellphones.

Care deeply about your kids' sports. Call the coach a lot. Attend every practice, constantly hollering instruction. If your kid is into hockey, get him on teams in three different parts of town, even if it means he has to eat dinner in the car every night. Remember, your kids are your second chance in life. Don't let them blow it for you.

If you're about to make a bet with a very tan stranger on the 1st tee and he says he's "about a 22," take his word for it.

Take yourself very, very seriously. It's crucial that the world remembers you after you're gone.

When the cameras are on you, pray louder than everybody else. God keeps track of this stuff.

If your team wins the big game, celebrate by picking up a Mini Cooper and throwing it through the window of a Denny's.

If your team loses the big game, console yourself by picking up a Mini Cooper and throwing it through the window of a Denny's.

And, most important, before making a decision, ask yourself these four words: "What would Rodman do?"

Remember, graduates, the future is in your hands.

Try to palm it off on somebody else.

89

The Power of 3

MAY 12, 2003

T HERE HE STOOD, TOUGHER THAN A $2 STEAK, NECK by Rawlings, a good 50 hard years behind him, tears dripping off his beard. ¶ J.W. Martin had driven eight hours for this—the late Dale Earnhardt's 52nd birthday, the one day of the year when worshipers of the NASCAR driver are allowed to enter his 70,000-square-foot Garage Mahal in Mooresville, N.C.—and now it was just too damn much for him.

Martin was standing between a row of four cars that Earnhardt had used to wax other drivers and the 1957 coral-pink street Chevy that Earnhardt had lovingly waxed himself, and the ol' boy was suddenly butter.

"People just don't understand what he meant," said a sniffling Martin, who back home in Lebanon, Tenn., has Earnhardt commemorative glasses and plates, blanket, wall decor, wet bar, truck, car, boat and grandbaby's car seat. "Racin' just ain't been the same without him."

On April 29 about 13,000 people like Martin made the pilgrimage to Dale Earnhardt Inc. headquarters on Dale Earnhardt Highway 3 in the town known as Dalesville to see some of the pistons the great man pumped, some of the hats he wore and some of the trophies he held over those hats.

There were men with Dale Sr.'s face tattooed on their right forearms and Dale Jr.'s on their left. There were women driving $31,000 Dale Earnhardt signature Monte Carlos, one with the plate DALESGR8. "See this pitcher?" said Elwood Jones of Rocky Mount, Va., showing an 11-by-14 photograph from the 2001 Daytona 500. "This was taken 20 minutes before Dale died. It's for sale, but I ain't sellin' to nobody but a true Dale fan. And I can tell."

Like Elvis's, Earnhardt's legend has only grown in death. It's been more than two years since he died in "the perfect crash," as it's called, the grisly combination of speed and angle of impact that killed him. "How long did I cry?" asked Jones. "Buddy, I ain't stopped."

This was the second birthday open garage, and fans slept outside the night before to be among the first in line. For what? For the gift shop, of course, a place they can get into most every other day of the year.

"Looks like you bought something," I said to Julie Weist, who drove 1,100 miles, from Dows, Iowa, with her husband, Mark.

"Yep," she said, wiping away tears. "I'm gonna frame it."

"You're going to frame a T-shirt?"

"Not the shirt!" she corrected. "The bag!"

A man got on his back and scooted under the 1994 Lumina that Earnhardt drove to clinch his seventh Winston Cup championship. He wanted to take a few snaps. Hey, if a close-up of Dale's drivetrain doesn't give you chill bumps, then you must not be from one of the five states—Florida, North Carolina, South Carolina, Texas and Virginia—that this year declared April 29 as Dale Earnhardt Day.

You wouldn't understand why three Mooresville-area hotels offered discount rates and shuttle-bus service to Earnhardt's muffler mecca. Or why the crowd there got eerily quiet when *The Dance*, by Garth Brooks, was played over the sound system. You probably wouldn't drive 13 hours just to stand on the street where Dale grew up—yeah, Sedan Street—the same place where his daddy died of a heart attack while fixing a carburetor. (Hell, you probably wouldn't fix your own carburetor, either.)

You wouldn't get why the minor league baseball team in Dale's hometown of Kannapolis, N.C., is called the Intimidators. Nor why people nearly cause traffic accidents pulling over to take pictures of themselves in front of DALE EARNHARDT BLVD. signs.

Three Nation still grieves. It holds three fingers to the sky at the start of every NASCAR race. It goes silent in the third lap of every race. It wears Earnhardt's trademark black jeans, black T-shirt and black hat whether it's 103° or 3°. Forty percent of NASCAR's souvenir sales are Earnhardt-related. A Navy sailor, Robert Butcher, begged for and received permission to take his reenlistment oath at the Earnhardt garage on this most holy day.

This obsession still amazes Dale Earnhardt Inc.'s 250 employees. Still amazes the family too. "What's funny is that Dale [never really wanted] us doing much for his birthday," says Dale's 50-year-old brother, Randy. The Intimidator was famous for skipping birthdays altogether—his age was something of a mystery. "All I know is, I started out younger than him," Randy says, "and ended up passing him somewhere along the line."

If that's true, his adoring fans want you to know something: It's the *only* damn time Dale Earnhardt liked gettin' passed.

If there was one moment that summed up the day, it was this: At about noon there was a sudden hush in the garage showroom, and a crowd gathered respectfully to peer down a hall, cameras to their eyes. "What's going on?" I inquired.

A woman holding a video camera whispered emotionally, "They're unloading some of Dale Jr.'s tools!"

The king is dead. Long live the king.

90

Why Wait to Go Postal?

NOVEMBER 14, 2005

Note to SI readers: We eliminated the middle man so that you would not have to wait a week between Rick Reilly's column and the hate mail that inevitably follows.

—THE EDITORS

L ET ME ASK YOU A QUESTION. IF I SAID, "THE SKY IS BLUE, water is wet and moose don't fit easily into coin slots," would you call for my dismissal? ¶ Well, then, why did Air Force football coach Fisher DeBerry get pure hell when he explained a bad loss to TCU by saying, "[They] had a lot more Afro-American players than we did, and they ran faster than we did. . . . It's very obvious to me [black players] run extremely well"?

Did DeBerry sneeze into the flag or put out a kitchen fire with a bunny? Besides butchering the phrase *African-American*, what exactly did the 67-year-old DeBerry say that was so wrong?

Hellllooo? In football, if you're looking for speed, 99.9% of the time you'll find it in a black athlete. All but one of the last 100 wide receivers taken in the first round of the NFL draft were black. Of the last 50 All-Pro corner-backs, only one was white. Only 48 men have broken 10 seconds in the 100-meter dash, and they're all black. You think that's a *coincidence*?

I have no clue *why* this is true. I just know it is true. Running fast is not the only thing these athletes are good at. Not by a million miles. But it is one thing.

And yet knees started jerking instantly. DeBerry was called into the athletic director's office for a tongue-hammering. He had to apologize. A sanctimonious Colorado state senator called for his immediate firing.

But get *this*: Almost no black people were upset! It was all PC whites freaking out *for* blacks. All my black friends were like, "Many blacks run fast? Duh!" Bill Johnson, a black columnist for Denver's *Rocky Mountain News*, couldn't understand the furor. "Was I missing something?" he wrote.

If I were DeBerry's boss, I'd have screamed at him, too. "You've been coaching here 22 years and you're just now realizing black guys run fast? No wonder we suck!!!"

DeBerry didn't insult blacks. If he'd have said, "Blacks are fast, but they can't grow orchids," or "Blacks are fast, but they stink at the accordion," then we'd have something.

Look, the only way we're ever going to deal with *real* racism is to throw out all the dumb crap that *isn't* racism—the stuff that gives racists ammo to toss at us.

Take it back? The only thing DeBerry should take back is his apology.

Letters: Reilly DeBuried

I think Rick Reilly just tested positive for stupid.
—Samuel Sosa, Baltimore

The only thing that SPORTS ILLUSTRATED should take back is Rick Reilly. Hey, Rick, what time does the Klan meeting start?
—Mr. Richard Feder, Fort Lee, N.J.

Hey, Rick. I'm enclosing a razor blade. Do the right thing.
—Spike Lee, Brooklyn

Cheerleaders, hunters, Bill Romanowski. Doesn't Rick Reilly *ever* get tired of being wrong? By defending a dinosaur like DeBerry, he's guilty of plantation-owner thinking—seeing an entire race merely for their bodies and not their minds. Reilly is dumber than a roomful of lint. This clown won Sportswriter of the Year? Now that's a mark that should have an asterisk next to it.

—Barry Bonds, San Francisco

Rush Limbaugh was right. You white guys in the media overhype the talents of black athletes.

—Donovan McNabb, Philadelphia

I agree. That state senator was totally out of line. He should be calling for Reilly to be fired.

—Gary Barnett, Boulder, Colo.

I, for one, am glad to see someone defend this fine Christian coach who really does want to reach out to the fast, Afro-American high-school-football-playing population.

—F. DeBerry, Colorado Springs

Couldn't Reilly just switch to tennis ball boy full-time and leave idiot sports-writing to somebody else?

—Conchita Martinez, Barcelona

Bravo! It's time somebody finally cut through the tyranny of ultrasensitive PC freaks and told the simple truth. Thank you, Rick Reilly!

—John Rocker, Atlanta

Postscript: I got the idea for this after a redesign of SI's column pages. They were broken up two-thirds/one-third. I thought, "It looks like the letters page." So I thought I'd skip the middle man by writing the column and going directly to the inevitable hate mail. The problem is hundreds of people thought they were actual letters. "Who the hell is Sammy Sosa to criticize you?" one guy wrote. I mean, did they think Sosa was learning over my shoulder as I wrote it and then dashed off an instant letter in protest? Oy.

91

Turning Losing
Into a Science

JANUARY 9, 2006

A T CALTECH, THE MOST EGGHEADED COLLEGE IN America, they love numbers the way moles love dirt, so here goes: ¶ Number of Nobel Prize winners on the faculty: 5. ¶ Number of players on the basketball team who had a perfect SAT score: 2.

Years since the hoops team won an NCAA game: 12.

Forget that. It's been 21 *years* since Caltech, a Division III school in Pasadena, won a Southern California Intercollegiate Athletic Conference game. Wouldn't you think just *once* a ball would bounce off a pocket protector and in for a win?

"We think too much," says Roy Dow, the Beavers' coach.

That's true. Every player on the team can tell you the optimum launch angle, parabola and velocity of a three-pointer. They just can't make one.

Not that Caltech doesn't have a rich athletic tradition. During halftime of the 1961 Rose Bowl thousands of kids in the Washington student section were duped into holding up flip cards that they thought would spell out HUSKIES but instead spelled CALTECH. At the 1984 Rose Bowl, Cal-

289

tech students hacked into the scoreboard by remote and changed it to read Caltech 38, MIT 9. There is a T-shirt you can buy in the university bookstore that reads CALTECH FOOTBALL: UNDEFEATED SINCE 1993. Possibly because Caltech hasn't had a football team since 1993.

But winning games instead of mocking them? They'll find the 10th planet before that happens. (Oops! A Caltech professor just did that.)

Do you have any idea how difficult it is to get decent basketball players into a school this hard?

"I search all around the country, trying to find a few good players who could get in here," says Dow, who has eight high school valedictorians on his squad, "but as soon as I hear they've gotten a B, it's, 'See ya!' "

Only six guys on his roster even played varsity ball in high school. Nobody on the team got an offer to play from any other college. None has dunked in his Caltech career.

The team's best player, senior Jordan Carlson, who's a theoretical physics major, figures he does schoolwork 14 hours a day. What's so important at school? "Well," he says, "an interesting question we're studying now is how mass is generated in terms of quantum field theory."

Oh, sure, the Kentucky players were discussing that the other day.

In his four seasons Dow has seen it all. One kid closed his eyes when he shot. One didn't know if he was left-or righthanded. One current player puts topspin on his jumpers. "Must be some sort of physics I'm not aware of," Dow says.

So I went to Pasadena last week to see the Beavers put their epic losing streak on the line against Rivier College of Nashua, N.H. Three things you notice right away:

1) Caltech has the world's most optimistic statistician. The stat sheet has a column titled WINNING STREAK. That's like Paris Hilton keeping track of how many Oscars she's won.

2) Caltech players are so skinny they look like they could be knocked over by a butterfly's burp.

3) Caltech has no cheerleaders. But wouldn't it be great?

Molecules, slide rules
Watt, ampere!
Fill that cylinder
With that sphere!

But the Beavers do hustle, make smart passes and run their motion offense as smoothly as a gyroscope. That's how, with 90 seconds left, they actually led Rivier by four. And the only thing the crowd could think was, *O.K., which of these brainiacs is messing with the scoreboard again?*

Alas, Rivier started pouring in threes, and Caltech started spitting out turnovers, and when Carlson's last-second 30-footer just missed, Caltech had lost its 181st straight NCAA game 55–54. (The Beavers have since lost two more.)

Hey, at least it was close. Two years ago they lost by an average of 59 points a game. "Winning any single game at Caltech," Dow says proudly, "has gone from impossible to improbable."

Not that it made the pizza afterward any easier to swallow. "I thought we were going to give you something to write about," Carlson said glumly.

You get the feeling, with kids as smart as this, they will. As an opposing player—whose team had just slaughtered the Beavers—said as he shook each Caltech player's hand, "Now go cure cancer for us."

Postscript: Poor brainiacs never won another game that season and went 0–25. In fact, their NCAA losing streak would reach 207 games before they buried Bard, another D-III team, 81–52, on Jan. 6. The geeks celebrated with commemorative headgear, but their record of 245 straight losses in the Southern California Intercollegiate Athletic Conference was intact. I'm glad. Keep studying, boys. Brilliant scientists we need. Jump shooters we don't.

92

The Play of the Year

NOVEMBER 18, 2002

JAKE PORTER IS 17, BUT HE CAN'T READ, CAN BARELY SCRAWL HIS first name and often mixes up the letters at that. So how come we're all learning something from *him*? ¶ In three years on the Northwest High football team, in McDermott, Ohio, Jake had never run with the ball. Or made a tackle. He'd barely ever stepped on the field. That's about right for a kid with chromosomal fragile X syndrome, a disorder that is a common cause of mental retardation.

But every day after school Jake, who attends special-ed classes, races to Northwest team practices: football, basketball, track. Never plays, but seldom misses one.

That's why it seemed crazy when, with five seconds left in a recent game that Northwest was losing 42–0, Jake trotted out to the huddle. The plan was for him to get the handoff and take a knee.

Northwest's coach and Jake's best friend, Dave Frantz, called a timeout to talk about it with the opposing coach, Waverly's Derek Dewitt. Fans could see there was a disagreement. Dewitt was shaking his head and waving his arms.

After a ref stepped in, play resumed and Jake got the ball. He started to genuflect, as he'd practiced all week. Teammates stopped him and told him to run, but Jake started going in the wrong direction. The back judge rerouted him toward the line of scrimmage.

Suddenly, the Waverly defense parted like peasants for the king and urged him to go on his grinning sprint to the end zone. Imagine having 21 teammates on the field. In the stands mothers cried and fathers roared. Players on both sidelines held their helmets to the sky and whooped.

In the red-cheeked glee afterward, Jake's mom, Liz, a single parent and a waitress at a coffee shop, ran up to the 295-pound Dewitt to thank him. But she was so emotional, no words would come.

Turns out that before the play Dewitt had called his defense over and said, "They're going to give the ball to number 45. *Do not touch him!* Open up a hole and let him score! Understand?"

It's not the kind of thing you expect to come out of a football coach's mouth, but then Derek Dewitt is not your typical coach. Originally from the Los Angeles area, he's the first black coach in the 57-year history of a conference made up of schools along the Ohio-Kentucky border. He'd already heard the n word at two road games this season, once through the windows of a locker room. Yet he was willing to give up his first shutout for a white kid he'd met only two hours earlier.

"I told Derek before the play, 'This is the young man we talked about on the phone,' " Frantz recalled. " 'He's just going to get the ball and take a knee.' But Derek kept saying, 'No, I want him to score.' I couldn't talk him out of it!"

"I met Jake before the game, and I was so impressed," Dewitt said. "All my players knew him from track. So, when the time came, touching the ball just didn't seem good enough." (By the way, Dewitt and his team got their shutout the next week, 7–0 against Cincinnati Mariemont.)

Into every parade a few stink bombs must fall. Mark Madden of the *Pittsburgh Post-Gazette* grumbled that if the mentally challenged want to participate in sports, "let them do it at the Special Olympics. Leave high school football alone, and for heaven's sake, don't put the fix in." A few overtestosteroned Neanderthals on an Internet site complained, "That isn't football."

No, it became bigger than football. Since it happened, people in the two towns just seem to be treating one another better. Kids in the two schools walk around beaming. "I have this bully in one of my [phys-ed] classes," says Dewitt. "He's a rough, out-for-himself type kid. The other day I saw him helping a couple of special-needs kids play basketball. I about fell over."

Jake is no different, though. Still happy as a frog in a bog. Still signs the teachers' register in the principal's office every morning, ready to "work." Still gets sent on errands, forgets where he's going and ends up in Frantz's office. Still talks all the time, only now it's to NBC, ESPN and affiliates from CBS and Fox about his touchdown that won the game.

Yeah, Jake Porter thinks his 49-yard run made for a comeback victory. He thinks he was the hero. He thinks that's why there were so many grins and streaks down people's faces.

Smart kid.

Postscript: After this hit, Jake won an ESPY and a Arete courage award and ESPN did a piece on him. But like a lot of these columns, the wonderful part of this story isn't so much the kid as the adults who acted so gracefully in his behalf. Former NFL coach Steve Mariucci called both coaches to congratulate them, and Oklahoma coach Bob Stoops sent a letter. And those were just two of dozens. As for Jake, he remains at Northwest High in McDermott, where he's the unofficial principal, athletics director and social director.

93

200-Dollar Babies

MAY 2, 2005

I T WASN'T EASY FOR MISS ANGELA TO TELL HER KINDERGARTNERS how she got a broken nose and a black eye, so she lied. "I got hit with a baseball," she told the class. ¶ What was she supposed to do, tell the truth—that she got it while making $200 in an underground L.A. street brawl known as Extreme ChickFights?

It wasn't easy for Laika de los Santos, a student at Santa Monica College, to tell her parents how she earned the $300 to fix her car, but she did. For five rounds, without gloves or headgear, she traded bare-knuckle punches in two Extreme ChickFights. "My dad thinks it's cool," she says, "but my mom won't let him come. So I let him see all my bruises afterward."

But it sure has been easy for the Extreme ChickFights' organizer, Marie (she won't give her last name), to sell more than 100,000 DVDs—"99.99 percent to guys," she says—at $19.99. "Some distributors think it's porn," Marie says, "but it's not." Hey, maybe they think it's *better*: lipsticked girls trying to whack each other's mascara off, many with no idea what they're doing. Now that's entertainment.

This was definitely going to be Becky Zerlentes's last fight. What's weird is, this was going to be Heather Schmitz's first fight. Before their Golden Gloves bout in Denver last month, the two women in their early 30s hit it off. They even set up a time to have lunch the following week. How could they know the lunch would never come off because one of them would be dead?

The Oscar-winning Best Picture for 2004—Clint Eastwood's *Million Dollar Baby*—has been a knockout for the women's fight game. In fact, if it weren't for all the blood, you'd swear an Extreme ChickFight was just a bad movie set.

The unsanctioned and unregulated fights are staged in private—usually in a backyard, a basement or a rented L.A. studio—and never in the same place twice. EXTREME CHICKFIGHTS sprayed on a wall like graffiti. A nurse in a low-cut, shiny vinyl uniform. Four rounds for street fighters. Three rounds for fighters in gloves or gloves and headgear. Thirty or 40 women, many with almost no clue how much $200 can hurt.

They come answering Marie's ads in L.A. papers and on her website: *Can you kick ass and take names?* One woman, calling herself Death Angel, came in mesh stockings and a miniskirt. She stopped fighting when she couldn't feel her face anymore. Another, Sugar Britches, came in frilly spanky pants and a camisole. Later she was swollen and scraped, and nothing looked sweet about her. One night a woman had her top and bra yanked off in a street fight yet kept swinging. Nobody comes to be a champion.

"The girls don't come for the money," explains Marie, who says she's a UCLA film school graduate who started all this as a way to make a "cool" documentary. "They come for the *fun* of it."

What's weird is the punch didn't even look nasty. No shoulders or hip in it. But Schmitz's straight right in the third round that night stiffened Zerlentes's legs and felled her like a new Christmas tree. Her head smacked the canvas. The doctor was over her within 15 seconds. But it was already too late.

The kindergarten teacher now runs a day-care center, but she still bleeds for Marie's cameras. "I do it for the adrenaline rush," says Angela Gabriel. "Sure, it's a risk. . . . But I'll be a cool grandma: 'Grandma, did you really fight other girls?' "

Her car is fixed, but de los Santos keeps fighting. "I don't know why," she giggles. "Someday I'll have kids, and I'll yell, 'No fighting!' They'll say, 'You did it!' And I'll say, '—unless you're paid!' "

Marie is shocked at the hunger for her videos—her million-dollar baby— out of which the fighters get zero percent. "This was supposed to be a one-off," she says. "Now it's a full-time business!" She hasn't seen Eastwood's movie yet. "How *does* it end?"

> *Zerlentes died the next day. Blunt force trauma. Believed to be the first female fighter to die in the ring. Schmitz crawled into her bedroom and hasn't spoken to reporters since. "She's devastated," says Julie Gold-sticker of USA Boxing. Her friends wonder if she'll ever fight again. That would be something, right? If it turned out to be the last bout for both fighters?*

Zerlentes died from a gloved punch that hit her headgear. She died with a doctor, an EMT and oxygen at ringside. What chance does a girl in a miniskirt have?

It will happen. One of these days blunt force trauma will come to Marie's little backyard brawls. In order to get paid, the fighters sign a waiver releasing Marie from liability. So if a girl comes in a camisole and goes home in a box, Marie says she can't be sued.

Besides, can you imagine the DVD sales of *that*?

Postscript: Sometimes you wonder if you're doing more harm than good. If you Google Extreme Chick Fights, it now says this: "Profiled in SPORTS ILLUSTRATED!"

Sigh.

94

Why Daddy Can't Write

MAY 5, 2003

T AKE OUR DAUGHTERS TO WORK DAY WAS LAST THURSDAY, so I took my 13-year-old, Rae, for the first time. Hey, a kid will do anything to miss a day of school. By noon she was begging to go back. ¶ Maybe she thought that at my office Shaq would be shooting Nerf hoops with swimsuit models while guys in fedoras clackety-clacked out metaphors in the back room.

Uh, nope.

It was a lot of conversations like this:

HER: Dad, what are you doing now?

ME: Planning my next column.

HER: With your eyes closed?

ME: Yes.

HER: Lying on the couch?

ME: Yes.

HER: How long does it take you to write a column?

ME: About two hours.

HER: And you only have to do one a week?

298

ME: Yes.

HER: Cool! What do you do with all the rest of the time?

ME: Worry about those two hours.

After about an hour of that, she was going out of her teenage mind, so I let her wade into a giant box of unopened mail.

HER: Why do all these Barry Bonds fans cut little letters out of magazines and make sentences out of them?

ME: I guess they get to do a lot of arts and crafts at the mental health center.

HER: What does this mean, "If I ever see you, run"?

ME: Uh, that's from my personal trainer.

After a while, she had called all her friends, e-mailed all her friends, faxed all her friends and text-messaged all her friends.

HER: What are you doing now?

ME: Planning my next column.

HER: Is it going to be about golf?

ME: No.

HER: Then why are you putting?

ME: It helps me think.

HER: Has it helped so far?

ME: No.

HER: Would it help more if one of the balls went in the thingy?

Nothing was coming to me, so I went and did a little planning at the driving range. I asked her to answer the phone while I was gone. When I came back, she was beaming.

HER: Daddy, a man called. Very nice. Said he's a hunter. He wants you to be sure you never walk alone.

ME: Uh, O.K.

HER: And a book reviewer from some New York paper called.

ME: Really?!

HER: Yeah, he said he got your new book and wants you to know he's going to waste no time reading it.

ME: Oh.

She's good at math, so I gave her a crack at my expense account.

HER: Hey, all these cabdrivers have handwriting like yours!

ME: Yeah. Weird, huh?

HER: "Cab to church, $27." Mom says it would take a team of Clydesdales to drag you to church.

ME: O.K., it was the racetrack. But people were praying.

HER: Who's Lamar Higgenbottom?

ME: Lamar Higgenbottom . . . Beats me.

HER: Says on this receipt you took him to dinner.

ME: Oh, sure! Nice fella.

After alphabetizing my books, rearranging my bottom-drawer ketchup packets and trying on all my hats, she sighed and said, "What do you think other dads are doing with their daughters?"

ME: Well, the Detroit Red Wings are doing the same thing as I am, lying around on the couch. And Hootie Johnson started the day by telling his daughter, "O.K., you stay in the parking lot, and I'll meet you at five." And whatever Jose Canseco and his daughter are doing, it's not more than 100 yards from their den, what with the court-ordered house arrest and all.

HER: Dad, are you trying lines out on me?

ME: Yes.

HER: Kimberly's probably having fun. Her dad works at the halfway house.

ME: Sometimes I write about the Portland Trail Blazers.

HER: Oh! Her dad wanted me to tell you he goes to sleep every week reading your column!

ME: Oh, well, thanks.

Finally, my wife, Linda, came by and asked how Take Our Daughters to Work Day was going. We both groaned.

RAE: I don't think Dad likes this part of town to work in.

MOM: Why?

RAE: He said the worst part about his job is this damn writer's block.

I leaped up and started typing furiously.

RAE: Did you get a good column idea?

ME: No, but I'm writing anyway.

Postscript: Rae is 18 now and a songwriter. Sometimes she'll be sitting at the piano, noodling around on the keys, trying to get a song just right, when I'll walk in, lean on it and say, "Whatcha doin'?" Payback is hell.

95

Stanley and Me

W HAT WOULD YOU DO WITH THE STANLEY Cup for a day? After a year of begging, I got the NHL to give it to me for one day to do anything I pleased. ¶ Well, not *anything*. The league vetoed taking it to a prison, seeing what I'd get for it at a pawnshop and eating Count Chocula from it. Other than that, Stanley and I had the day to ourselves.

I wanted to take it crazy places, places that the Cup would not normally go. Naturally, I chose Chicago, the NHL city that has gone the longest—39 years—without winning the Cup.

It arrived at O'Hare in a blue crate covered with FRAGILE stickers. It also arrived with a burly redhead in a blue suit and white gloves named Paul Metzger-Oke, who went everywhere the Cup went. "It can't go anywhere of ill repute," Paul warned me. "No casinos, no strip clubs, no skydiving." Rats.

When Paul took it out of its velvet-lined box, I got chill bumps. The Stanley Cup is the greatest trophy in sports, because it's the *people's* trophy. When a team wins the Cup, each of its players actually wins the Cup—for

301

a day. It's been on mountaintops and pool bottoms, at the White House and a Waffle House. It's got more dings than a driving-school Pinto, but those are battle scars that make it more handsome.

So on a chilly October day I rented a cherry-red convertible, put the top down, buckled Stanley into the backseat with Paul and set sail down the freeway. Almost nobody noticed.

We took it down Michigan Avenue, where most people figured it was a fake. "Where's the real one?" we heard a lot. Once someone said, "That ain't the Cup! The Cup *never* comes here!"

We took it to a convent, where the sisters touched it reverently. One sister reminded us that Colorado Avalanche defenseman Sylvain Lefebvre had his daughter baptized in the Cup. The sisters figured it for a good save.

We took it to the Billy Goat Tavern, the greasy spoon made famous by the "cheeseboiger, cheeseboiger!" skit on *Saturday Night Live*. The fry cooks all had their pictures taken with it while the burgers burned.

We took it to a children's hospital, where the Blackhawks' star wing, Tony Amonte, met us and showed it to the kids in the burn unit. Some of them could barely turn their heads to see the Cup and yet smiled at it, as painful as it was. All of us had a lump in our throat, which was why it was a relief when a nurse asked Tony, "Have you spent much time around the Cup?" and he replied, "You obviously haven't seen my stats."

We took it to a Mite hockey practice, where six-year-olds swarmed it, applauded by banging their sticks on the ice and bragged about who would win it first, while their parents begged them to skate still for a moment so they could get a picture. By then, of course, the kids were flying around the rink, pretending to be Jaromir Jagr.

We showed it to 21-year-old J.J. O'Connor, a quadriplegic whose spinal injury came in a hockey game five years ago. We set it on the armrests of his wheelchair, and his grin was the size of a Buick grille. J.J. still loves the game, doesn't blame it or his best friend, who checked him into the boards that day. In fact J.J. loved the Cup more than anybody else we met. Knew more about it, too. He guided us to all kinds of odd stuff on the Cup, misspellings and X-outs, and it hit us that physical perfection is way overrated.

Right then, a junior league player walked in and just couldn't deal with bumping straight into the Cup. He kept rubbing his hair and staring at it, walking all around it, getting within an inch of it but not touching it. I asked him why. "Not worthy," he whispered.

But the best place we took the Cup was a place where most of the people couldn't see it—the Chicago Lighthouse. More than 200 people who were blind or visually impaired came up and felt it. Their hands started low, thinking the Cup was, well, a cup. The higher they felt, the wider their mouths opened. "It's huge!" one boy said. A woman gasped and said, "It feels like a wedding cake!"

It was my privilege to take their hands on a quick tour of hockey history, letting their fingers touch the great names, from M. RICHARD to W. GRETZKY. They hugged it. They kissed it. They rubbed their faces on it. One man whose eyelids didn't open wouldn't let it go. "Never seen anything like this," he said.

Agreed.

Postscript: And it hasn't been back to Chicago since.

96

Wishful Thinking

JULY 1, 2002

J UST ONCE, BEFORE YOU DIE, WOULDN'T YOU *LOVE* TO SEE . . . ¶ . . . Bud Selig and Donald Fehr crushed by the same meteorite? ¶ . . . a Chinese fan inform an NBA superstar that his cool, eight-inch Chinese-character tattoo means, literally, "I enjoy dating chickens"? ¶ . . . an NFL player beat his chest after tackling a running back for a two-yard gain, then point to the sky, thanking God, and get struck by lightning?

. . . every book publisher refuse to print Jose Canseco's autobiography on the grounds that a person must first read a book before writing one?

. . . a pack of jubilant football players sneak up from behind the gnarled old coach on a freezing night and dump a cooler of icy Gatorade on him, and the coach cut them on the spot?

. . . a World Cup soccer player forget what he's doing and flop to the ground during the postgame jersey swap?

. . . coach Lou Holtz describe South Carolina's next opponent as "worse than pitiful. These guys couldn't beat the Asthma Institute. We're looking *way* past them to Alabama two weeks from now"?

... a major league player call a press conference to demand the club negotiate his contract—downward? "I'm barely hittin' my damn weight," he'll say, his agent nodding by his side. "Either start paying me a whole lot less or I'm leaving for Pawtucket right now!"

... Alex Rodriguez, ahead of you in line at Wal-Mart, getting his Visa rejected?

... a reporter stick a tape recorder in the face of the linebacker, say, "Talk about the game, Tank," and Tank reply, "Wait a minute. You sat in that press box for 2½ hours, toasty warm, with stats handed to you, replays on 50 TV sets, prime rib buffet—with two desserts—and you can't think of *one single question* to ask me?"

... some megamillionaire athlete take MTV's *Cribs* on a tour of his mansion and get *lost*?

... Rasheed Wallace stick his hand in the air after being called for a foul?

... genius manager Joe Torre try to win a game with the Kansas City Royals' lineup?

... radio bad-boy Jim Rome say to a caller, "Hey, there's no need to be nervous. Take your time. Nobody's judging you here. You're among friends!"

... the superstar outfielder go on and on in a press conference about how he needs a trade closer to his home so he can drive the carpool, when his wife stands up in the back and yells, "Really? You want to drive the carpool? How about November? I hear you're pretty free then! How come you never drive the carpool in November? You're going to force a trade to Atlanta so you can drive the carpool? That'll be some trick, since we live in Orlando!"

... two WWF wrestlers actually land haymakers and go bawling off to their dressing rooms?

... the winning Super Bowl quarterback holler, "I'm going to Disney World! And after that, we're taking a *real* vacation!"

... a belligerent hockey fan screaming bloodthirsty insults at a 6' 6" goon in the penalty box when he suddenly realizes there's no glass between them?

... Kobe Bryant's run-jump-land-and-jump-again move get called for what it is: traveling?

... a Wimbledon ball boy say to Pete Sampras, "Well, bloody hell, aren't you going to go pick up *any* of them?"

... someone on *SportsCenter* say, "Detroit defeated Atlanta 101–99," and *nothing else*?

. . . Al Davis show up at the 50-yard line in a bright blue Perry Ellis blazer, matching ascot and bleach-blond Brad Pitt bangs?

. . . Bob Costas look straight into the camera and say, "At this very moment in the Olympic Games, the women's softball final, the men's 100-meter-dash final and the excruciating finish of the marathon are all taking place. That's why it sickens me to have to send you to the three o'clock practice session of the U.S. women's gymnastics team"?

. . . all the manicured, blown-dry, poof-poof dogs at the Westminster Kennel Club Dog Show suddenly see a vendor spill a box of wieners and go tearing off all at once?

. . . Ahmad Rashad smear on red lipstick before sucking up to Kobe?

. . . your kids sit down to dinner and tell you about that *afternoon*'s World Series game?

. . . Mo Vaughn say, "I think I'll have the salad, please."

. . . the puck?

97

Doing the Hustle

JULY 4, 2005

THE BLACK WIDOW IS TO POOL WHAT BEN FRANKLIN is to kites, Wallenda is to heights and Google is to sites. Her ink-black Rapunzel hair, Asian beauty and killer stroke make her the most famous player in the world. ¶ So why doesn't anybody in this Indianapolis pool hall recognize her?

Because she's in disguise.

See, I had this sinister idea: Could I walk into a pool hall with the most famous player in the world and hustle people for money?

Hey, it's not like Jeanette Lee hasn't done it before. The daughter of Korean parents, she started hustling at 18. "I never hustled people," she says. "I just gambled against them. Every guy thinks he can beat a woman. The only disguise I needed was showing up female."

The most she's ever taken off a guy? "Well, $90,000, years ago," she mumbles.

But now that she's on TV more than Larry King, she needs a disguise. A slender 5' 9", she has spent most of this day getting her nose widened, her bust stuffed, her butt and thighs padded, her head wigged and her eyes covered in cheap sunglasses. Suddenly, at 33, she's a hoochie mama.

The disguise is so good that a guy sidles up to her at the bar in the pool hall and asks, "You workin'?"

I laugh out loud, and she responds in perfect hoochie style, wagging her index finger in my face. "Donchu even disrespec' me like that!"

I'm playing Billy, her stake horse, and I'm wearing a wife-beater, a bad hat and cheap gold. I'm pretending to be drunk and throwing hundred-dollar bills on the felt, the traditional bait for pigeons.

Speaking of pigeons, the one we're after just walked in.

Our hustling guru, George Breedlove—reformed hustler, one of the best players in the world and the Black Widow's husband—told us the guy would show up. He's a local shark, and as soon as he hears (by way of George's anonymous call) that there are a couple of drunks and a hoochie betting Benjamins over at Claude & Annie's poolroom, he double-times it straight into the trap.

The mark unpacks his cue and goes, "You guys wanna play for a little money?"

Ahh, music to the hustler's ear. It's like a chubby man wandering into a cannibal convention and asking, "Anybody know how I can lose all this fat?"

Pretty soon, the mark is playing $100 nine ball against George, and George is dumping like crazy. Meanwhile, Jeanette is at the next table, banging balls as though she's a rank amateur, her mouth wide open, butt out, head poking up in the air like a sea turtle's.

"Hell, let's play for some real money," George says. "How about you play our girl here?" Well, the mark figures he can beat Jeanette with the wrong end of his stick, so he puts up $700 to my $500. Best of five. Nine ball.

Sometimes you'd kill for a video camera—the No. 4–ranked women's player in the world itching herself with her cue, primping in the window and holding the stick like a nail file. She tries to throw the first game, but the mark scratches on the 9 ball.

In the second game Jeanette starts burying balls off two and three cushions. Even when she purposely misses, she leaves him blocked in like it's 5 p.m. on an L.A. freeway. She wins the game.

Now the pigeon is frying. He's got $700 riding on the third game, and this hoochie is getting luckier than Paris Hilton's Chihuahua. Now she combos the 1 into the 9, sending the 9 off the far cushion and back the entire length of the table into the corner pocket. "Yo, Billeeeee!" she screeches. "So, like, I win, right?"

Game over. Match over. Hustle over.

The mark is so hot you could bake a calzone on his forehead. "Double or nothin'?" asks George. Jeanette pinches my side, hard. "We have to let this guy off the hook now," she whispers.

Party pooper.

I take the Black Widow up to him and say, "Do you know who this is?"

He can barely stand to look at her. "No," he grunts.

Jeanette takes off the crazy sunglasses and the wig. "Now?" I say.

His eyes go all Runaway Bride. "The Black Widow?" he groans.

He is a good sport, furniture salesman Jim Calder is. A lot of guys would've cracked the bridge over somebody's skull for this. "I've lost more than that before," he admits, "but never to a girl."

The hardest part for us is giving the $700 back. "Do we have to?" George whines.

As we leave, the bartender, Scott Hart, scratches his head at the end of a very odd night. "I knew we had a pro in here tonight," he says. "I just didn't realize which kind."

Postscript: One of my alltime favorite athletes. Who else would spend the day in makeup, wear fat pads, and help me con somebody? And it's not just me. Guys melt over her. One time, she signed a guy's head and he had it traced over by a tattoo artist. After our little sting operation, we all went back to her ranch and she stayed up half the night, teaching me trick shots and playing 3-cushion. And that's when I learned my favorite Black Widow trivia: To this day, her father runs a tiny smoke shop across the street from the Empire State Building. And he' can't shoot a lick of pool.

98

Dear Derek . . .

THE LOCKER NEXT TO DEREK JETER'S IN THE NEW YORK Yankees' home clubhouse throbs with his unopened mail. It piles up in feet. Spills onto the carpet. Gives off odd smells. *Aches* to be opened. So I asked him if I could open it all. He said yes. Here's what I found in 261 pieces of mail.

Despite pleas of URGENT! and IMPORTANT! and TAPE THIS ASAP TO DEREK JETER'S LOCKER! on the envelopes, most of the letter writers wanted only his autograph—141 to be exact, including 52 on Jeter photos they sent, 13 on baseballs they sent, the rest on all kinds of stuff, like a book report and a baby photo. To aid their cause, eight people even sent pens. One, seeking an autograph for her sailor husband, wrote, "Think of the publicity you'll get!" *Tonight on the 11 o'clock news: Derek Jeter signs autograph for sailor!*

Jeter is one of the rare athletes who tries to respond to all his mail himself, but he admitted, "I'm a couple road trips behind." It's no wonder. Reading his mail for one day is more depressing than watching the NASDAQ Composite. Most requests came from people who "wouldn't normally ask for something like this," except that they were hearing-impaired; had lost a grandfather, a best friend or their appendix; had a brain tumor, an aneurysm, a breach baby, essential tremor disease, breast cancer, colitis, cerebral palsy, Down syndrome or colon cancer; had gone through a rough divorce or fallen off a bike; were abandoned or unloved.

One hopelessly doomed woman needed an autograph because she had "lost four close friends, a father-in-law and almost an alcoholic father, had an apartment fire, had a miscarriage of twins and has to take care of my loser husband." Lady, you don't need an autograph; you need Montel Williams.

There were three out-and-out come-ons from women, including one jaw-dropper that would make a dead man straighten his tie. She included her photo and her phone number "as a long shot that you might call me." Jeter wasn't going to. "I never date anybody that way," he said. (However, I am selling the number on eBay, beginning on Tuesday.)

People *really* needed Jeter at their movie premieres (3), auctions (6), Playboy Mansion party, Eagle Scout ceremony, third-grade play, backyard BBQ ("and bring all your teammates"), boat ride and birthday parties (3, including one in Tampa from a boy who wrote, "Make sure you bring your swimsuit").

There were four pitches from real estate agents—including a man who was standing by "for all your real estate needs in the greater Akron area"—and two people begging for money. One guy wanted $20,000. "That's only .002 of your income," he wrote, for "a small addition on our house . . . a car loan and . . . upgrading the musical equipment I have." Well, as long as it's an emergency!

Too bad Jeter doesn't *have* any money. Otherwise, why would Master-Card have sent a letter that read, "We regret to inform you that we are unable to approve your application at this time"? Jeter's average salary is only $19 million a year. Perhaps he should try for a debit card. Luckily, there was also a notice from an insurance group informing him that he might be "eligible for worker's comp benefits under Florida statute 440." Not only that, but he was entitled to "29 cents a mile" for doctor's visits.

It would mean "so, so much" if Jeter would accept people's gifts of bubble gum, poems (2), cookies (by the 100s), audio letters (2), shoes (wrong size), needlepoint, novels (2), rambling seven-page essays about Pokemon

(6, all from the same woman) and a dead woman's favorite Yankees T-shirt and shorts, which, after three weeks in a plastic bag, stank to wherever she is now. "It was her final wish," wrote her daughter. "I'm hoping they bring you luck."

Nearly every request came with the phrase, "It'll only take a minute," except for the one from the kid who wanted Jeter to send a lot of baseball tips and the one from the mother who instructed Jeter to "write a brief, encouraging letter" to her Little Leaguer. What, no song?

Only nine people out of the 261 wanted nothing except to tell Jeter how much they loved watching him play ball. There was even a small, handwritten thank-you note—from David Letterman for appearing on his show.

Jeter had a game to play, so I asked him what he wanted me to do with it all. "Just stick it back in that locker," he said. I trucked the letters back in, only to find something awful sitting there.

The new mail.

Postscript: It's been long enough now that I think it's O.K. to add this story. One of the envelopes contained a scented handwritten letter from a Miss Universe I won't name. It even included a picture of her so hot I'm surprised it didn't take off the glue. I remember one line: "My friends say you and I would really hit it off!" Jeter had famously dated the 2000 Miss Universe, Lara Dutta, but this was somebody different. So I said, "Derek, there's a total come-on from a Miss Universe in here." And he grumbled, "Dude, I'm not going down that Miss Universe road again." Now, what exactly do you say to that? I mean, has that sentence ever been uttered before? So I replied, "I'm with you, brother. Meeeeeee, neither!"

99

War Games

OCTOBER 27, 2003

THAT BALL IS BACK! THAT BALL IS WAY BACK! THAT BALL IS over the tarmac and the weeds and the tactical truck for a home run! ¶ Only it's not really a baseball. It's an old tennis ball wrapped in toilet paper and then smothered in duct tape. ¶ And, true, the slugger isn't circling the bases; he's circling the paper plates left over from chow.

And he isn't using a bat to squeeze the Charmin; he's using a wooden tent stake. And he's not in spikes; he's in combat boots. And the outfielders don't have gloves, but they've got something that Sammy Sosa doesn't have—rifles. "Over here," says Army specialist Jeremie Johnson, "you just never know."

And this isn't Pro Player Stadium; this is a homemade ballpark in Tall 'Afar, Iraq, 250 miles north of Baghdad and a million miles from cold beer and La-Z-Boys and the wife's sweet lips. This isn't the World Series; it's a pickup game played by a bunch of American soldiers stuck in a withering kind of hell and boredom and terror that only politicians can dream up.

And that's why Johnson and his buddies of the 101st Airborne Division built a little piece of sanity.

They put a diamond on the bubbling-hot tarmac where day after sunburned day they service the thirsty copters that come whirling through. If you hit it into the sticky weeds, it was a double; over the fuel truck, a dinger. And God help you if you slid.

Then 1st Sgt. Randy Lange and his Delta Company Desperados decided to build a better ballpark in their rare hours off. He flattened a field of wheat by dragging a metal shower frame behind a tractor. To put weight on the frame he asked one of his privates to stand on it, and after each trip around the field the soldier in back was covered in so much dirt "he looked like a sugar-coated cookie," Lange says. Somebody put up dugouts—two cots with camouflage netting for cover—and somebody else found lime for the baselines. Some guys donated the seat cushions from their Hummer for bases. Some grunts rigged up a load of plastic mesh and bamboo poles for an outfield fence.

Then they looked up at the searing sun on a typical 110° day and wondered, Why not play night games? So they rolled out maintenance lights and generators. And suddenly there it was, a slice of America: Field Afar, a Yankee Stadium with real Yankees, a place as beautiful to these men as Fenway Park is to a Dorchester dentist.

And that's when they realized that they were having something rarer than a sirloin around there: fun.

Lord knows they could use some. According to *The Stars and Stripes*, a third of U.S. troops in Iraq say their morale is low. Since the war began in March, 10 soldiers have committed suicide and another 15 deaths are being investigated as possible suicides.

Hopelessness comes with this kind of conflict: You can't quite figure out why it started and can't quite figure out how it can end, but guys are getting sent home in body bags in between. More American soldiers have been killed since President Bush declared an end to major combat operations on May 1 than died in the war itself. Most of the 101st were supposed to leave Iraq by September. Now it's looking like January at the earliest.

That's why if you built it, they would come and hang around. Guys like specialist Ronald Hancock of Alpha Company, who doesn't play baseball but spends his downtime at the field keeping score. "It gives me something to do," he says. "It keeps my mind off the fact that we're never going home."

"It's so fun to fly back to our airfield in the evening and see the ball field lit up with guys running the bases," says Capt. Hunter Marshall. "Surreal."

And they don't spend game days at their cribs, kickin' it with their peeps, then bouncin' to the park in their Escalades. Most of them spend their day gassing Chinooks and Apaches and Black Hawks, keeping the trucks rolling and burning out latrines.

They can play only four nights a week, so they always do—sometimes until 1 a.m. But instead of New York City cops providing security, they have infantry posted on all sides, which is what you need in a war with no front lines against an enemy who doesn't care about saving his own flesh, only splattering yours.

"So far," says Johnson, "we've been lucky enough not to have to call a game because of an enemy attack."

But don't all those lights make these guys a well-lit bull's-eye? "It does make us a little nervous," says Capt. Adam Kamann, "but we're all too en-grossed in the game to worry about all the what-ifs."

And that's how much these guys need this field, this game, this break: Getting blown to St. Peter qualifies as a *what-if*.

Anyway, when Yankee Stadium P.A. announcer Bob Sheppard asks the crowd before the seventh-inning stretch to remember our servicemen and women around the globe, at least you know who he's talking about. Guys like this—homesick, sandsick, deathsick Americans who would give any-thing right now just to be waved home.

100

Trumpeting the Father of the Year

OCTOBER 16, 2006

QUESTION: *What has four wheels, four feet, two eyes and one horn?*
ANSWER: *Trumpet position number 7 in the Louisville marching band.*

EET PATRICK HENRY HUGHES AND HIS DAD, Patrick John Hughes—the only two-person marching-band member in college football. ¶ Patrick Henry, 18—born with a rare genetic disorder that left him without eyes, and with arms and legs that won't straighten—plays the trumpet from his wheelchair. Patrick John, 45, pushes the wheelchair. You can watch them roll during the halftime show at Cardinals home games. "I was a little worried about the endurance factor at first," says band director Greg Byrne. "Not Patrick's. His dad's."

You think it's easy pushing a 165-pound man, in full uniform, around a spongy artificial-turf field, trying to keep up with 213 other band members and get to your spot in the *A* in CARDS and the *L* in U OF L, while not getting slammed by the person marching behind you—all on four hours' sleep because you work the graveyard shift loading planes for UPS? You try it.

"My job is just to get, say, to the 32½-yard line at the exact right time," says the older Patrick, who doesn't wear the band uniform. "Every now and then I'll take a mellophone in the back, but mostly it's been a blast!"

"He hasn't dumped me yet," young Patrick says, grinning.

Dad also pushes his son to classes, sits with him and whispers anything written on the blackboard. After band practice they go home and eat dinner, then Dad goes to work at 11 p.m., gets off at 5 a.m., sleeps a little and gets up at 11 for breakfast, classes and band. If this guy isn't Father of the Year, I'm Liberace.

Patrick John and Patricia Hughes, a sales assistant in a brokerage firm, have been going full-Patrick-ahead since he was born. "My wife and I were sort of devastated at first," the father says. "I mean, we played by all the rules. We worked hard. She didn't have any alcohol during the pregnancy. Why us?" But then they started finding out why them. Dad, a violinist and pianist, found that he could calm his baby boy by laying him on top of the piano and tickling the ivories. By nine months young Patrick was tapping keys on the piano, mimicking his dad in a listen-and-play exercise. By two years old he was playing *Sesame Street* songs.

Now the kid's a killer pianist and a monster trumpet player. Even though people have tried to stop him—like the ones at a performing-arts school in Louisville who discouraged the Hugheses from even applying—he has done nothing but succeed. Was all-state in band and chorus at Atherton High. Had a 3.99 GPA. Sang a duet with Pam Tillis at the Grand Ole Opry. Played piano at the Kennedy Center in Washington, D.C. Put out a CD of 23 songs.

So when he enrolled at the university, young Patrick asked to join the pep band, which guaranteed a precious seat at Cardinals basketball games. But director Byrne crossed him up. He asked him, "Why don't you join the marching band?"

Next thing you know, the teenager and his father were at band summer camp—12-hour days with only 90-minute breaks for lunch and dinner. Dad pushed like crazy, and young Patrick played the theme from *Superman* while being whirled around in his own giddy darkness.

It about killed Pop. "I was whipped," he says. So he took the chair to a mechanic friend, who rigged it with bigger, wider wheels. That helped them get through the triple Axel of marching-band maneuvers: the dreaded Diamond. Two battalions of marchers come at each other in full stride, intersect, reverse, then split apart again. To pull it off, Dad has to pop a wheelie, spin the chair, try not to wipe out the entire wind section, then peel off the other way. "It takes everything I've got to make sure I'm in step," the older Patrick says. "If I don't get there quick enough, or cut quick enough, I'm the lone cowboy out at the end of this thing. I don't want people to remember us as the kid in the wheelchair whose dad couldn't keep up."

"I'm so jealous," says Byrne. "My father-son time with my dad is golf, twice a year. Patrick gets to be with his dad all the time."

Don't you love pushy parents?

Life with this kid just keeps getting more fun. "We still say, Why us?" says the father. "But now it's, Why us—how'd we get so lucky?"

I asked young Patrick what he thought his dad looked like, this man who's devoting his life to him. "Tall, skinny, muscular and bald," he said, laughing.

Yeah, there are lots of ways to play Superman.

Postscript: People can't get enough of these two. They were featured all over the cable and network news shows. They even appeared live on ESPN's College Game Day. And then the topper: Young Patrick won Disney's 2006 Wide World of Sports Spirit Award, given each year to college football's most inspirational figure.